A GREEN DIMENSION FOR THE EUROPEAN COMMUNITY: POLITICAL ISSUES AND PROCESSES

A Green Dimension for the European Community: Political Issues and Processes

edited by

DAVID JUDGE

FRANK CASS

First published 1993 in Great Britain by
FRANK CASS AND COMPANY LIMITED
Gainsborough House, 11 Gainsborough Road,
London E11 1RS, England

and in the United States by
FRANK CASS
c/o International Specialized Book Services Inc.
5804 N.E. Hassalo Street
Portland, OR 97213-3644

Copyright © 1993 Frank Cass & Co. Ltd

British Library Cataloging in Publication data

Green Dimension for the European
Community:Political Issues and Processes.
– (Special Issue of "Environmental
Politics" Series, ISSN 0964-4016;Vol.1,
No. 4)
  I. Judge, David   II. Series
  333.7094

ISBN 0-7146-4510-9 (hb)
ISBN 0-7146-4096-4 (pbk)

Library of Congress Cataloging-in-Publication Data

A Green dimension for the European community : political issues and
  processes / edited by David Judge.
     p.   cm.
  Includes bibliographical references and index.
    ISBN (invalid) 071464510 : £35.00. — ISBN 0-7146-4096-4 (pbk.) :
£16.00
    1. Environmental policy—European Economic Community countries.
  2. Green movement—European Economic Community countries.
  I. Judge, David.
  HC240.9.E5G73   1993
  363.7'056'094—dc20   92-21174
                                   CIP

This group of studies first appeared in a Special Issue: A Green Dimension for
the European Community: Political Issues and Processes, of *Environmental
Politics*, Vol. 1, No. 4, published by Frank Cass & Co. Ltd.

Typeset by Regent Typesetting, London
Printed in Great Britain by Antony Rowe

Contents

A Green Dimension for the European Community?

DAVID JUDGE

The introduction of the 'Single Market' marks a particularly appropriate time to consider the political issues and processes affecting environmental policy in the European Community (EC). In Britain the '1992 project' designated 31 December 1992 as the date for the *completion* of the 'single market': for the removal of physical, technical and fiscal barriers to the free movement of goods, services, capital and people within the EC. The French on the other hand, whilst talking of the same thing, see the '1993 programme' as marking the *start* of the single market. Irrespective of whether the 'single market' was 'completed' in 1992 or 'starts' in 1993 its impact on environmental policy within member states will be considerable. As the European Commission states:

> Under the Single Act, the EC has taken on the task of preserving and protecting a sound environment and improving its quality, safeguarding human health, and ensuring the prudent and rational use of natural resources. It intervenes where these objectives can be better achieved at Community level than by Member States acting individually. The basic principle is to prevent and remedy environmental damage [*EC Commission, 1991: 17*].

This statement in itself is sufficient justification for a volume concerned with the *politics* of environmental policy-making within the EC, for it raises fundamental questions. What is sound environmental policy? What forms of intervention serve to 'preserve and protect' a sound environment? At what level is a sound environmental policy to be formulated and implemented? And who decides what constitutes 'prudent and rational' policy? These questions go to the heart both of studies concerned with policy making in the EC and of those concerned with the substantive policy area of the environment itself.

A second justification for this volume, however, is that 'environmental politics' and the 'politics of the European Community', until fairly recently, have been Cinderella subjects in the United Kingdom. Significantly, in recent years, both have been transformed from being the preserve of small but dedicated groups of scholars and teachers into the status of mainstream university courses and research areas [*Rüdig, 1990:*

3; Weale, 1991: 198; George, 1991: x]. None the less, as emergent subjects, they have tended, perhaps not surprisingly, to develop discretely with few systematic connections made between the politics of the EC and environmental policy. One notable exception to this tendency is provided by the Institute for European Environmental Policy which has long recognised the interconnectedness of the nature of environment policy with the 'system that exists to develop and implement EC policies' [*Haigh and Baldock, 1989: 47;* also *Haigh, 1991; Wilkinson, 1992*]. This 'exceptional' concern with the interconnectedness of environmental policy and EC political processes provides the directional pointers for the present volume.

Why EC Environmental Policy?

The 1957 Treaty of Rome, the founding treaty of the European Economic Community, made no reference to the environment and had no conception of 'environmental policy' as an integral part of a 'common market'. Some 35 years later, however, environmental policy is indisputably a major part of the EC's activities; and moreover, in the opinion of two respected commentators, is 'not only a major Community policy, but also an undeniable success, despite certain gaps and weaknesses' [*Johnson and Corcelle, 1989: 2*].

So the first, related, questions to ask are: why, and how, has the EC developed a major environmental policy role? The answer to the first question is often treated as self-evident: because of an increased recognition of the political salience and the international dimension of environmental problems. Pinder [*1991: 111*] implicitly accepts this logic in his statement that: 'Pollution carried by air or water does not recognise frontiers, so member states have a common interest in its mutual control. As ecological deterioration has become aggravated and public concern correspondingly sharpened, this aspect of Community activity (environmental policy) has become increasingly important.' But, as Philipp Hildebrand's contribution to the present volume demonstrates, the reasons for the development of EC environmental policy were far more complicated than a spontaneous recognition of 'common interest' by member governments. Indeed, in the period before 1972 the driving force behind environmental protection in western Europe was a few environmentally conscious national governments (most particularly Holland and West Germany) rather than the EC itself. In part, this was because of the absence of legal competence for EC institutions in this area, with legal opinion divided over whether the EC had *any* competence in environmental matters [*Lodge, 1989: 320*]; but also, in part, because many member governments conceived of environmental protection primarily in relation to intra-Community non-tariff barriers. In this sense, as McGrory [*1990: 304*] points out, until 1973, 'Community environmental policy was incidental to measures to harmonise laws in order to abolish obstacles to trade between the Member States'.

What transformed environmental policy from an incidental to an essential part of the EC's policy programme, starting in the 1970s, was a heightened awareness of the environmental consequences of unregulated economic growth; the trade distortions attendant upon uncoordinated pollution standards; two environmental disasters in EC states – in 1974 at Flixborough in the UK and in 1976 in Seveso in Italy; and increased public sensitivity to environmental issues (see Hildebrand in this volume). Once the Community's heads of state and government acknowledged in 1972 that 'economic expansion is not an end in itself ... it should result in an improvement in the quality of life as well as the standard of living' (quoted in COM (92) 23 final, Vol.2, 27 March 1992, p.17), and asked the Commission to draw up an Action Programme for the Environment, then the legitimacy of the EC as a coordinator and harmoniser of environmental programmes rapidly became political, if not legal, reality. Legal recognition was to come later in 1987 with the Single European Act (SEA), and its belated recognition and symbolisation of what had been happening anyway [*Haigh and Baldock, 1989: 20*].

But the very mention of the SEA points to the second of the two initial questions raised above: 'How has EC environmental policy developed?'. In part, this question is answered in considering why EC policy developed. But a fuller answer requires an analysis of the dynamic process of institutional and substantive policy development within the EC. Thus, as Hildebrand, Boons, Mazey and Richardson, and Judge in this volume make clear, interactions within and between institutions impact upon the scope and nature of policy itself. In the case of EC environmental policy, for instance, the differential and changing power bases and institutional relations within and amongst the Commission, the European Parliament, the Council of Ministers, member states and organised interests have impacted, over time, upon the form and content of environmental policy. Understanding how EC environmental policy has developed, therefore, is crucial to understanding the nature of that policy.

The Nature of EC Environmental Policy

As several of the contributors to this collection of essays note, the nature of EC environment policy has changed over time. Albert Weale and

Andrea Williams, in examining the concept of 'ecological modernisation' note how EC policy makers contributed to the idea that environmental protection and economic development could be complementary rather than conflicting objectives. In successive Action Programmes the Commission moved from an emphasis on preventive action in the First Action Programme of 1973 and the protection of the environment at 'the lowest cost to the Community' [*Johnson and Corcelle, 1989: 13*], to the statement in the Third Action Programme, some ten years later, that 'the resources of the environment are the basis of – but also constitute the limit to – further economic and social development and the improvement of living conditions'. The 1983 Programme then went on to state that environment policy should be incorporated into other major EC policy programmes.

By the Fifth Action Programme (COM (92) 23 final, Vol.2, 27 March 1992) the emphasis upon the integration of environmental considerations into the formulation and implementation of economic and sectoral policies was paramount alongside the concept of 'sustainable development'. This concept was defined in terms of policies and strategies to secure 'continued economic and social development without detriment to the environment and the natural resources on the quality of which continued human activity and further development depend' (COM (92) 23 final, 27 March 1992, p.3).

Hence, the approach adopted by the Fifth Action Programme differs from its predecessors in its stress on long-term objectives and its recognition that success is dependent upon an informed evaluation of the risks to the environment and the monitoring of Community actions taken to alleviate those risks. Moreover, the latest programme identifies a number of specific issues – climate change, acidification and air pollution; depletion of natural resources and biodiversity; deterioration of the urban environment; deterioration of coastal zones; and waste – as being of sufficient seriousness to warrant Community-wide action. The Fifth Action Programme also marked a departure in its emphasis upon the need for 'satisfactory implementation of community rules' which will 'require better preparation of measures, more effective co-ordination with and integration into other policies, more systematic follow-up and stricter compliance-checking and enforcement' (COM (92) 23 final, Vol.2, 27 March 1992, p.9).

Indeed, it is precisely these issues that are addressed in this collection of essays. The contributions by Albert Weale and Andrea Williams, and by Jan van der Straaten, examine the extent to which environmental considerations have been integrated into EC economic policies thus far. Van der Straaten argues that the latest Action Programme is 'a plan on paper and nothing more' and draws upon a discussion of economic theory to illustrate the difficulties in operationalising the concept of a 'sound European environmental policy'. Similarly, Weale and Williams invoke, as part of an explanation of the continuing disjunction between the EC's economic and sectoral policies and its environmental policy, the deficiencies of neo-classical economic analysis. The intellectual assumptions of mainstream economics are insufficient in themselves to account for this disjunction, and Weale and Williams argue instead that it is the *combination* of intellectual, organisational and political factors that has served to prevent the successful integration of environmental policy, and that needs greater attention in the future.

In introducing the concept of 'network analysis', Frank Boons' contribution provides a direct bridge between the issue-focused papers in the first section of this volume and the process-oriented pieces in the second section. Indeed, one organising theme of this volume is that the substance of EC environmental policy can only be properly understood in relation to the processes through which policy is made. Boons' paper is useful in this respect for it demonstrates, in the context of the control of the chemical industry, how corporate strategies, the nature of national policy communities and international networks, alongside the formal national and EC-level decision-making structures, all impact upon the formulation of EC environmental policy. Indeed, it is significant that the Fifth Action Programme itself records the Commission's concern to improve decision-making processes to 'make the programme work':

> Up to the present, environmental protection in the Community has been based on a legislative approach ('top–down'). The new strategy advanced in this Programme implies the involvement of all economic and social partners ('bottom–up'). The complementarity and effectiveness of the two approaches together will depend, in great measure, on the level and quality of dialogue which will take place in pursuance of partnership (COM (92) 23 final, Vol.2, 27 March 1992, p.9).

To this end the Commission proposes to establish three ad hoc 'dialogue groups': a 'general consultative forum' of functional representatives, non-governmental organisations, regional and local authorities; an 'implementation network' of representatives of relevant national authorities and of the Commission; and an 'environmental policy review group' 'comprising representatives of the Commission and the Member States at Director-General level' (COM (92) 23 final, Vol.2, 27 March 1992, p.9). The significance of this proposal is emphasised by Sonia Mazey and Jeremy Richardson in their conclusion that if the proposed consultative forum promotes 'collective responsibility' for policy between the social partners and the Commission then 'the two competing interests will have been incorporated into the policy process as joint partners – with all the constraints and responsibilities that that entails'. These proposals are thus seen as evidence of the Commission, as an 'adolescent bureaucracy', attempting to 'rationalise' the process of interest intermediation. Using the analytical frame of 'policy networks' and 'lobbying styles', Mazey and Richardson proceed to assess the prospects afforded to environmental groups by recent developments. These concerns link the contribution of Mazey and Richardson in the 'processes' section with that of Boons in the 'issues' section, and, in so doing, demonstrate that 'lobbying *styles* may be as important as the content and objectives of the lobbying itself'.

If the development of international policy networks and increased lobbying of EC institutions has had a profound effect in the environmental field, then so too did the electoral success of green parties in the 1989 European elections. One senior member of DG XI noted in interview (Brussels, 20 May 1992): 'The Green vote in 1989 was a shock to the Community's system. Certainly, it helped to raise the profile of "green" issues within the Commission and to assist those parts of the EC's decision making process committed to environmental improvement and protection to press forward'. In this sense the green vote was of importance for its impact upon the perceptions of decision makers after 1989; but, equally, it was of importance in raising a number of important questions about the character of green politics in European Community countries. And it is these questions that Mark Franklin and Wolfgang Rüdig consider in their contribution to this volume. They approach the important questions of who green voters are; to what extent green voting is a 'protest vote'; and what explains the support for 'ecological' and 'left' green parties. In answering these questions Franklin and Rüdig assess some of the most important theories that have underpinned the analysis of green voting.

Elizabeth Bomberg provides a logical stepping stone from the analysis of green voters to an examination of the activities of one of the major green parties – the German Greens – in the European Parliament. Bomberg applies the theoretical model of 'movement-parties' to explain the contradictions and tensions apparent within the strategy and goals of the German Greens within the European Parliament. It is apparent from her analysis that they still remain sharply divided over the proper role of the EC as a means of achieving green goals in Europe. Bomberg's more general conclusion is equally sobering: 'Without a comprehensive and comprehensible conception of Europe, the impact of the growing green consciousness in Europe will remain muted.'

Indeed, one current in the debate within green parties concerns the efficacy and justification of parliamentary action as a means of promoting green objectives and policies. Certainly established parties within the European Parliament (EP), especially since 1989, have taken on board many green issues. However, this has not appeased those within the green movement who remain opposed to what they see as the un-democratic and popularly unresponsive institutions of the EC. 'Fundis' outside the EP and 'oppositionist' green MEPs within it have adopted a hostile and disruptive approach to the European Parliament specifically and the institutional structure of the EC generally. 'Realos' within the green movement and 'reformists' and 'constructive co-workers' (see Bomberg in this volume) within the EP have recognised the potential of the Parliament to insert itself into the EC policy process and to raise green issues and so bring a 'green dimension' to EC legislation.

The internal debate within green parties and the movement echoes the wider discussion amongst political scientists as to the policy impact made by the European Parliament. It is this wider theme that David Judge pursues through a detailed examination of the work of the EP's Committee on Environment, Public Health and Consumer Protection. In analysing the committee's contribution to environmental policy-making the general theme of the interconnectedness between the *substance* of EC policy and the *process* of policy-making is pursued. In other words, the 'what' (the content) of EC environmental policy reflects the 'how' (the process) of policy making. Judge concludes that any explanation of 'how' EC environmental policy is made needs to acknowledge the input of the European Parliament and its Environment Committee.

The importance of 'implementation' to the success of policy has been recognised for some considerable time by political scientists (see, for example, Pressman and Wildavsky [*1973*]; Hogwood and Gunn [*1984*]). Moreover the institutions of the EC have rapidly come to recognise that:

> Satisfactory implementation and enforcement of ... policy (is) imperative if the objectives of environmental protection, sustaina-bility of socio-economic activity and development of the integrity of the Internal Market are to be achieved ... the effectiveness of implementation (is) closely related to the quality of the measures themselves and of the arrangements for their enforcement (COM (92) 23 final 27 March 1992, p.75; also PE 116.085 fin, 11 Nov. 1988, PE 152.144, 28 Aug. 1991).

The problems and complexities associated with the implementation and enforcement of EC environmental legislation are reviewed by Ken Collins and David Earnshaw. Speaking with the combined authority of 'insiders' in the EC policy process as well as former social science academics, Collins and Earnshaw reveal the inextricable connection between the quality of policy formulation and deliberation, and successful policy implementation. Viewed systemically the 'problem of implementation' provides insights into the relationships amongst EC institutions themselves and between the Community and the national interests of member states.

A Green Dimension? Or Green Dimensions?

This volume seeks to investigate the conditions under which environmental issues are raised and policies made at the EC-level. In this respect it is concerned with several dimensions of the EC and is not, therefore, monofocal but poly-focal in its approach. One advantage of this approach is that it allows consideration of specific issues from different perspectives and different theoretical vantage points. Hence, for example, the various Environmental Action Programmes of the Commission are mentioned in nearly every contribution to this volume as a reflection of how the same policy documents can be refracted through different analytical prisms to reveal both the multifaceted nature of those documents themselves and of the diverse theoretical concerns of the contributors to this volume.

Similarly the Commission and the Council of Ministers feature prominently in most chapters in both sections of this volume. In this way, many of the issues which might have been covered in discrete chapters dedicated to the Commission or the Council are covered in a more logical and a less structurally contrived manner than otherwise might be case. In viewing the Commission and Council from the perspectives provided in the contributions to this volume – especially on lobbying, the European Parliament, and the process of implementation – the theme of how institutional interactions and interconnections impact upon the scope and nature of EC environmental policy can thus be more fully developed.

It is perhaps unoriginal to invoke S.E. Finer's famous rallying call for political scientists: 'Light! More Light!'. But, what is needed with regard to environmental issues and processes at the EC-level is precisely 'Light! More Light!'. What is required are more detailed and theoretically sustained studies: of voters and voting; of parties at the EC-level; of environmental groups; of policy networks; of the European Parliament; of the Commission; the Council; the Court of Justice; and of the implementation process. Equally, more rigorous analyses of the key issues of sustainability, subsidiarity, and strategies for environmentally-sound economic development within the EC, need to be encouraged. This need can only be heightened in the face of such statements as those made by Michael Howard, the UK's Secretary of State for the Environment, who pledged the UK government – within a week of its assuming the EC presidency in July 1992 – to 'pursue vigorously the principle of subsidiarity – devolving regulation (including some environmental matters) back from the EC to national governments where possible' (*Financial Times*, 7 July 1992). The headline of the *Financial Times* article left no doubts as to the Secretary of State's intention: 'EC "Green" Laws Face UK Threat'. At such a time, and in the face of such threats, an understanding of the 'green dimension' of the EC is more than an academic exercise.

REFERENCES

EC Commission (1991), *The European Community 1992 and Beyond*, Luxembourg: Office for Official Publications of the EC.

Finer, S.E. (1966), *Anonymous Empire* (2nd edn.), London: Pall Mall Press.

George, S. (1991), *Britain and European Integration Since 1945*, London: Blackwell.

Haigh, N. (1991), *The European Community and International Environmental Policy*, London: Institute for European Environmental Policy.

Haigh, N. and D. Baldock (1989), *Environmental Policy and 1992*, London: Institute for European Environmental Policy.

Hogwood, B. and L. Gunn (1984), *Policy Analysis for the Real World*, Oxford: Oxford University Press.

Jacobs, F. and R. Corbett (1990), *The European Parliament*, London: Longman.

Johnson, S.P. and G. Corcelle (1989), *The Environmental Policy of the European Communities*, London: Graham & Trotman.

Lodge, J. (1989), 'Environment: Towards a Clean Blue-Green EC?', in J. Lodge (ed.), *The European Community and the Challenge of the Future*, London: Pinter.

McGrory, D.P. (1990), 'Air Pollution in the United States and the Community', *European Law Review*, Vol.15, pp.298–316.

PE 116.085/fin. (1988), Report of the Committee on the Environment, Public Health and Consumer Protection on the Implementation of European Community Legislation Relating to Water, Luxembourg: European Parliament Session Documents.

PE 152.144 (1991), Report of the Committee on the Environment, Public Health and Consumer Protection, on the Implementation of Environmental Legislation, Luxembourg: European Parliament Session Documents.

Pinder, J. (1991), *European Community: The Building of a Union*, Oxford: Oxford University Press.

Pressman, J.I. and A. Wildavsky (1973), *Implementation*, Berkeley CA: University of California Press.

Rüdig, W. (1990), 'Editorial' in W. Rüdig (ed.), *Green Politics One: 1990*, Edinburgh: Edinburgh University Press.

Weale, A. (1991), 'The Greening of the European Polity', *West European Politics*, Vol.14, No.4, pp.193–8.

Wilkinson, D. (1992), *Maastricht and the Environment*, London: Institute for European Environmental Policy.

PART I: ISSUES

The European Community's Environmental Policy, 1957 to '1992': From Incidental Measures to an International Regime?

PHILIPP M. HILDEBRAND

This contribution reviews the environmental policy of the European Community from the Treaty of Rome to the Maastricht Treaty, tracing its evolution and outlining the determining factors. An international institutional framework is applied to the analysis in order to come to terms with the dynamic nature of the policy. Through the process of institutionalisation, the participants' behaviour has gradually converged around a set of established rules. These rules, in turn, evolve as a reflection of the participants' experiences during the process of institutionalisation. The tradition of neo-liberal institutionalism provides the conceptual tools to understand how a number of ad hoc environmental measures can, over time, evolve into an international regime or a 'negotiated order'. The European Community's environmental policy can indeed be interpreted as having reached the state of an international regime. This is no reason for complacency, however. In order to address the urgent environmental problems facing the European Community, its member states must respond to the dictates of the regime and comply with the institutional requirements. In order to build on the guideposts set up by the advocates of international institutional approaches and determine when and to what extent international environmental regimes matter, systematic compliance studies will be needed that take into account both domestic and international variables.

This contribution describes and analyses the evolution of the European Community's environmental policy. The chosen time frame covers the period from January 1958, when the Treaty of Rome came into effect, to '1992', the target-date for the completion of the Single European Act (SEA) which entered into force on 1 July 1987.[1] The Treaty of Maastricht and its environmental consequences will be considered briefly in a final section. In light of the difficulty of a reliable interpretation so shortly after

The author wishes to thank Andrew Hurrell, Andrew Walter, David Wartenweiler and David Judge for their helpful comments on earlier versions of this study.

the treaty's signature and the fact that it is unlikely to go into effect before the middle of 1993, the reviewed legislative acts are drawn from the pre-Maastricht period.

It is often stated that, prior to 1973, there was no EC environmental policy. In principle this assessment is correct. Nevertheless, a number of pieces of environmental legislation had been adopted during that period. For that reason and in order to present an historically and analytically complete picture, the entire period will be assessed here.

At the outset it is necessary to ask two questions. First, how did the EC environmental policy evolve? Secondly, what were the determining factors of this evolution? At a time when the EC's environmental policies are increasingly being followed by the public, private corporations as well as various interest groups [*Sands, 1990: 2*], it is important to gain a thorough understanding of the historic evolution of European[2] environmental policies as a whole. The introduction of the Single European Act has brought about significant changes. Yet, relatively little has been written on the subject and, although '1992' has become every European's catchword, few seem to be aware of the potential environmental consequences of these recent developments.

Before laying out the structure of this study, it is necessary to discuss briefly the legal instruments that the relevant Community institutions are equipped with, in 'order to carry out their task'.[3] They are applicable to all issue-areas within the competence of the European Community and have not been changed by the amendments introduced by the Single European Act or the Maastricht Treaty creating the European Union. Article 189 of the EEC Treaty sets out five different types of legal instruments. The first paragraph states: 'In order to carry out their task the Council and the Commission shall, in accordance with the provisions of this Treaty, make regulations, issue directives, take decisions, make recommendations or deliver opinions.' The last two have no binding force and should therefore not 'properly be regarded as legislative instruments' [*Haigh, 1990: 2*].

A regulation has general application and is 'binding in its entirety and directly applicable in all Member States' (Article 189/2). It has generally been used for rather precise purposes such as financial matters or the daily management of the Common Agricultural Policy (CAP). Only rarely has it been used for environmental matters [*Haigh, 1990: 2*].

A directive is 'binding, as to the result to be achieved', while it leaves it to the national authorities as to the 'choice of form and method' (Article 189/3). According to Nigel Haigh, 'it is therefore the most appropriate instrument for more general purposes particularly where some flexibility is required to accommodate existing national procedures and, for this reason, is the instrument most commonly used for environmental mat-ters' [*Haigh, 1990: 2*].[4]

Finally a decision is 'binding in its entirety upon those to whom it is addressed' (Article 189/4). With respect to environmental protection, decisions have been used in connection with international conventions and with certain procedural matters.

For analytical purposes I have divided the period to be covered here into three different phases. The first one begins with the entry into force of the Treaty of Rome and the establishment of the European Economic Community in 1957 and ends in 1972 with the Stockholm Conference on the Human Environment. With the approval of the first Community Action Programme on the Environment by the Council of Ministers in November 1973, the second phase begins which, according to this chronology, lasts until the adoption of the Single European Act in Luxembourg in December 1985. On 17 and 28 February the SEA was signed in Luxembourg and The Hague and, after ratification by the twelve national parliaments (and referenda in Denmark and Ireland), it came into force on 1 July 1987. The ratification of the SEA represents the onset of the third phase, in the midst of which the European Community's environmental policy is presently unfolding.[5]

I have attempted to describe and label each of the three phases in a distinct manner. According to this typology, the first one, from 1956 to 1972 is best understood as a time of pragmatic measures as opposed to proper policy. The overriding objective of the European Community during that time was to harmonise laws in order to abolish trade impedi-ments between the member states. The pieces of environmental legisla-tion that were adopted throughout those years were, as one observer has described them, 'incidental' to the overriding economic objectives [*McGrory, 1990: 304*].

After 1972 one begins to witness the emergence of an EC environmen-tal policy. Specific actions and measures were initiated in a response to a number of circumstances and events. First, mounting public protest against environmental destruction exerted a considerable degree of pressure upon elected government officials. This pressure, in turn, seems to have had a positive effect on the dynamics and innovation of official EC policy. Secondly, during the 1970s and the early 1980s the world was witness to a number of environmental disasters which provided a dramatic backdrop to the emerging environmental sensitivity. Last but by no means least, member states became concerned about uncoordinated local environmental protection measures causing intra-community trade distortions.

With the third phase, which essentially coincides with the SEA, EC environmental policy becomes more substantive. The Title VII amendment to the original Treaty of Rome introduced important new ideas and methods of environmental policy. Within this context, it is important to keep a proper perspective and avoid a sense of 'europhoria'. The new provisions of the Single European Act are, although potentially far-reaching, rather abstract. Dirk Vandermeersch [*1987: 407*] describes them as giving a 'constitutional' base to the Community's environmental policy, and as defining its objectives. Nigel Haigh and David Baldock [*1989: 20*] take this line of thought one step further arguing that, depending on how one views the relevant articles of Title VII, they may 'do no more than legitimise what was happening anyway'. Yet, at the end, their final judgement is a positive one. They conclude that the new provisions contain interesting elements and result in subtle consequences. Ernst von Weizsäcker [*1989: 49*] arrives at a similar, though slightly more optimistic, conclusion. According to him, it will be up to us Europeans to convert the formal provisions into legal and economic reality.

This brings me to the concept of an international regime, to which I referred in the title of this contribution. Throughout the past decade, a significant amount of international relations and political science literature has been concerned with the concept of international regimes. As a result, a whole range of different definitions and approaches has emerged. Arguably, the most promising path is the one that perceives an international regime as a form of international institution or 'persistent and connected sets of rules (formal and informal) that prescribe behavioural roles, constrain activity, and shape expectations' [*Keohane, 1989: 3*]. Within this tradition, Robert Keohane defines international regimes as institutions with explicit rules, agreed upon by governments, that pertain to particular sets of issues in international relations'. Similarly, Oran Young [*1992: 165*] defines international regimes as 'institutional arrangements that deal with specific issue-areas'.

Another recent and related definition stems from Otto Keck [*1991: 637*] who views an international regime as an institutional arrangement for the collective management of problematic interdependencies of action, meaning problems that simultaneously touch upon the interests of several states and that cannot, or only inadequately, be resolved by individual states without resorting to coordination or co-operation with other states.[6] Applying this kind of concept of an international regime to the EC's environmental policy allows us to embark upon a dynamic analysis. Regimes do not just come into existence; they develop over time. The same applies to the EC's environmental policy. This development takes place via a process of increasing institutionalisation, which is the gradual recognition of participants that their behaviour reflects, to a considerable extent, the established rules, norms and conventions and that its meaning is interpreted in light of this recognition [*Keohane, 1989: 1*].

Throughout the following discussion of the evolution of the environmental policy of the European Community I shall pause at the end of each of the three phases mentioned above in order to assess to what extent this process of institutionalisation can be said to have taken place. In the conclusion I shall briefly address the question of the benefits of using a regime or institutional framework in an analysis of the European Community's environmental policy.

1957–72: 'Incidental' Measures

When the Treaty of Rome, establishing the European Economic Communities (EEC), was signed on 25 March 1957, it did not include any explicit reference to the idea of environmental policy or environmental protection. The primary aim of the six founding Member States was to establish a 'common market' in which goods, people, services and capital could move without obstacles (Article 3). There are two articles in the original treaty that can be regarded as a direct indicator that, as Rolf Wägenbaur [*1990: 16*] has pointed out, 'the ambitions of the founding fathers went far beyond' the objective of the common market. First, Article 2 of the Treaty of Rome calls for the promotion throughout the Community of 'a harmonious development of economic activities, a continuous and balanced expansion, an increase in stability, an accelerated raising of the standard of living and closer relations between the states belonging to it'. The Community institutions tend to interpret this mandate to include not only an improved standard of living but also an improved quality of life [*Rehbinder and Steward, 1985: 21*]. Although this interpretation, which suggests that environmental protection might be among the Community's objectives, is not uncontroversial, the general view of the literature seems to be that it is 'reasonable to interpret the Preamble and Article 2 of the EEC Treaty as including economic concepts of environmental pollution, such as those of external cost and of the environment as a common good' [*Rehbinder and Steward, 1985: 21*].

Secondly, Article 36 refers, at least implicitly, to the protection of the environment. It states that it is justifiable to restrict imports, exports or goods in transit on grounds of 'public morality, public policy or public security; the protection of health and life of humans, animals or plants; the protection of national treasures possessing artistic, historic or archaeological value'. In both cases, therefore, there exists a certain obligation to safeguard the environment. However, given the very general phrasing of Article 2 and the negative provision of Article 36, allowing for trade restrictions for reasons of public health and the protection of humans, animals and plants only as a derogation from the supreme principle of freedom of exchange, it is obvious that it was the 'common market' and the four 'freedoms' that constituted the core of the treaty's objectives [*Wägenbaur, 1990: 16*]. Within this context it is worth noting that the European Court of Justice made an attempt to define the substance of the common market, stating that it involves 'the elimination of all obstacles to intra-Community trade in order to merge the national markets into a single market bringing about conditions as close as possible to those of a genuine internal market'.[7] Again, there is some room to perceive environmental protection as being related to the objective of such a common market but only insofar as it touches upon intra-Community trade obstacles, particularly non-tariff barriers.

During those early years, EC environmental legislation was therefore subject to a twofold restriction. First, there were no explicit, formal legal provisions to support any Community-wide action and, secondly, whatever action could be taken under the available general provisions had to be directly related to the objective of economic and community harmonisation [*McGrory, 1990: 304*]. This meant that the pace of environmental protection was essentially set by strongly environmentally-oriented member states as opposed to anyone on the Community level.

As a result of the uncertainty about the jurisdictional basis for Community environmental protection measures, the Community institutions have, at least until the Single European Act, based their environmental policy primarily on Article 100 and, to a lesser extent, on Article 235 of the Treaty of Rome. Article 100 authorises the Council, provided it acts unanimously, to 'issue directives for the approximation of such provisions laid down by law, regulation or administrative action in Member States as directly affect the establishment or functioning of the common market'. Article 235 is also based on unanimous decision. It accords the Council the authority to take 'appropriate measures' to 'attain, in the course of the operation of the common market, one of the objectives of the Community' where the 'Treaty has not provided the necessary powers' to do so. Obviously the 'justification for using these two articles as the foundation of a common environmental policy depends ultimately on basic Community goals' [*Rehbinder and Steward, 1985: 20*]. According to Article 3 of the EEC Treaty, 'approximation of the laws of the member states' is to 'promote the proper functioning of the Common Market and the Community's objectives set out in Article 2' [*Rehbinder and Steward,*

1985: 20]. As a result, the use of Article 100 and Article 235 was essentially dependent on a generous reading of Article 2.[8] To sum up, while politically it was possible to use Article 100 and Article 235 for environmental objectives, these provisions were, as Rehbinder has pointed out, originally 'designed to give Community institutions powers to ensure the establishment and functioning of the Common Market as an economic institutions and were not aimed at environmental protection as such' [*Rehbinder and Steward, 1985: 16*].

Despite the absence of a coherent framework, the Council passed several concrete pieces of environmental legislation prior to the First Action Programme on the Environment. Between 1964 and 1975 a number of initiatives were adopted under Articles 30, 92, 93 and 95 of the EC Treaty to prevent excessive subsidisation of the regeneration or incineration of used oil [*Rehbinder and Steward, 1985: 16*]. In 1967 a directive was used for the first time to deal with environmental matters, establishing a uniform system of classification, labelling and packaging of dangerous substances.[9] The jurisdictional basis for Directive 67/548 was Article 100 of the Treaty of Rome. In March 1969 this directive was modified, again on the basis of Article 100.[10] In 1970, Directives 70/157, regulating permissible sound level and exhaust systems of motor vehicles, and 70/220, limiting vehicle emissions, were again passed with reference to Article 100 of the EEC Treaty, while Regulation 729/70 with respect to countryside protection in agriculturally less favoured areas was based on Articles 43 and 209. In 1971, the only 'environmental' directive that was passed extended the deadline for the implementation of the 1967 directive on dangerous substances. In the last year of the first phase, the Council passed three directives that can be considered to have an environmental impact, two of which were related to agricultural issues and therefore took their jurisdictional basis from Articles 42 and 43 of the EEC Treaty. Directive 72/306, regulating vehicle emissions caused by diesel engines, once again referred to Article 100.

While environmental measures were not altogether absent during the first fifteen years of the European Community's history, they cannot be regarded as adding up to any sort of proper and coherent policy. Only nine directives and one regulation were adopted during that time and, on the whole, these measures were incidental to the overriding economic objective [*McGrory, 1990: 304*]. This is reaffirmed by the fact that all 'environmental' directives, with the exception of the ones pertaining to agriculture, were adopted on the basis of Article 100 and thus perceived as approximation measures with respect to the 'establishment or functioning of the common market'.

During this first phase, it is inappropriate to speak of an institutionalisation process in terms of environmental protection. A limited number of pieces of legislation were passed but these were not based on an established set of rules pertaining to the protection of the environment. In fact, the issue-area of the environment did not yet exist *per se*. It was therefore impossible for the participants to perceive their behaviour as a reflection of a set of rules within this issue area.

1972–86: The 'Responsive' Period

The Paris Summit Conference on 19 and 20 October 1972 marks the onset of the second phase in the evolution of Community environmental policy. In Versailles, the heads of state or government of the six founding member states and of the new members (United Kingdom, Denmark and Ireland) called upon the institutions of the Community to provide them with a blueprint for an official EC environmental policy by 31 July 1973. Accordingly, the Commission forwarded a 'Programme of environmental action of the European Communities' to the Council on 17 April 1973. Pursuant to this Commission initiative, the First Community Action Programme on the Environment was formally approved by the Council and the representatives of the member state on 22 November 1973.[11] The programme must be regarded as a landmark in the evolution of Community environmental efforts. It marked the beginning of an actual policy in that it set the objectives, stated the principles, selected the priorities and described the measures to be taken in different sectors of the environment for the next two years. As Eckhard Rehbinder [*Rehbinder and Steward, 1985: 17–18*] states, it 'opened up a field for Community action not originally provided for in the treaties' and, according to the Commission, 'added a new dimension to the construction of Europe'.[12]

The objective of Community environmental policy, as expressed in the First Action Programme, was 'to improve the setting and quality of life, and the surroundings and living conditions of the Community population'.[13] In order to achieve this objective, the Council adopted 11 principles, determining the main features of the policy. Three of these principles deserve particular mention here. First, the emphasis was laid on preventive action. Secondly, it was asserted that 'the expense of preventing and eliminating pollution should, in principle be borne by the polluter'.[14] Finally, the programme stipulated that 'for each different type of pollution, it is necessary to establish the level of action' befitting the type of pollution and the geographical zone to be protected.[15] With respect to the Commission this meant that it had the authority to act 'whenever lack of action would thwart the efforts of more localised authorities and whenever real effectiveness is attainable by action at Community level'.[16] Overall, the First Action Programme called for measures in three different categories: the reduction of pollution and nuisances as such; the improvement of the environment and the setting of life as well as the joint action in international organisations dealing with the environment. The second category of measures essentially fell under common policies, such as the common agricultural policies (CAP), social policy, regional policy, and the information programme.[17]

The first Action Programme was followed in 1976 by a second, more encompassing programme covering the period from 1977 to 1981. It was approved by the Council on 9 December 1976 and formally adopted on 17 May 1977.[18] With the transition from the first to the Second Action Programme coincided the publication of the first report by the Commission on the state of the environment in the Community, as provided for in the 1973 programme, reviewing all the environmental measures taken up to the end of 1976.[19] The aim of the Second Action Programme was to continue and expand the actions taken within the framework of the previous one. Special emphasis was laid on reinforcing the preventive nature of Community policy. Furthermore the programme paid special attention to the non-damaging use and rational management of space, the environment and natural resources. With respect to the actual reduction of pollution, the programme accorded special priority to measures against water pollution. Prior to the adoption of the third environmental programme in 1983, the second programme was extended by one and a half years. Due to the problems of institutional transition caused by the accession of Greece and the upgrading of the Environment and Consumer Protection Service to a Directorate-General for Environment, Consumer Protection and Nuclear Safety, the extra time was needed to make the necessary adjustments [*Rehbinder and Steward, 1985; 18*].

The continuity of Community environmental policy was assured on 7 February 1983 when the Council adopted a resolution on a Third Community Action Programme covering the years 1982 to 1986.[20] While the third programme certainly remained within the general framework of the policy as outlined in the previous two, it introduced a number of new elements. Most importantly, it stated that, while originally 'the central concern was that, as a result of very divergent national policies, disparities would arise capable of affecting the proper functioning of the common market',[21] the common environmental policy is now motivated equally by the observation that the resources of the environment are the basis of – but also constitute the limit to – further economic and social development and the improvement of living conditions. It therefore advocated 'the implementation of an overall strategy which would permit the incorporation of environmental considerations in certain other Community policies such as those for agriculture, energy, industry and transport'.[22] According to the resolution, the EC environmental policy could, in fact, no longer be dissociated from measures designed to achieve the fundamental objectives of the Community.

This acceptance of environmental policy as a component of the Community's economic objectives was fundamental in that it was the first attempt to do away with the clear subordination of environmental concerns vis-a-vis the overriding economic goal of the common market. Admittedly, the wording of the resolution was carefully chosen. Yet, with the Third Action Programme, environmental policy had clearly gained in terms of its political status. Besides the integration of an environmental dimension into other policies, the programme again reinforced the preventive character of Community policy, specifically referring to the environmental impact assessment procedure. It also established a list of actual priorities, ranging from atmosphere pollution (Directive 89/779/EEC), fresh-water and marine pollution (Directive 76/464/EEC; Directive 78/176/EEC), dangerous chemical substances (Directive 79/831/EEC; Directive 67/548/EEC), waste management (Directive 78/319/EEC) to the protection of sensitive areas within the Community and the co-operation with developing countries on environmental matters. Finally, the programme also included a commitment by the Commission to use certain considerations as a basis for drawing up their proposals such as, for instance, the obligation to evaluate, as much as possible, the costs and benefits of the action envisaged.[23]

Not surprisingly, these novelties resulted in a significant increase in terms of environmental legislation. Between February 1983 and the adoption of the SEA in December 1985, over 40 directives, eight decisions and ten regulations that all had at least some regard to the environment were adopted by the Council.

1986 was the designated final year of the Third Action Programme. The negotiations about a follow-up fourth programme were well under way by 1985, at which time it had become clear that the EEC Treaty would be supplemented by the SEA by way of which a separate chapter on the environment would be introduced in the Treaty. Although the Fourth Action Programme was not formally adopted until October 1987,[24] a new phase in the evolution of Community environmental policy was about to begin by the end of 1985, the legal basis of which would be provided by the Single European Act.

The preceding paragraphs have outlined how the Community's environmental policy evolved quite significantly during the second phase; both in terms of the underlying political attitude towards environmental protection as well as the actual number of adopted pieces of legislation. It must be remembered, however, that the actual legal basis for the policy remained relatively weak. In other words, even by the mid-1980s the Community lacked the formal competences to deal with many environmental problems. Two writers have evoked the image of a 'grey zone' of Community competences in this respect [*Teitgen and Mégret, 1981: 69*]. Rehbinder and Steward [*1985: 19*] have gone even further by stating that the 'Community's expansion into this policy area is a considerable extension of Community law and policy at the expense of member states without any express authorisation'. To put it differently, until the SEA, the evolution of Community environmental policy took place in the absence of an evolution of its formal legal basis. Articles 2, 36, 100 and 235 of the Treaty of Rome were discussed within the context of the first phase. Of these, Article 100 and Article 235 continued to serve as the principal legal instruments to forward EC environmental policy. There are other specific provisions in the Treaty of Rome which can be regarded as a source of Community competence with respect to environmental policy. Article 43(2) has been used in connection with the common agricultural policy while Article 75(1)(c) and Article 84(2) had some relevance to the common transport policy. Their relevance, however, is marginal, since their scope is too limited to have any significant impact on the general evolution of Community environmental policy.

All said, the second epoch of the EC environmental policy portrays a peculiar image. On the one hand, the jurisdictional basis, being limited from the outset, did not evolve until the adoption of the SEA. On the other hand, the development towards a common environmental policy framework was, though arguably far from satisfactory, remarkable. Within the context of this dichotomy, I shall, in the following paragraphs, make an attempt to shed some light upon the driving forces behind Community environmental policy during these years.

With the unequivocal establishment of economic growth as the goal for post-war Europe, there was simply no room for environmental concerns at the time of the foundation of the European Economic Communities. This situation was accentuated by the fact that, at the time, the majority of the public and certainly most politicians probably did not perceive the need for particular efforts in the domain of the environment. The general degree of environmental degradation had not yet reached today's dimensions and even where that was not necessarily true, relatively little reliable scientific information was available. Within this context, it is interesting to note that even progressive politicians such as, for example, Lester Pearson had little doubt as to the political supremacy of economic growth.[25]

By the early 1970s, this premise was no longer uncontested. In many parts of the developed world, environmental concerns started to surface on political agendas. In the United States, the Environmental Protection Agency was founded in 1970, accompanied by the Clean Air Act and the subsequent Clean Water Act of 1972. American public opinion was mobilised through organisations such as Friends of the Earth and the Conservation Foundation which later merged with the WWF USA. During the late 1960s Europe witnessed the emergence to prominence of environmentalists such as Bernhard Grzimek in Germany and Jacques Cousteau in France. They made effective use of the mass media to sensitise the public to their causes. Greenpeace International also started to make an important impact with its much publicised and often spectacular missions on behalf of the environment. In the Federal Republic, Willy Brandt put environmental protection on his 1969 election platform. As Chancellor, he then set a precedent by granting environmental protection a high political priority. In fact, in October 1971, his government launched an official environmental programme [*Hartkopf and Bohme, 1983: 84–118; Bechmann, 1984: 55–65; Müller, 1986: 51–96*]. At least formally, France went even further, becoming the first European country to establish its own environmental ministry. Finally, in the summer of 1972, the United Nations convened the Stockholm Conference on the Human Environment with the extensive acid rain damage to a large number of Swedish lakes as a dramatic backdrop. Under the leadership of Maurice Strong the conference succeeded, despite diplomatic isolation of the West, in establishing a United Nations Environmental Programme (UNEP).

Within the context of this newly emerging international sensitivity towards environmental protection, France seized the opportunity of her EC presidency to bring about the decision to establish the first Environmental Action Programme on the Environment at the 1972 Paris Summit in Versailles. Juliet Lodge has pointed out that the Member States' interest in an EC environmental policy was

> spurred not so much by upsurge of post-industrial values and the Nine's[26] endeavours to create a 'Human Union' or to give the EC a 'human face' as by the realisation that widely differing national rules on industrial pollution could distort competition: 'dirty states' could profit economically by being slack [*Lodge, 1989: 320*].

It is clearly in light of the fear of trade distortions that the Federal Republic of Germany and the Netherlands were among the strongest supporters of a concerted Community environmental policy. Their actual and foreseen national environmental standards were relatively strict, causing some concern about the resulting economic burdens. The German and Dutch industrial lobbies therefore argued for equal economic cost of environmental protection throughout the EC via the adoption of their standards on a Community-wide basis.

To sum up, the impetus for the First Action Programme was essentially threefold. First and, as we have seen, most importantly, there prevailed an increasing concern among the Member States about the relationship of environmental protection and trade distortions. Secondly, governments felt the need to initiate a coherent response to the increasing political pressure from environmentalists both on the national as well as on the international level. Finally, considering the inherently transnational characteristics of much of Europe's pollution, it was recognised that, in order to be effective, concerted supranational efforts were needed which could be based on the existing political structures of the European Community [McCarthy, 1989: 3].

In the years following the 1972 'turning point', there is another factor that affected the further course of Community environmental policy. Environmental disasters demonstrated the urgent need for further strengthening of the existing principles of environmental protection. Flixborough in 1974 and Seveso in 1976 were perhaps the most dramatic representations of the 'daily environmental abuse by petro-chemical and other industries, urban programmes and "high-tech" agricultural methods' that grew exponentially during the 1970s and 1980s [Lodge, 1989: 319]. The oil shocks of the 1970s resulted in a temporary deceleration of environmental policy.[27] At the latest by the late 1970s, however, environmental protection had once again become an important item on Europe's political agenda. Several European countries experienced fierce debates about the expansion of civil nuclear capacities and by 1982, with the disclosure of the widespread forest destruction in Germany, environmental policy had become a matter of first priority, a status that even surpassed the one it enjoyed in the early 1970s [Weizsäcker, 1989: 27].[28]

Not surprisingly, the 1983 Stuttgart European Council reacted to these developments. Reviewing the state of Community environmental policy, it concluded that there is an 'urgent need to speed up and reinforce action', drawing special attention to the destruction of the forests [Johnson and Corcelle, 1989: 3]. With the 1985 Brussels session of the European Council, the status of environmental protection policy was once again upgraded in so far as it was now perceived as a fundamental part of economic, industrial, agricultural and social policies within the Community [Johnson and Corcelle, 1989: 3]. What this meant is that, by the mid-1980s, the view had emerged that environmental protection was an 'economic and not simply a moral imperative' [*Lodge, 1989: 321*]. This final step in the evolution of Community policy during the second phase must be understood as a result of the increasing realisation of the link between economic growth stimulated by further integration and the resulting costs in terms of adverse environmental encumbrances [*Haigh and Baldock, 1989: 45*]. The ensuing integrated approach towards environmental protection leads directly to the last of the three phases that were outlined at the outset.

The second phase of Community environmental policy can be summarised as an active one that undoubtedly furthered environmental protection in the European Community. At the same time, however, it was characterised by a considerable degree of uncertainty. It lacked the truly integrated approach based on a sound legal basis that emerged in the third phase with the Fourth Action Programme and the SEA. The policy until 1985 was a 'responsive' one in that it evolved according to the momentary economic, political and social circumstances. Its initial and probably most important impetus was, as described above, the general concern of environmental protection as a potential cause for trade distortions. Public pressure and the direct effects of environmental accidents later accelerated the process. Finally, there was the realisation that economic progress and the protection of the environment are so closely interlinked that one cannot be considered without the other. The nature of the policy evolved at each stage depending on the given set of circumstances. Generally speaking, the circumstances as they presented themselves during the second phase favoured a progressive evolution of the policy although, in the case of the 1973 oil shock, they temporarily worked in the opposite direction.

This type of policy had certain advantages. As a whole it remained flexible, not having to rely on rigid principles that quickly become outdated. In other words, it was possible to readjust quickly the policy to a newly arisen situation or set of circumstances. The disadvantage rested in the fact that under these conditions, environmental protection would always be relegated to a subordinate position in relation to Community economic aims. Whether this disadvantage has successfully been eliminated without undermining some of the positive aspects of the second phase will be discussed in the following section. Before that, however, I shall briefly review the most important pieces of legislation of the second phase. Given the significant number of environmental directives, regulations and decisions between the First Action Programme and the Single European Act, it would, of course, exceed the limits of this study to review them all. I have therefore chosen a small representative selection.

Ernest von Weizsäcker [*1989: 42*] has identified just over 20 directives as being the most important pieces of Community environmental legislation between 1973 and 1985. For the sake of simplicity I shall base my review on this selection.[29] The relevant directives can conveniently be grouped together in six different categories according to the environmental problem they are addressing:

(1)   Water
(2)   Air
(3)   Noise
(4)   Waste
(5)   Emissions
(6)   Lead in petrol.

In addition there are a number of other directives that do not readily fit into any of these categories: the 'Seveso' directive, a directive on chemicals, one on birds and their habitat and one on sewage sludge. Weizsäcker's selection of directives is useful in that it more or less represents the full spectrum of EC environmental activities.

In the fight against water pollution, there are four directives, all of which are based both on Article 100 and Article 235 of the EEC Treaty. Directives 75/440 and 80/778 are concerned with drinking water while directive 76/160 regulates bathing water.[30] Directive 76/464 deals with dangerous substances in water.[31] The air quality efforts are represented by three directives: 80/779 on smoke and sulphur dioxide, 82/884 on lead and 85/203 on nitrogen dioxide.[32] Again the legal basis for all three directives rests in Article 100 and Article 235 of the Treaty of Rome. The same applies to the three directives on waste: 75/442 outlines a general waste framework while 78/319 and 84/631 deal with toxic waste and transfrontier shipment of waste respectively.[33] In terms of emission standards, Directive 83/351 on vehicle emission only refers to Article 100, whereas Directive 84/360 on emission from industrial plants is again based on Article 100 and Article 235.[34] The two directives on the approximation of laws of Member States concerning lead content in petrol (85/210 and 78/611) are solely based on Article 100 of the Treaty of Rome.[35] The same is true of directive 79/831, amending for the sixth time directive 67/548 on the approximation of the laws, regulations and administrative provisions relating to the classification, packaging and labelling of dangerous substances, as well as directive 79/117 on use restrictions and labelling of pesticides.[36]

Directive 79/409 on birds and their habitat, on the other hand is exclusively based on Article 235. This is, of course, to be expected, since animal protection has hardly any direct effect on the 'establishment or functioning of the common market' as expressed in Article 100 of the Treaty of Rome.[37] Finally, there are two more directives that need to be mentioned here, both of which were adopted under Article 100 and 235. Directive 82/501 on the major accident hazards of certain industrial activities was a Community response to the dioxine disaster in Seveso, and Directive 85/337 on the assessment of the effects of certain public and private projects on the environment set out an important new priority of Community environmental policy.[38]

This selective review of EC environmental 'legislation' between 1973 and 1985 reemphasises a point made earlier. Although the Community institutions were engaged in a considerable amount of environmental activity, the available legal foundations remained limited. There was no explicit jurisdictional mandate for the protection of the environment; the Community therefore proceeded with its environmental efforts on the basis of what Ernst Weizsäcker has called a 'Kunstgriff', or knack, using Articles 100 and 235 of the original EEC Treaty. This is, of course, the most fundamental difference with respect to the final phase of Community environmental policy as it has been unfolding since the adoption of the SEA.

During this second phase, the institutionalisation process mentioned at the outset is becoming discernible. Member states begin to understand that certain collective actions are necessary in order to address a more or less specific set of problems in the newly defined issue-area of the environment. As I have pointed out, however, the environment does not stand on its own feet yet. It is still at least partly subordinated to the paramount objective of economic growth. Furthermore, although explicit rules exist in form of the various directives passed, their ability to prescribe behavioural roles, constrain activity and shape expectations is limited because of the absence of an unambiguous legal foundation. Despite an ongoing gradual process of institutionalisation, no proper EC environmental regime can therefore be in place. Though explicit and agreed upon by the member states' governments, the rules in fact remain weak and exert little independent compliance pull.

1985–'92': The 'Initiative' Phase

An analysis of EC environmental policy after 1985 is rendered more complicated by the fact that, although there exists an element of continuity, it would be too simplistic to regard it as a mere continuation of previous policy developments. In terms of its general approach, the Fourth Action Programme is certainly related to the previous one, despite the fact that it was differently structured and that it initiated a number of new policy directions such as environmental educational efforts and a focus on gene-technology. It essentially completed and formalised the notions of earlier Community policy. In fact, EC policy, as laid down in the programme, is virtually all-encompassing. It demands integration of social, industrial, agricultural and economic policies, an objective that, as mentioned earlier, began to emerge with the Third Action Programme in 1983. Besides this factor of continuity, however, post-1985 EC environmental policy is shaped by a second strand of influence which manifests itself in the SEA amendment to the Treaty of Rome. Interestingly enough, the forces behind the emergence of the SEA have little to do with the environment. As Rolf Wägenbaur [*1990: 17*] has stated, the impetus stemming from the original EEC Treaty gradually weakened in the 1980s and 'it was felt that a new initiative was necessary. The so-called Single European Act came to the rescue'. The initiative was also related to the enlargement of the Community from the original six Member States to the present 12 (UK, Ireland, Denmark: 1973; Greece: 1981; Spain and Portugal: 1986). In light of the extended membership, the original treaty was clearly in need of revision. There were intensive discussions as to what sort of reform the treaty should undergo: a social charter, an environmental chapter, research and development programmes, a regional policy, the strengthening of the European Parliament, majority voting in the Council: all these issues were brought onto the agenda. The most important outcome of these negotiations, however, was the decision to go ahead with the completion of the internal market.

The commitment to achieve this goal within a specific time limit was laid down in Article 8a of the Treaty. This states that the Community 'shall adopt measures with the aim of progressively establishing the internal market over a period expiring on 31 December 1992'. The internal market is defined as 'an area without internal frontiers in which the free movement of goods, persons, services and capital is ensured'. In Lord Cockfield's White Paper, the Commission presented a plan as to what it perceived to be the specific measures that needed to be adopted in order to complete the internal market (*COM 85/310*).[39] This relatively sudden acceleration in the process of European integration put an end to perceptions of 'eurosclerosis' and caused great optimism as to the economic effects of the Single European Market.[40] The Cecchini Report on 'the economics of 1992' estimated that the internal market would result in an economic gain of 4.5–7 per cent of the Community's GNP. Such an increase in economic activities would affect the state of the environment. In the absence of any changes in policies or technologies, the environment could clearly be expected to deteriorate. It is within this context that, in 1989, a Commission Task Force published a report on 'The Environment and the Internal Market' in which it stated that the creation of a single market, as well as the need to decouple economic growth from environmental degradation requires a fundamental review of existing environmental policy at EC level and in the Member States' [*Wägenbaur, 1990: 18*]. By including Title VII on 'Environment' in the new EEC Treaty, the authors of the SEA provided the formal legal foundation on the basis of which such a fundamental review could take place.

Figure 1 shows the two strands that define the post-1985 EC environmental policy. As mentioned earlier, it is the formal legal foundation as expressed in the SEA that distinguishes Community policy after 1985 from the earlier one. The chart indicates that the dynamics of the first and second phase are still operating (b). However, it is strand (a) that is the primary determinant of the third phase of Community environmental policy.

Obviously the distinction between the two strands is somewhat schematic and therefore not entirely correct. The connecting line between the two strands suggests that the SEA amendment is also a result of Community environmental policy as it had been developing since 1972, culminating in the Fourth Action Programme in 1987. Nigel Haigh and David Baldock [*1989: 20*] make this point, arguing that the lack of a clear legal base for the EC's environmental policy had been much criticised. Within this context they see the 'Environment' title as a 'response to this criticism'. Nevertheless, the distinction is analytically useful if one works with the hypothesis that the adoption of the SEA had a significant effect on the nature of EC environmental policy. The following pages attempt to shed some light upon the question of whether or not this hypothesis is valid.

The SEA affects Community environmental policy in three different ways: First, through the general institutional changes – majority voting and the co-operation procedure; secondly, through the objective of completing the internal market; and thirdly through the new legal provisions that actually define Community environmental policy [*Haigh and Baldock, 1989: 12*].

Institutional Changes

The first of the two institutional changes instigated by the SEA is the 'co-operation procedure' with its second reading by Parliament as expressed in Article 149 of the EEC Treaty. In response to criticism of lack of

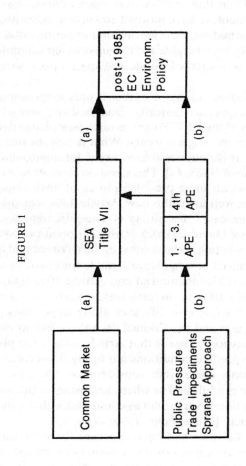

FIGURE 1

openness of the EC legislation process and charges of a 'democratic deficit', the 'cooperation procedure is designed to allow the European Parliament to play an effective but qualified role in the legislative process' [*Lodge, 1989: 69*].[41] In terms of environmental protection, there is some significance to Article 149 in that it effectively allows public opinion, represented by the Parliament, to have more of an impact on the process of environmental policy formation. Considering that environmental consciousness has undoubtedly been heightened throughout the Community in the past few years, this source of public influence could prove to become quite relevant.[42]

The co-operation procedure is limited in that it only applies when a vote is taken in Council by qualified majority. Qualified majority voting, as laid down in Article 148 of the EEC Treaty, is not a new phenomenon; it was already contained in the original treaty. What is new, however, is that under Article 100A, it is now possible to use it for environmental purposes [*Haigh and Baldock, 1989: 14*]. This stands in contrast to Article 100 and Article 235 on which most pre-1985 pieces of environmental legislation were based, as well as to the new Article 130s which I will discuss below. In all three cases, unanimity is a requirement for any action. As Nigel Haigh and David Baldock [*1989: 15*] point out, one of the problems with majority voting in the context of the environment is the uncertainty that prevails about how 'a choice is made for environmental measures between Article 130s (unanimity) and Article 100a (majority voting)'. Although Article 100a is, in principal, reserved for traded products, it is difficult to categorise all cases along these lines. Not surprisingly, the Commission and the Council do not see eye to eye on this question. The Commission's view is that Article 100a is the proper legal base whenever the specified conditions are fulfilled. According to this view, Article 130s 'only comes into consideration when the conditions of Article 100a are not fulfilled or when, for instance, the impact of the product on competition is very small as compared with the impact on the environment as such' [*Wägenbaur, 1990: 21*].

The European Court of Justice had been expected for some time to clarify the legal confusion arising out of the tension between these two articles. With the June 1991 ruling in the titanium dioxide[43] case 300/89, it has finally done so. The Court clearly gives preference to Article 100a, thus supporting majority voting. This could well set the path for future EC environmental legislation. In anticipation of the actual effect of the Court's position, Nigel Haigh's conclusion can be accepted that, while majority voting may not have revolutionised environmental policy, it has made it more difficult for one or two countries to block certain proposals as Denmark had to experience when it failed to prevent the adoption of

Directive 88/76 on emission from large cars [*Haigh and Baldock, 1989: 15*].

Completion of the 'Internal Market'

In order to achieve the objective of completing the internal market by 31 December 1992 (Article 8a), the SEA has introduced Articles 100a and 100b concerning the harmonisation of national laws, including environmental laws. Article 100a(3) states that the Commission essentially takes as a base a 'high level of protection' in its harmonisation efforts. Article 100a(4) allows member states to apply more stringent national environmental standards provided they are 'not a means of arbitrary discrimination or a disguised restriction on trade between member states'. There is also a safeguard clause (Article 100a(5)) that allows member states to opt out of harmonisation efforts in appropriate cases as provided for in Article 36. Article 100b requires the Community to draw up an inventory of national measures 'which fall under 100a and which have not been harmonised pursuant to that Article'. By majority voting, the Council then is to decide which of these can 'be recognised as being equivalent'. All others presumably have to be harmonised at that point [*Haigh and Baldock, 1989: 18*]. These harmonisation measures designed to complete the internal market have an impact on environmental policy to the extent that most environmental protection standards that affect the functioning of the internal market will be set at EC level. Whether or not the EC will seek to harmonise standards for emission (to air or water) or for environmental procedures (eg safety requirements at factories, disposal standards at vast sites), which 'have the potential to affect the "functioning of the common market" (Article 100) or the "establishment of the internal market" (Article 8a) remains uncertain' [*Haigh and Baldock, 1989: 19*].

Environmental Title

The SEA has inserted Title VII entitled 'Environment' in part III of the EEC Treaty which is concerned with the 'policies' of the European Community. This is worth noting since it suggests that with the SEA it is no longer just de facto but de jure correct to speak of an environmental policy. The relevant treaty provisions are numbered 130r to 130s. Article 130r specifies the objectives of Community environmental policy and lays down the principles and guidelines that such a policy must follow. It also deals with member state versus Community competences in terms of environmental protection and finally calls for co-operation with third countries and international organisation in matters involving the environment. Article 130s, as discussed earlier, stipulates the legislative process for the formulation of environmental laws and Article 130t allows states to introduce more stringent protective measures as long as they are compatible with the rest of the treaty.

There are a number of ways in which these new provisions have affected Community environmental policy. First, title VII has given symbolic importance to environmental protection policy, reinforced by the preamble to the SEA in which the Community commits itself to 'promote democracy on the basis of the fundamental rights recognised in the constitutions and laws of the Member States'. As Haigh and Baldock [1989: 21] have pointed out, 'more than a third of the member states have accorded constitutional status to the protection of the environment or recognise environmental rights'. Secondly, the Community environmental policy objectives outlined in Article 130r(1) are sufficiently broad – to preserve, protect and improve the quality of the environment; to contribute towards protecting human health; to ensure a prudent and rational utilisation of national resources – to bring almost any environmental issue within the competence of Community legislation. Thirdly, Article 130r(2) gives legal force to the principle which, as discussed earlier, gradually evolved in the 'Action Programmes on the Environment': principle of prevention, rectification at source and polluter pays. In addition, Article 130r(2) formalises the new principle that environmental 'protection requirements shall be a component of the Community's other policies'. Fourthly, Article 130r(3) states four basic factors that the Community needs to consider in its policy adoption: (a) available scientific data, (b) environmental coordination in the various regions of the Community, (c) the potential benefits and cost of action or lack of action and (d) the economic and social development of the Community as a whole and the balanced development of its region. Fifthly, Article 130r(4) lays down the principle of subsidiarity which determines whether appropriate action is to be taken at the Community or at the member states level. The article states: 'The Community shall take action relating to the environment to the extent to which the objectives referred to in paragraph I can be attained better at Community level than at the level of the individual Member States', thus expressly reserving residual jurisdiction to the Member States [Vandermeersch, 1987: 422].

Before addressing the question of whether or not these effects are negative or positive in terms of actual environmental protection, I shall, once again, turn to a brief review of environmental legislative measures of the third phase. As was the case for the second phase, this review is highly selective. I have, however, tried to make the selection as representative as possible of the totality of measures adopted. The survey begins with the entry into force of the SEA on 1 July 1987 and ends in August 1990.

Of the nine directives and two regulations that I have selected to review, there is not a single one that is based on Article 100 and/or Article 235. Regulation 3143/87, amending Regulation 3626/82 on the implementation in the Community of the convention on international trade in endangered species of wild fauna and flora, and Directive 88/302, amending for the ninth time directive 67/548 relating to the classification, packaging and labelling of dangerous substances, make no reference to any specific legal foundations at all. They simply have 'regard to the Treaty of the EEC'.[44] There are four directives and one regulation that take Article 130s as their legal basis: Directive 87/416 amending Directive 85/210 on approximation of the laws of the member states concerning lead content of petrol;[45] Directive 88/347, an amendment of Directive 86/280 on DDT, carbon tetrachloride and pentachlorophenol;[46] Regulation 3322/88 on certain chlorofluorocarbons and halons which deplete the ozone layer;[47] Directive 90/219 on the contained use of genetically modified micro-organisms[48] and Directive 90/415 on dangerous substances in water.[49] The remaining four directives – 88/76 and 88/77, both on emissions from vehicles; 88/436, amending an earlier directive on vehicle emission (70/220); and 90/220 on the deliberate release into the environment of genetically modified organisms[50] – were adopted on the basis of Article 100a of the EEC Treaty which, of course, implies that they were essentially harmonisation measures agreed on by qualified majority voting and subject to the co-operation procedure.

This limited survey reveals a number of interesting points. First, it is clear that the legal basis used during the first and second phase – mainly Article 100 and Article 235 – have been replaced by the new provisions provided by the SEA amendments to the Treaty of Rome. Secondly, it reaffirms the fact that, prior to the titanium dioxide case, there reigned uncertainty about which article – 100a or 130s – was to serve as the legal foundation for a given piece of environmental legislation. The range of problems that qualify as having an effect on the 'establishment of the internal market' does not seem to have been rigorously established. Finally, the evidence from our review indicates that Article 100a, implying majority voting and the co-operation procedure, was not used as frequently as one might have expected. Thus, at least until late 1991, much of the Community's environmental policy continued to be contingent on a unanimous decision by the Council.

Whilst it is difficult to assess unfolding events, there are, however, a number of observations about European Community environmental policy since the Single European Act that can already be made. For this purpose it is useful to recall that I set out to examine the hypothesis that the SEA is likely to result in a dramatic change of EC environmental policy. There are a number of indications that would validate such a hypothesis. Community environmental policy has undoubtedly gained momentum since the SEA. Title VII of the EEC Treaty has important symbolic consequences. The protection of the environment is now formally of equal or even superior status to all other Community objectives. The possibility of majority voting provides a framework for adopting a much greater amount of environmental legislation. The principle of subsidiarity, as expressed in Article 130r(4), may well have significant psychological effects on member states. Using the example of the United Kingdom, Nigel Haigh and David Baldock [*1989: 24*] have demonstrated how, in terms of the environment, Europe, including its sub-national units, is likely to increasingly perceive itself as a whole, thus moving ever closer to the 'union among the peoples of Europe' called for in the preamble to the Treaty of Rome. From such a point of view, the SEA has indeed had dramatic effects; not only in terms of a much broader and more effective environmental policy but also in terms of accelerating the process of integration among the European people in general.

As so often in international politics, there is, however, a perspective that points in the opposite direction. It is conceivable that the new provisions on majority voting could have negative effects in that they allow some member states to overrule others which will then, in the absence of an effective European enforcement agent, be tempted to simply ignore their implementation obligations. Anxiety has also been expressed with respect to the subsidiarity principle, arguing that, from a Community perspective, it is clearly a step backwards [*Vandermeersch, 1987: 422*]. While, prior the the SEA, 'the issue was whether or not the EC had competence to act or not, now measures can be challenged in terms of whether or not the EC or the member states could better deal with the issue' [*Lodge, 1989: 323*]. In that sense, the SEA has widened the possibilities for challenging EC environmental action which could result in an overall weakened and less effective Community environmental policy.

These examples should suffice to demonstrate that there is indeed significant potential in the Community environmental policy as laid down in the SEA amendments to the EEC Treaty. At the same time, many of the provisions are abstract and leave much room for manoeuvering the thrust of the policy in either direction. Much will therefore depend on the political interpretation of the policy and the nature of future amendments to its jurisdictional basis.

Maastricht and Beyond

The signing of the Maastricht treaty represents the first step towards such an amendment. It introduced important institutional and jurisdictional changes to the foundation of the European Community's environmental policy. The traditional economic growth ethos of the community has been 'greened' considerably. According to the preamble, the European Community is now determined 'to promote economic and social progress for their peoples within the context of the accomplishment of the internal market and of reinforced cohesion and environmental protection'. Title I, Article B sets the objective 'to promote economic and social progress which is balanced and sustainable'. Article 2 of the Treaty of Rome has been amended. It no longer simply refers to a 'continuous and balanced expansion', but 'a harmonious and balanced development of economic activities, sustainable and non-inflationary growth respecting the environment'. Finally, article 3(k) stipulates that the activities of the Community shall include 'a policy in the sphere of the environment'. With Maastricht, the environment has therefore 'acquired full status as a policy falling within the Union's priority objectives'.[51]

Specifically, the environment is covered by title XVI of the new treaty, articles 130r to 130t. Again, the reference is to 'Community policy on the environment' as opposed to 'action by the Community relating to the environment' under the previous article 130R. The concept of making environmental consideration a part of the other community considerations has been strengthened by the obligation to integrate environmental policy requirements into other Community policies as opposed to merely making them components.

More importantly, qualified majority voting has been introduced for most matters of environmental policy. The exceptions are provisions that are primarily of a fiscal nature, policies with limited transnational effects such as town and county planning, some aspects of water pollution control as well as measures that affect a Member State's choice between different energy sources and the general structure of its energy supply. With that, another step has been taken to reduce the prevailing uncertainty under the SEA amendments to the Treaty of Rome between unanimity and qualified majority voting as the proper procedure for environmental legislation.

The Maastricht treaty also increased the European Parliament's say over environmental standards. In addition to the cooperation procedure, introduced by the Single European Act, it contains the new 'co-decision procedure' under article 189b.[52] The new procedure for the adoption of an act is characterised by a Conciliation Committee which can be convened at two different stages as well as the possibility for a total of three different readings by the Council and the Parliament.

It will be some time before a reliable judgement on the new environmental provisions can be made. On the one hand, there are indications that the EC's environmental regime has been strengthened by the new treaty. Environmental policy has gained in prestige with respect to the other, particularly economic, objectives of the Community. The new voting rules and the additional power of the European Parliament have increased the policy's political potential. Indeed, one observer judges that 'the notions of sovereignty in the area of environmental policy have become increasingly irrelevant' [*Wilkinson, 1991*]. On the other hand, the possibility of overruling recalcitrant states could once again amplify the already existing implementation problems. Also, the new procedures are so complicated that the objective of increasing legislative transparency has slipped away further than ever. Beyond that, the wording concerning the exceptions to the qualified majority voting procedure is 'sufficiently vague to allow many exceptions and endless wrangles' [*Wolf, 1991*].

Rather than trying to give a positive or negative verdict on the new provisions, it is perhaps more important and more relevant to emphasise once again the dynamic characteristics of the European Community's environmental policy. The Maastricht treaty has not created an unambiguously powerful Europe-wide environmental regime. Neither has it made a radical departure from the environmental objectives as set out in the SEA amendments. It has, however, moved the policy yet another step on the road towards an institutional framework which will, sooner or later, have to be taken seriously by the Member States. Clearly this road is covered with obstacles, one of which could soon prove to be the ratification processes in some of the Member States. Nevertheless, it is bound to evolve further. The Fifth Action Programme was presented by Commissioner Carlo Ripa di Meana in March 1992. There are now well over 100 new environmental proposals in the policy pipeline, covering a wide range of issues. This will entail significant costs to the business communities of the member states. At the same time, there are new opportunities opening up as a result of the new policy thrusts. There will be community funding to support companies investing in new environmental standards, not to speak of the investment opportunities in environmental protection industries. It is also important to keep in mind that the treaty itself states 1996 as the date for a new intergovernmental conference. This will almost certainly set off another reform round in the European Community. By then, the discussions will need to take into account the membership of Austria, Sweden and possibly other EFTA states. All these factors will influence the further development of the EC's environmental policy. Therefore, while it might be too early to predict the exact course the policy will take, it appears safe to conclude that it will play an increasingly important role in the future development of Europe.

But is it possible to argue that the institutionalisation process as described at the start of this study has progressed to the point where it is useful to describe the present state of the European Community's environmental policy in terms of an international regime? Let us once again look at Robert Keohane's definition of an international institution as 'persistent and connected sets of rules (formal and informal) that prescribe behavioural roles, constrain activity, and shape expectations'. The rules are clearly established. There is a large and growing body of legislation in the various areas of European environmental protection. This legislation is based on a relatively unambiguous jurisdictional basis. Formally, there is no doubt that it prescribes behavioural roles, constrains activities and shapes expectations. In fact, its tendency to shape expectations has even reached beyond the present Community member states. The central and eastern European countries which are aspiring to an eventual accession to the European Community are already involved in adjusting or, in some cases, establishing their domestic environmental legislative bodies in such a way as to make sure that they will eventually be compatible with the expectations as expressed in the Community rules. Within this context the conclusion imposes itself that the institutionalisation process of the European Community's environmental policy, notwithstanding the above-mentioned weaknesses, has progressed far enough to warrant the description of an international environmental regime.

Conclusions

As mentioned above, the question imposes itself whether there is any added value in introducing the potentially ambiguous concept of an international regime in this attempt to describe the evolution of the European Community's environmental policy up to the most recent amendments. Critical voices might, after all, point out that all it does is to bring conceptual confusion to what amounts to a relatively simple task of description.

Such criticism is inappropriate for two reasons. The first one I have already discussed. An institutional framework is useful to assess the dynamic nature of the Community's environmental policy. Through the process of institutionalisation, the participants' behaviour gradually converges around the established rules. These rules, in turn, evolve as a reflection of the participants' experiences during the process of institutionalisation. In that sense, what has been labelled the tradition of neo-liberal institutionalism provides us with the conceptual tools to understand how a number of ad hoc environmental measures can, over time, evolve into an international regime or, what Oran Young calls a 'negotiated order' [*Young, 1983: 99*].

The second reason why regime or institutional approaches are useful is perhaps even more significant. To study and explain the formation and the maintenance of an international institutional arrangement is important. Many students of international relations have, in recent years, been preoccupied with this problem. It is now time, however, to move on to the next stage and assess the effectiveness of international regimes. Do regimes matter? This is a fundamental question. In the long term, the emphasis on international institutions can only be justified if it is possible to demonstrate that there is a link between 'institutional arrangements on the one hand and individual and collective behaviour on the other' [*Young, 1992: 160*].

Very little work has been done in this area. The ideas emerging out of the institutional literature are probably the most promising ones to follow up. As Oran Young has pointed out,

> 'we must look at the behaviour of states not only in responding to the dictates of international institutions on their own behalf but also in implementing the provisions of regimes in such a way as to ensure that those operating under their jurisdiction (for example, corporations, non-governmental organizations, and even individuals) comply with institutional requirements as well' [*Young, 1992: 161–2*].

This brings the concept of compliance to the forefront of future international institutional studies. To determine when and to what extent international regimes matter, systematic studies need to be undertaken that take into account both domestic and international variables. The conclusion that the European Community's environmental policy has reached the state of an international regime is therefore no cause for complacency. In many ways the task has only just begun. We are, after all, not dealing with an obscure intellectual puzzle. The issue at hand is the increasing threat to our environment. It is in our immediate interest to start examining the effectiveness of the European Community's environmental regime as one of the available institutional arrangements to address this situation. The first set of conceptual guideposts has been provided by the advocates of international institutional approaches. It certainly seems worthwhile and, for the time being, promising to try to build on them.

NOTES

1. The first time '1992' was officially mentioned was in the Commission president's statement to the European Parliament on 14 January 1985. Referring to the next European Council, he said: 'now that some Heads of State and Government have decided to set an example ... it may not be over-optimistic to announce a decision to eliminate all frontiers within Europe by 1992 and to implement it' (Commission, of the European Communities (1985b), 'The Thrust of Commission Policy', Bulletin of the European Communities, Supplement 1/85, 14 and 15 January. The idea was formally approved by the Brussels European Council on 29–30 March 1985 and adopted in December 1985 in Luxembourg. See Lodge 1989: 9.
2. The terms 'European' and 'European Community' are used interchangeably throughout this article. When referring to other parts of Europe, the proper specification will be made; i.e. 'Eastern European', 'Southern Europe', and so on.
3. Article 189, Treaty Establishing the European Economic Community as Amended by Subsequent Treaties. Rome, 25 March, 1957; subsequently referred to as Treaty of Rome.
4. See also, House of Lords' Select Committee on the European Communities Transfrontier Shipment of Hazardous Wastes, 9th Report Session 1983–1984, HMSO.
5. It remains to be seen whether the changes incorporated in the Maastricht treaty, creating a European Union will, in itself, represent a new phase of Community environmental policy or follow in the footsteps of this third phase. I will briefly comment on this question in the final section on Maastricht.
6. Citation translated by author
7. Gaston Schul Judgement of 1982, Case 15/18, 1982 ECR 1409, p.1431.
8. For a thorough discussion of the legal details of Article 100 and Article 235 see Rehbinder and Steward [1985: 21–8].
9. Directive 67/548 EEC of 27 June 1967 on classification, packaging and labelling of dangerous substances, JO No.196, 16.8.1967, p.1 (French ed.).
10. Directive 69/81 EEC of 13 March 1969 modifying the directive of 16.8.1976 on classification, packaging and labelling of dangerous substances, JO No.L68, 19.3.1969, p.1 (French ed.).
11. OJ No.C112, 20. 12. 1973, p.3. See also Seventh General Report of the EC (Brussels, 1973), point 258; Bulletin of the EC, 11–1974, point 1203, pp.11–12.
12. 7th Report EC, 1973, point 258, p.235.
13. See OJ No C112, 20. 12. 73, p.5.
14. 7th Report EC, 1973, point 262.
15. OJ No.C112, p.7.
16. 7th Report EC, 1973, point 263.
17. Ibid., point 264.
18. OJ No.C139, 13.6.1977; Bulletin EC 5–1977, point 2.1.40.
19. See, 'State of the Environment: First Report', 1977.
20. Action Programme of the European Communities on the Enviroment (1982 to 1986) in OJ No.C46, 17. 2. 1983, p.1.
21. OJ No.C46, 17. 2. 1983, p.3.
22. Seventeenth General Report on the Activities of the European Communities, 1983, point 372, p.158.

23. See OJ No.C46, p.2.
24. In December 1986, the Council adopted a resolution on the strengthening of Community action in favour of the environment in which it welcomed 'the submission by the Commission of detailed proposals for a Fourth Environmental Action Programme and considers that such a programme provides an opportunity to strengthen decisively Community action in this area, building on the achievements of the past, and to determine a coherent framework within which specific Community actions can be formulated, coordinated and implemented over the period of 1987–1992'. It also refers to the SEA which 'will constitute a new legal basis for the Community environmental policy'. OJ No.C3, 7. 1. 1987, p.3.
25. See, Pearson Report, Bericht der Kommission für Internationale Entwicklung, Wien, München, Zürich, 1969, pp.48–51.
26. By the time of the Paris Summit, the adherence to the Community of the United Kingdom, Ireland and Denmark was already decided. Weizsäcker argues that one of the objectives of the 1972 Action Programme was to get it through and then present it to the new Member States as a 'fait accompli'.
27. For a discussion of the German example see Müller [1986: 97–102].
28. It is worth noting that 1982 was also the year when the Greens were first elected to the German 'Bundestag'.
29. The total number environmental legislative pieces for the entire second phase amounts to 120 directives, 27 decisions and 14 regulations.
30. Directive 75/440, OJ No.L194, p.26; Directive 80/778, OJ No.L229, 30. 08. 1980, p.11; Directive 76/160, OJ No.L31, 05. 02. 1976, p.1.
31. Directive 76/464, OJ No.L129, 18. 05. 1976, p.23.
32. Directive 80/779, OJ No.L229, 30. 08. 1980; Directive 82/884, OJ No.L378, 31. 12. 1982; Directive 85/203, OJ No.L87, 27. 03. 1985, p.1.
33. Directive 75/442, OJ No.L194, 25. 07. 1975, p.39; Directive 78/319, OJ No.L84, 31. 03. 1978, p.43; Directive 84/631, OJ No.L326, 13. 12. 1984, p.31.
34. Directive 83/351, OJ No.L197, 20. 07. 1983, p.1; Directive 84/360, OJ No.L188, 16. 07. 1984, p.20.
35. Directive 85/210, OJ No.L96, 03. 04. 1985, p.25; Directive 78/611, OJ No.L197, 22. 07. 1978, p.19.
36. Directive 79/831, OJ No.L259, 15. 10. 1979, p.10; Directive 67/548, OJ No.L196, 16. 08. 1967; Directive 79/117, OJ No.L33, 08. 02. 1979, p.36.
37. Directive 79/409, OJ No.L103, 25. 04. 1979, p.1.
38. Directive 82/501, OJ No.L230, 05. 08. 1982, p.1; Directive 85/337, OJ No.L175, 05. 07. 1985, p.40.
39. Commission of the EC, Completing the Internal Market: White Paper from the Commission of the European Council (the Cockfield White Paper), Luxembourg, 1985.
40. Although the phrase 'Single European Market' has come into widespread use, it is not used in the SEA. It simply combines the SEA and the internal market, at the expense of conferring the original meaning of the word 'Single' in the SEA 'which was so called because it combined in a single legal instrument two texts that had different origins, one amending the Treaty of Rome (Title II) and one dealing with cooperation in the sphere of foreign policy'. See Haigh and Baldock [1989: 10].
41. For a detailed discussion of the 'cooperation procedure' see Lodge [1989: 68–79].
42. This is illustrated by the case of Directive 88/76 on Emissions from small cars. See Haigh and Baldock, 1989: 51–54.
43. Titanium dioxide is a white pigment, generally thought to be harmless. It is used in paints, plastic and other products in order to reduce reliance on toxic substances such as lead and zinc. The problem is that its manufacture results in the discharge of acid waste contaminated by metals. EC legislation on titanium dioxide dates back as far as the early 1970s.
44. Regulation 3143/87 OJ No.L299, 22. 10. 1978, p.33; Regulation 3626/82 OJ No.L384, 31. 12. 1982, p.1; Directive 88/302 OJ No.L133, 30. 05. 1988, p.1.

45. Directive 87/416 OJ No.L225, 13. 08. 1987, p.33; Directive 85/210 OJ No.L96, 03. 04.
     1985, p.25.
46. Directive 88/347 OJ No.L158, 25. 06. 1988, p.35; Directive 86/280 OJ No.L181, 04. 07.
     1986, p.16.
47. Regulation 3322/88 OJ No.L297, 31. 10. 1988, p.1.
48. Directive 90/219 OJ No.L117, 08. 05. 1990, p.1.
49. Directive 90/415 OJ No.L219, 14. 08. 1990, p.49.
50. Directive 88/76; Directive 88/77; Directive 88/436; Directive 70/220; Directive 90/220.
51. Bulletin of the European Community, Supplement 1/92, p.30.
52. On British insistence, the term of 'co-decision procedure' has been dropped from the
     treaty. Interestingly enough, this has not deterred Jacques Delors from using it. See
     Bulletin of the European Community, Supplement 1/92, p.31.

REFERENCES

Bechmann, Arnim (1984), *Leben wollen*, Köln.
Haigh, Nigel (1990), *EEC Environmental Policy and Britain*, 2nd revised edition, Essex:
    Longman.
Haigh, Nigel and David Baldock (1989), *Environmental Policy and 1992*, London: British
    Department of the Environment.
Hartkopf, Günther and Eberhard Bohme (1983), *Umweltpolitik, Band 1: Grundlagen,
    Analysen und Perspektiven*, Opladen.
Johnson, Stanley P. and Guy Corcelle (1989), *The Environmental Policy of the European
    Communities* (International Environmental Law and Policy Series), London: Graham
    & Trotman.
Keck, Otto (1991), 'Der neue Institutionalismus in der Theorie der Internationalen Politik',
    Politische Viertelsjahresschrift, 32, Jahrgang, Heft 4, pp.635–53.
Keohane, Robert O. (1989), *International Institutions and State Power: Essays in Inter-
    national Relations Theory*, Boulder, Co: Westview Press.
Lodge, Juliet (1989), 'Environment: Towards a Clean Blue-Green EC', in Juliet Lodge
    (ed.), *The European Community and the Challenge of the Future*, London: Pinter.
McCarthy, Elmaire (1989), *The EC and the Environment*, European Dossier Service II.
McGrory, Daniel P. (1990), 'Air Pollution Legislation in the United States and the
    European Community', *European Law Review*, Vol.15, No.4, Aug.
Müller, Eda (1986), *Innenwelt der Umweltpolitik*, Opladen.
Rehbinder, Eckard and Richard Steward (eds.) (1985), *Environmental Protection Policy,
    Volume 2, Integration Through Law: Europe and the American Federal Experience*,
    Firenze: European University Institute.
Sands, Philippe (1990), 'European Community Environmental Law: Legislation, the ECJ
    and Common Interest Groups', *Modern Law Review*, Vol. 53, No. 5, Sept., p.685.
Teitgen, Pierre-Henri and Colette Mégret (1981), 'La fumée de la cigarette dans la "zone
    grise" des competences de la C.E.E.', *Revue Trimestrielle de Droit Européen*, 68.
Vandermeersch, Dirk (1987), 'The Single European Act and the Environmental Policy of
    the European Economic Community', *European Law Review*, Vol.12, No.6.
Wägenbaur, Rolf (1990), 'The Single Market Programme and the Protection of the
    Environment', in *Environmental Protection and the Impact of European Community
    Law*, Papers from the Joint Conference with the Incorporated Law Society of Ireland,
    Dublin: Irish Centre for European Law.
Weizsäcker, Ernst U. von (1989), *Erdpolitik. Oekologische Realpolitik an der Schwelle zum
    Jahrhundert der Umwelt*, Darmstadt: Wissenschaftliche Buchgesellschaft.
Wilkinson, David (1991), 'Eurovision Conquest', *The Guardian*, 29 Nov.
Wolf, Julie (1991), 'Environmentalists Bemoan Watered Down Draft Chapter', *The
    Guardian*, 7 Dec.
Young, Oran R. (1983), 'Regime Dynamics: The Rise and Fall of International Regimes',

in Krasner, Stephen (ed.) (1983), *International Regimes*, Ithaca, NY: Cornell University Press.

Young, Oran R. (1992), 'The Effectiveness of International Institutions: Hard Cases and Critical Variables', in James N. Rosenau and Ernst-Otto Czempiel (eds.) (1992), *Governance without Government: Order and Change in World Politics*, Cambridge: Cambridge University Press.

Between Economy and Ecology?
The Single Market and the Integration of
Environmental Policy

ALBERT WEALE and ANDREA WILLIAMS

For a number of years influential voices in the international environmental policy community, including policy-makers in the European Community, have been calling for the integration of environmental considerations into the making of economic policy. Despite acknowledgements in formal statements of the importance of environmental policy integration in the Community and the attempt by policy-makers to argue that environmental protection was a precondition for sustainable economic growth, the programme to complete the single European market was developed without consideration of its environmental implications. The reasons for this involve a complex mix of intellectual, organisational and political factors. Moreover, the failure to achieve an integration of environmental considerations into the making of economic policy creates its own political dynamics, having three main features: disjointed decision-making in the formulation of common technical standards across the EC; pressure from countries who are environmental leaders to bring laggards up to common standards; and the search by environmental policy-makers for bureaucratic alliances to reinforce their position.

As environmental policy developed over the 1970s and the 1980s an increasing number of influential voices began to call for its integration or coordination with other sectors of public policy.[1] Recognising that many environmental problems have their origins in activities like transport, agriculture and tourism, as well as in manufacturing processes, the argument was that successful environmental policy was not simply a matter of environment ministries implementing their own policies and priorities, but also of other ministries recognising that there was an environmental dimension to their work. This line of argument received authoritative endorsement by the World Commission on Environment and Development in its report *Our Common Future*, usually known as the 'Brundtland Report', which in its discussion of the institutional changes needed to secure sustainable development, urged that 'the major central economic and sectoral agencies of governments should now be made directly responsible and fully accountable for ensuring that their policies, programmes, and budgets support development that is ecologically as well as economically sustainable' [*World Commission on Environment and Development, 1987: 314*].

Although the theme of environmental policy integration had become a popular one with many policy elites during the 1980s, there is in fact no canonical statement of what precisely it might involve and those concerned to advance the idea of integrated environmental policy have typically had a range of rather disparate problems in mind [*Weale, O'Riordan and Kramme, 1991: 5–13*]. However, for our present purposes, we shall follow Arild Underdal and refer to a policy as integrated when the consequences for that policy are recognised as decision premises, aggregated into an overall evaluation and incorporated at all policy levels and into all government agencies involved in its execution [*Underdal, 1980: 162*]. On this definition, environmental policy is integrated into public policy generally when decision-makers in other policy sectors take into account environmental consequences in the making of their decisions and make suitable adjustments to their plans and the execution of those plans when environmental implications are recognised.

The endorsement offered by the Brundtland Report for environmental policy integration is only one expression, albeit a highly influential one, of arguments that had been advanced by a range of official bodies over a number of years. Thus, as early as 1969, in his message establishing the US Environmental Protection Agency, President Nixon asserted that for the purposes of pollution control the environment should be perceived as a single interrelated system, and that the task of policy was to identify pollutants, trace their paths through the ecological chain and intervene to prevent damage at the most appropriate point (cited in Council on Environmental Quality [*1985: 10*]). In its First Action Programme on the Environment, the European Community (EC) asserted that Community activities in different sectors, including agriculture, social policy, industrial policy and energy policy should take account of concern for the protection and improvement of the environment [*Official Journal of the EC, 1973: 11*]. Subsequent action programmes became more explicit, so that one of the top priorities listed in the Fourth Programme, covering the period 1987 to 1992, was the integration of environmental considerations into other policy sectors [*Official Journal of the European Communities, 1987*].

By the late 1990s these concerns were finding their way into definite plans by governments to reform environmental administration and policy. The UK government stressed the need for environmental policy integration in its 1990 white paper on environmental policy [*Cm 1200, 1990*], and in the previous year the Dutch government launched perhaps the most ambitious attempt to integrate environmental considerations into the making of public policy with its *National Environmental Policy Plan [1989]*, which set quantitative targets for the reduction of pollution flows over a 20-year period and which was signed by the economics, transport and agriculture ministries in addition to the environment ministry (for a discussion see Weale [*1992: 125–53*]).

During the 1980s this well-established theme of environmental policy became associated with a new twist in the logic of environmental discourse. This new twist, we would argue, was to relate the theme of integration to a wider set of ideas, which may be identified by the term 'ecological modernisation'. Ecological modernisation is a complex belief system which, for a variety of reasons, became attractive to many policy elites in Europe and elsewhere in the 1980s. One of its chief tenets is that environmental protection should be seen not as being in competition with economic growth and development, but instead as an essential precondition for such growth and development. In terms of this argument, 'sustainable development' was defined in the Brundtland Report as development which met the needs of present generations without compromising the ability of future generations to meet their own needs [*World Commission on Environment and Development, 1987: 43*]. On this account, economic and other public policies that ignored harmful environmental effects on grounds of cost did not in the end avoid those costs but merely displaced them across space or time, so that, for example, lax pollution controls applied in one generation meant that subsequent generations had to incur increased clean-up costs. Policies for economic development and policies to protect the environment, on this analysis, should be seen as complementary to one another rather than as rivals.

Environmental policy makers in the EC were among the main contributors to this ideology of ecological modernisation among European policy elites. As successive environmental action programmes were developed within the Commission, those framing the policy began to stress the importance of stringent environmental standards in a period of global economic competition, in which standards were determined by Japan and the United States of America, as well as underlining the importance of quality of life considerations for skilled workers.

The development of the theme is apparent in the contrast between the initial Action Programme of 1973, which was largely concerned with the problems that different national environmental regulations might cause for the creation of a single EC market, and the Third Action Programme, which was motivated 'by the observation that the resources of the environment are the basis of – but also constitute the limits to – further economic and social development and the improvement of living standards' [*Official Journal of the European Communities, 1983: 3*].

In adopting the Third Action Programme, the Council explicitly recognised the benefits that environmental protection could offer the EC in terms of greater competitiveness, stressing that 'account should be taken of the economic and social aspects of environmental policy, and particularly of its potential to contribute to the easing of current economic problems, including unemployment' [*Official Journal of the European Communities, 1983: 1*]. This theme was taken up and developed in the Fourth Environmental Action Programme, with the claim that 'the protection of the environment can help to improve economic growth and facilitate job creation' [*Commission of the European Communities, 1986: 4*], a view that had been argued by representatives of the Commission to the House of Lords enquiry on the Fourth Programme in its 1986–87 sittings [*HL 135, 1987: 53–4*].

According to the logic of ecological modernisation, an essential element in the marriage of environmental and economic concerns is the integration of environmental considerations into the making of public policy across a number of policy sectors. In the Council's resolution on the Third Environmental Action Programme, it was asserted that 'making the most economic use of the natural resources offered by the environment requires the preventive side of environmental policy to be strengthened in the framework of an overall strategy and environmental considerations to be integrated into other Community policies' [*Official Journal of the European Communities, 1983: 2*]. The programme went on to assert the need to integrate concern for the environment into the planning and development of economic activities as much as possible in order to promote an overall strategy making environmental policy a part of economic and social development, with the intention that such integration should result in a greater awareness of the environmental dimension of developments in other policy sectors, most notably agriculture, energy, industry, transport and tourism. Moreover, by the time of the Fourth Programme, the Community was able to rely upon the Single European Act, which laid down not only that environmental policy should be based on the principles of prevention and the polluter pays, but also on the principle that environmental protection requirements 'shall be a component of the Community's other policies ...' [*Official Journal of the European Communities, 1987: 3*].

In adopting these principles policy makers within the EC, particularly in the directorate-general responsible for environmental policy, DG XI, were both responding to and contributing towards the development of the ideology of ecological modernisation. Yet, despite the formal stress placed upon the integration of environmental concerns into the making of a wide range of EC policies, it can be argued that the implementation of integration has been a faltering and haphazard affair, without serious resonance in the central policy activities of the EC. The most striking example of this implementation deficit is provided by the Commission's programme to complete the single market by the end of 1992. The policy processes associated with the planning and implementation of the completion of the internal market went ahead without any consideration being paid to its environmental implications until 1989, when a task-force was hastily assembled to report on the matter. Although it is clear that the completion of the single market will have both positive and negative environmental consequences, these were not recognised as decision premises in the creation of the single market programme nor were these anticipated consequences aggregated and evaluated along with the other dimensions of the programme. In this sense there was no integration of environmental policy in the programme to create the single market.

This absence of an environmental dimension to the single market programme is particularly striking given the fact that regulations on products and processes are potentially one of the ways in which non-tariff barriers to trade can be erected between member countries of the EC. By imposing environmental protection standards on the supply of goods and services it is possible for governments to protect their own national industries at the expense of foreign competitors. Hence, any programme concerned with the removal of non-tariff barriers to trade ought logically to be concerned with environmental protection and pollution control policies. In practice, the environmental concerns of the Community were placed at the margins of the single market programme.

In this study we seek to identify the character of the processes that led to the marginalisation of environmental considerations in this way, despite the formal recognition of the importance of environmental policy integration in the Single European Act. We aim also to examine what the effects of the process so far are likely to be upon the political dynamics of environmental policy-making within the EC. We argue, in particular, that the creation of the single market has implications not only for the environment itself but also for the way in which policy for the environment is made and that for this reason attention needs to be paid as much to the processes by which the rules of the policy game are formulated and developed as to the substantive development of environmental policy within those rules.

The Single Market Programme

The programme to complete the internal market has as its aim the intention to remove barriers to trade between member states of the EC. In essence the idea is that the movement of goods, capital and labour should be no more difficult between any two member states of the EC than it currently is between, say, Scotland and England. The elements of the programme were set out in the Commission's 1985 White Paper [*Commission of the European Communities, 1985*]. The White Paper contained both the rationale of the programme in terms of the anticipated benefits that the Commission believed would flow from the completion of the internal market, as well as a timetable according to which the individual measures that make up the programme should be handled.

Although obviously a matter of the highest political priority within the EC in the 1980s, the single market programme is less remarkable for the substance of its policy measures than for the way in which those measures were organised and packaged. Virtually all of the substantive measures had been under discussion for some time, and the commissioner responsible for the programme, Lord Cockfield, would not have been able to present the white paper within a few months of taking office had the various specific proposals not been under active development within the EC bureaucracy [*George, 1991: 163*]. Thus, the political success of the Commission was in taking a number of disparate and often rather specific measures and building momentum and political capital around their implementation. One way in which this packaging is accomplished is in terms of a threefold classification of the individual measures by reference to whether they are aimed at physical, fiscal or technical barriers to trade. As Pelkmans and Winters [*1988: 10*] point out, the third of these groups is a residual category into which everything else is fitted that cannot be classified as either physical or fiscal.

Two key political changes were necessary in order to sustain the momentum for the single market programme. The first of these was the acceptance of the principle of mutual recognition. According to this principle if agreement cannot be secured on uniform rules to govern trade within the Community, then any standard that is acceptable in one country should be acceptable in all. Although there are one or two exceptions to the scope of this principle (lawyers for example will still be required to gain qualifications in the country in which they intend to practise), its broad application has succeeded in breaking the deadlock that was implicit in the attempt to harmonise a wide range of national standards. The second key political change was the switch to qualified majority voting in the Council of Ministers for measures aimed at the completion of the internal market. This change of voting rules has enabled the Community to escape the conservative consequences of the Luxembourg compromise, under which any country could effectively veto a proposal that it thought to be against its vital national interest [*George, 1991: 11–12*].

The project to complete the internal market has undoubtedly contributed to its major aim, namely to provide the EC with direction and momentum at a time when, in the early 1980s, it was widely felt that progress had slowed. Its intellectual rationale was provided by the Commission's research programme on the costs of non-Europe, although the research was undertaken after the main lines of the single market programme had been laid down in the 1985 White Paper. This research programme ran from 1986 to 1988, and was headed by Paolo Cecchini, hence the naming of the published research as the 'Cecchini Report'. The report itself comprises a series of studies carried out by consultants under commission. The overall aim of the report was to establish the economic costs of the EC's market fragmentation, thus providing an estimate of the potential benefits from their removal, by analysing the impact of market barriers and by comparing Europe's position with North American experience [*Commission of the European Communities, 1988f*]. The report offers both an analysis by specific sectors of the economy (public procurement, telecommunications and so on) and a general estimate of the economic losses associated with the absence of a single market.

According to the Cecchini Report existing barriers to trade added to the costs of European production, and the removal of those barriers would add something like seven per cent per annum to the Community's gross domestic product. Removal of these barriers was therefore justified on grounds of economic efficiency. The sources of existing inefficiencies were to be found in transactions costs created by the existence of non-Europe, of which the most obvious example is the time and expense of border crossings, as well as the failure to exploit economies of scale that could be secured within a market of 340 million persons.

In 1989 the Commission established a task-force whose aim was to complement the Cecchini Report with a study of the environmental dimensions of 1992, and which reported in the same year in a document entitled *1992: The Environmental Dimension [Task-Force on the Environment and the Internal Market, 1989]*. The task-force report can thus be regarded as Chapter 17 of the Cecchini Report. The task-force followed the train of thinking that is implicit in the ideology of ecological modernisation, and asserted that the modernisation of the economy implied by the single market programme could be turned to the advantage of environmental protection:

the Single Market will set in train a fundamental restructuring of the Community economy which will involve a modernisation and renewal of its infrastructure. In a sense this constitutes a 'new beginning' since the Community will have a historic opportunity to ensure that these changes take full account of the environmental dimension [*Task-Force on the Environment and the Internal Market, 1989: II*].

This quotation provides a good example of how those concerned with environmental policy seek to appropriate the language of economic modernisation and harness it to the cause of environmental protection. Yet, despite this assertion, the task-force was able to identify a number of negative environmental implications from the implementation of the programme to complete the internal market as well as positive ones that it asserted would flow from the completion of the internal market.

The first of these negative implications relates to the increase in production that would be generated by the internal market. In the absence of any countervailing measures, an increase in production could be expected to increase waste flows proportionately. This stress upon waste flows reflects the general experience of policy-makers in the 1980s. One of the disappointing features of existing legislative attempts to curb pollution is that measures that are successful in reducing pollutants from a particular source may not reduce the aggregate pollution burden, because the point-source reduction is more than outweighed by increases in volume. Thus, German policy-makers found that air quality in respect of nitrogen oxides did not improve in the 1980s, despite the introduction of controls, because of increased traffic flows. From a perspective of ecological modernisation therefore it is appropriate to lay stress on these volume aspects, and the Dutch *National Environmental Policy Plan [1989: 105]* has as one of its principal goals an increase in the quality of products rather than an increase in their quantity.

The removal of physical barriers provides another area where the task-force anticipated negative environmental effects. Along with other elements of the 1992 package, the removal of customs and border controls would increase road haulage and road traffic more generally, with transfrontier lorry traffic likely to increase by 30–50 per cent. Moreover, the removal of border controls would involve rethinking the controls on trade in endangered species, as well as reducing the constraints on the transfrontier shipment of hazardous waste.

Both fiscal harmonisation and the breaking down of technical barriers have implications for environmental policy. In some countries the harmonisation of taxes would lead to a reduction in the tax burden on potentially polluting products, and in other countries harmonisation might lead to the elimination of tax advantages that environmentally friendly products now enjoy – for example, on cars fitted with catalytic converters. Moreover, the elimination of technical barriers carries the possibility that countries would not be able to prevent environmentally damaging products from being sold in their national markets without being in breach of Community policy.

The conclusions of the task-force about the likely effects of the completion of the internal market are, of course, self-confessedly estimates about what is likely to happen. The amount of time and the resources that it had available were not sufficient for it to undertake a proper environmental impact assessment. The process of policy-making for the single market illustrates vividly therefore the failure of the Commission to integrate environmental considerations with other sectors of public policy. The example is not unique. The common agricultural policy, with its tendency to encourage intensive farming leading to nitrate pollution, provides another example. However, given the centrality of the single market to the Commission's policy strategy in the late 1980s, the example of the single market is a particularly telling one. In the next section we offer a tentative account of the structural and institutional conditions under which this lack of integration could arise.

The Failure of Integration

In seeking to account for the failure of the Commission to integrate environmental considerations into the creation of the single market programme, it is useful to consider the relevant factors in three distinct categories: intellectual, organisational and political [*Weale, O'Riordan and Kramme, 1991: Ch. 3*].

Intellectual Factors

The role of intellectual factors in the making of public policy has been recently stressed in a number of studies. In particular, Majone [*1989*] has shown that intellectual and cognitive factors play a crucial role in the shaping of public policies by defining the core assumptions in terms of which problems are defined and constructed. Similarly, Sabatier [*1986*] has argued that implementation failures often occur in public policies because of mistakes in cause and effect assumptions made by policy makers about how the world works. The Cecchini Report itself acknowledges the importance of intellectual factors:

> the overall outcome of the research, which points to very significant gains to be derived from European integration, seem to be both

accurate and reasonable. It is highly unlikely that the intellectual input of so many leading consultants, academics, officials and independent experts would unanimously be pointing in the wrong direction. [*Commission of the European Communities, 1988a: 561*].

This suggests that we should look at the intellectual assumptions that underlay the logic of Cecchini, and in particular at the characteristic policy biases to be expected from those assumptions.

The general failure of the Cecchini Report to consider the environmental dimensions of its analysis can be documented in a number of examples. Ernst and Whinney's examination of the road haulage sector [*Commission of the European Communities, 1988b: 183–272*] was intended to evaluate the cost of empty journeys and the effects of permitting cabotage (the ability of the carrier from one country to carry goods in other countries) and easing permits restrictions. The environmental consequences in terms of increased noise and pollution from a growth in the volume of heavy transport are not discussed at all, nor are the potentially positive environmental consequences mentioned if cabotage managed to cut the number of heavy goods vehicle journeys. The section on public procurement looked at building and civil engineering, mentioning the likely cost savings in specialist activities like tunnelling and airport building, without making any references to environmental impact assessments [*Commission of the European Communities, 1988c: 32*], whilst the case studies focused largely on industries related to the generation of power, such as coal and turbine generators, without any mention of environmental standards [*Commission of the European Communities, 1988c: 611–39*].

However, the most significant influence of intellectual factors is not to be found in the simple neglect of particular topics within the scope of what was covered, but instead in the analytical techniques in terms of which the policy problems are constructed. The intellectual assumptions of the Cecchini Report derive from the mainstream of applied neo-classical economics, in which economic welfare is conceptualised as the sum of the market value of goods and services. As has been stressed on a number of occasions, such assumptions make no allowance for the valuation of environmental goods like clean air or biodiversity. Since these goods are not privately owned, their valuation does not enter conventional national income accounts and in consequence their degradation is not assigned an economic value. Thus, Pearce, Markandya and Barbier [*1989: 4–7*] argue that the integration of environmental and economic concerns is necessary to prevent overconsumption of natural resources that provide economic services. But they also point out [*Pearce, Markandya and Barbier, 1989: 116*] that national income accounting in the UK, in common with all other developed economies, has made no real effort to deal with the issues of valuing changes in the natural resource base.

The critique by Pearce *et al.* may seem like a relatively technical question to be discussed among economists particularly since their work is within that tradition of neo-classical economics which goes back to Pigou's [*1920*] discussion of corrections for externalities. None the less it raises fundamental issues about the conventional practices of national income accounting as these have been developed over the course of the twentieth century and as they were presupposed in the Cecchini Report. To insist, as do Pearce *et al.* that the valuation of environmental resources needs to be incorporated into national income accounting is to allow for the possibility of market failure in the securing of economic welfare, and it therefore introduces a rationale for public regulation of markets to correct such failure. The Cecchini Report, by contrast, is premissed on the proposition that it is barriers to trade that need to be reduced and, in this context, public intervention in markets to protect perceived national economic interests is a problem to be overcome. In short, the difference of emphasis is between that version of neo-classical economics that draws attention to market failure in achieving maximum social welfare and that version that draws attention to government failure, particularly as a result of interventions in the functioning of markets.

From the point of view of the Pigovian tradition in economic analysis, the most subtle bias of the Cecchini Report was, therefore, not in overlooking the environmental dimensions of the creation of the single market, but in failing to note that estimates of the gains in economic welfare to be expected from the single market would need to be corrected for the increasing externalities that would thereby be produced. One consequence of this is that at various points the Cecchini Report is critical of just the corrective measures for externalities that a broader Pigovian approach would encompass. An example of this is contained in the discussion of fiscal barriers to trade in the automobile sector [*Commission of the European Communities, 1988d*]. This was critical of the practice in The Netherlands and Germany of tax incentives to encourage consumers to buy vehicles that conformed to high emission standards. Similar shots are aimed at packaging laws to encourage recycling, most notably the Danish law requiring beer and other beverages to be sold in returnable bottles [*Commission of the European Communities, 1988e: 368–93*].

Organisational Factors

Organisational constraints on decision-making and policy formation are all pervasive, stemming from basic social psychological features of the policy-making process. Among these features the most important are the limited time and attention that policy-makers have to scan problems with which they are familiar, and the practice of handling business according to standard operating procedures. Moreover, since the efficiency of bureaucracy depends upon the breaking down of activity into distinct and separate spheres of competence, it is hardly surprising that no part of the bureaucratic machine is capable of taking a synoptic viewpoint. Looked at in this way, the simplest model of organisational process in policy making, as developed in the work of Simon [1957], Lindblom [1959] and Allison [1971] is sufficient to explain the failure to integrate environmental policy into other sectors of public policy, including the single market process.

Limits on attention span are reinforced by the predispositions of training and orientation that policy-makers have experienced, and the collective authors of the Cecchini Report were unlikely to perceive the importance of environmental factors, given their own technical backgrounds. The Steering Committee was largely staffed by economists, whilst Commission representatives and economic analysts came from the Directorate-General on Economics and Financial Affairs. Some Commission representatives came from the Directorate-General concerned with the Internal Market and Industrial Affairs, and two of the economic analysts came from the Directorate-General on Science, Research and Development. There was no representative from DG XI, the directorate-general responsible for environmental affairs. Given the composition of the Steering Committee it is hardly surprising that the focus of the report stressed the economic advantages of the removal of barriers to trade without engaging with the complications involved in environmental protection as a result. The Steering Committee thus provides another illustration of Allison's [1971: 176] aphorism to the effect that where you stand depends on where you sit.

In environment policy in the 1980s there were other factors at work that reinforced these general organisational constraints. The general increase in environmental concern among mass publics and policy-makers led the Commission to formulate a number of specific environmental measures in the 1980s that were handled as straightforward issues of policy development within DG XI. During the 1980s a whole series of new directives were passed on matters of urgent environmental priority including the discharge of dangerous substances to water, the transfrontier shipment of toxic waste, the use of sewage sludge in agriculture, air pollution from industrial plants, air quality standards for nitrogen dioxides and lead, the monitoring of forest damage, the control of asbestos and the regulation of major hazards (see Haigh [1989] for details). Moreover, many existing directives needed either amendment or supplementation. Thus organisational pressures of time and administrative resources would have made it difficult for DG XI to conduct the necessary inter-departmental diplomacy to secure the integration of environmental policy into other aspects of the Commission's work.

Moreover, as soon as Germany moved from the defensive to the offensive phase of its environmental policy in the early 1980s, it sought to use the European Community as a principal forum within which to pursue the international control of pollution [*Boehmer-Christiansen and Skea, 1990; Mueller, 1986*]. In consequence, much energy within DG XI and the Council of Environment Ministers was taken up with negotiation and bargaining over such issues as the Large Combustion Plant Directive, the politics of which dominated EC environmental debate in the 1980s.

The organisational pressures of business combined with the limitations of bureaucratic resources to reinforce the sectorisation of environmental policy. By the end of November 1991 DG XI had only about 160 officials working full time, and some 200 persons working on contract or secondment. Since the overall staff of the Commission is 15,000, the number of those responsible for the environment is relatively small [*HL 53-II, 1992: 2*]. In these circumstances it would be surprising if DG XI could mount an effective campaign to ensure that its concerns were included in the process of implementing the internal market.

Political Factors

The completion of the single market was a matter of high political priority for the EC during the 1980s. It was important not simply for its perceived effects, but also for the political role that it played in reestablishing the forward momentum of the Community after the apparent stagnation of the 1970s. Enlargement of the Community and the stagflation of the 1970s with its associated budgetary problems meant that in the 1970s the original impetus towards the completion of the internal market, which had had a propitious beginning with the early elimination of customs barriers and the erection of the common external tariff by 1968, had slowed down [*George, 1991: 158–60*]. The completion of the internal market promised, by contrast, to provide the EC with goals that were both challenging and achievable and thus promote the cause of European integration.

This political imperative was reinforced by a number of policy changes that were taking place within member states of the Community. The 1980–82 recession created in the minds of many members of national policy elites worries about European competitiveness in relation to Japan and the United States. In the post-Keynesian period of economic management, there was an increasing emphasis upon a supply-side approach to economic growth and improving the allocative efficiency of markets, instead of macroeconomic fiscal and expenditure stimulation. And business interests expressed their commitment to the development of the single market in the form of the Round Table of European Industrialists [*Pelkmans and Winter, 1988: 6–7*]. Behind these converging trends in policy thinking there lay longer-term developments in the structure of the European and global economies, leading to increased economic and industrial interdependence and the rise of global competition [*Garrett, 1992: 538–9*]. On the basis of these factors it became possible for European leaders in the early 1980s to construct a complex intergovernmental contract under which the completion of the internal market, representing the liberal programme of Mrs Margaret Thatcher, could go hand in hand with reform of the Community's decision-making powers favoured by France and Germany.

With this background, the single market programme was accorded high political priority at the Copenhagen meeting of the European Council on 3 December 1982. No doubt it also helped that the commissioner responsible for the programme was Lord Cockfield, who was not only temperamentally sympathetic to its liberal credentials but also close to Mrs Thatcher. Unlike many other Commission projects the single market programme would not encounter UK opposition; indeed, the UK was committed to taking a leading role in forwarding the policy. With this background it would be surprising if any attempt politically to question some of the premisses of the single market programme would have got very far. There was simply too much weight pushing in the opposite direction.

There are also difficult considerations of bureaucratic politics involved in the relations between the environment section of the bureaucracy and other sections. By common consent, environment departments are not heavyweight political actors. Though growing in importance in the 1980s, the environmental portfolio of the Commission is still relatively junior, whereas those directorate-generals responsible for the development of the single market programme were at the traditional centre of the Commission's activities – finance and industry. Neither at the level of practising politicians nor at the level of bureaucratic actors therefore is it realistic to expect representatives of environmental concerns to match the influence of other actors.

An illustration of these differences in bureaucratic power is provided by the struggle over the 1981 Danish drinks packaging law. This law requires that beer, soft drinks, mineral waters and lemonade only be marketed in returnable bottles, except for a fixed quota agreed in 1984 which allowed up to 300,000 litres per year to be sold in non-approved containers. The question was referred to the European Court of Justice by the Commission, after an internal bureaucratic dispute between DG XI on the one hand and DG III, with the responsibility for the internal market, on the other [*ENDS Report, 1988: 3–4*]. As it turned out, the Court, to everyone's general surprise, ruled that the Danes were not in breach of the Treaty of Rome, and that the 1987 Single European Act provided grounds for holding that the protection of the environment took priority over rules of free trade. The importance of the incident, in the present context, however, is that the internal power struggle within the Commission was won by DG III in the initial decision to refer Denmark to the Court. Thus, political factors made it difficult to challenge a programme whose essential features had already been established by powerful actors within the policy-making system.

General Features

Putting these three sets of factors together, it is clear that there are a number of factors that inhibit the integration of environmental concerns in the making of economic policy, and many of these factors combined in the case of the EC's single market programme. In essence, the analysis shows that whereas the ideology of ecological modernisation has served to justify more stringent environmental policy in its own traditional domain of the imposition of standards on the performance of polluting plant or processes, it is a wholly different matter to persuade policy makers outside the traditional domain of environmental policy to adopt environmental considerations as the premisses of their own decision-making.

But what are the likely consequences of the existence of this continuing disjunction between the demands of economic policy making on the one hand and environmental policy on the other? In the next section we look at the structure of the political dynamics that are being established in the relationship between the single market and environmental policy, in order to analyse how this question is likely to be answered in the future.

The Political Dynamics of Environment and the Single Market

In May 1991 the then EC Commissioner for the Environment, Mr Ripa di Meana, claimed that a turning-point had been reached in the EC, so that the Community was at 'a point where environment and the single market are on an equal footing', substantiating his assertion by reference to the plans for a carbon tax and for company environmental audits [*Gardner, 1991: 22*]. The failure of EC ministers to support Mr Ripa di Meana's proposals for a carbon tax to take to the UN summit in Rio and the evidence we have reviewed so far suggests that this assessment somewhat exaggerates the extent to which environmental policy is seen as on a par with economic policy. Yet, it is clear that the relationship between environmental policy and the single market is not one of simple antagonism. Three features of the Community's policy-making process stand out as being particularly relevant to this assessment.

First, the rule-making process provides scope for complementarity between the harmonisation provided by the policies for a single market and the imposition of high environmental standards. Before the Single European Act environmental policy competence had been based either on article 100 of the Treaty of Rome, dealing with harmonisation measures affecting the single market, or the catch-all article 235, which gave the Community competence in residual areas [*Macrory, 1991: 15*]. After the Single European Act, environmental measures could be passed either under the majority voting procedure of article 100A for measures dealing with the completion of the single market or under the unanimous voting procedures of article 130s. Because of the role of environmental policy in harmonising standards, the Commission has sometimes been able to present environmental measures to the Council of Ministers as part of the single market programme. Thus, in March 1991 four out of the nine measures considered by the environment ministers fell under this heading [*Gardner, 1991: 22*].

However, this potential for complementarity is not always so clearly realised. In 1991 the European Court of Justice determined a dispute between the Commission and the Council of Ministers when it decided that a directive on the control of pollution from titanium dioxide plants properly fell within the scope of article 100A, as the Commission had argued, rather than article 130s, as the Council of Ministers had held [*Macrory, 1991: 51*]. The substance of this judgement offers a generous interpretation of the single market harmonisation rule, but its political implications are as significant as its legal ones. The case clearly establishes that one of the principal issues in the process of rule-making is establishing the basis under which legislation can be passed. The Single European Act has thus provided an institutional basis in which competition can take place not simply over the substance of rules but also over the procedure for their adoption. One effect of this process will be to increase the influence of the Court in determining EC policy in those areas of contest between the internal market and environmental protection.

The second important feature of the political dynamics is that even a body of harmonised rules is subject to pressure. One source of this pressure is that public attitudes towards the environment and the political organisation of the environmental movement are not evenly distributed within member states. Countries like Denmark, Germany and The Netherlands in particular are subject to strong pressures from their domestic publics for ever greater stringency in the making of environmental policy, and this pressure is enhanced by the increasing political weight of environment ministries in those countries. Hence, even when there are agreed standards at the European level, there is pressure within those countries for tighter standards to be applied, especially when the EC standards have been the result of political compromise under the unanimous voting procedure in the Council of Ministers. The Danish bottles case illustrates one facet of this process, as does the practice by The Netherlands and Germany of granting tax concessions to cars fitted with a catalytic converter.

Moreover, public and policy pressure in these 'northern' states creates conditions in which new environmental standards are adopted that threaten access to domestic markets by firms from other countries. The most important contemporary example of this process is the German Packaging Ordinance, which establishes a compulsory elaborate system of control and responsibility for the packaging of goods, making suppliers of packaged materials responsible for the life cycle of the packaging. This has generated considerable fears in the European packaging industry outside Germany that the new legislation will establish barriers to trade. Meanwhile, the German packaging industry, anxious that it will be at a competitive disadvantage when the new packaging law is fully operational, is making moves to ensure that the EC adopts a version of the European law, thus replaying the game of the 1980s when the electricity supply industry pressured the German government into persuading the EC to adopt the Large Combustion Plant Ordinance.

The third feature of the political dynamics of the policy making process is the attempt by DG XI to create alliances between itself and other directorate-generals within the Commission. This was particularly important in the case of the proposals for the carbon tax, where the relationship between Mr Ripa di Meana and Mr Antonio Cardoso e Cunha, the commissioner responsible for energy, was important in the development of the policy [Lascelles, 1992: 16]. Similarly, the recent green paper on transport and the environment reveals this tendency to form alliances on the part of DG XI with other directorate-generals. It can be argued that the position of DG XI makes such a strategy almost imperative. Lacking the weight of a finance department, an environment department needs to develop collaborative working relationships between itself and those departments whose policies it is seeking to influence. Certainly, if the experience of the Dutch National Environmental Policy Plan is anything to go by, the necessity for collaborative relationships is essential to the prospects for successful policy integration.

The idea of environmental policy integration has been a central concept in the changing ideology of the environmental movement, and policy analysts have stressed its importance for the future development of environmental policy. The example of the single market programme shows that there are a number of intellectual, organisational and political barriers to its implementation. Thus, despite attempts by policy makers with responsibility for environmental policy to develop an ideology of ecological modernisation that could overcome the tension between economy and the environment, there is still an ambiguous and ambivalent relationship between the demands of economic competitiveness on the one hand and the demands of environmental protection and sustainable development on the other. This is not to say necessarily that environmental policy integration is a forlorn hope. It may merely be that the conditions for its success still need to be discovered. On the other hand it may be that the failure of the European Community to act in accordance with the principles of ecological modernisation shows that whatever its rhetorical appeal for policy elites, the aspiration to provide a middle way between economy and ecology cannot succeed. For better or worse, we shall only discover the answer once the single market and European integration have taken a few steps further forward.[2]

NOTES

1. The terminology varies from time to time and from place to place. Some people talk of 'integration', others of 'coordination' and yet others of 'harmonisation'. In Dutch policy discourse there is also the distinction between 'internal' integration (that is, ensuring that environmental policies cohere with one another) and 'external' integration (that is, making sure that environmental policies cohere with non-environmental policies). We prefer the term 'integration' and use it in the sense in which the Dutch speak of 'external integration'.
2. This study is the product of research funded by the Economic and Social Research Council under its Single European Market initiative. The project is entitled 'Environmental Standards and the Politics of Expertise in the Single European Market' (grant no. W113251025) and is being conducted jointly with Dr Pridham and Ms Michelle Cini of the University of Bristol. We should like to thank David Judge and Geoffrey Pridham for comments on an earlier version.

REFERENCES

Allison, Graham T. (1971), *Essence of Decision*, Boston, MA: Little, Brown & Co.
Boehmer-Christiansen, S. and J. Skea (1990), *Acid Rain*, London: Belhaven.
Cm 1200 (1990), *This Common Inheritance*, London: HMSO.

Commission of the European Communities (1985), *Completing the Internal Market*, COM(85) 310 final.

Commission of the European Communities (1986), *Fourth Environmental Action Programme*, COM (86) 485 final.

Commission of the European Communities (1988a), *Research on 'The Costs of Non-Europe', Vol.1, Basic Studies: Executive Summaries*.

Commission of the European Communities (1988b), *Research on 'The Costs of Non-Europe', Vol.4, Border-Related Controls and Administrative Formalities: An Illustration in the Road Haulage Sector*.

Commission of the European Communities (1988c), *Research on 'The Costs of Non-Europe': Basic Findings, Vol.5, 'The Costs of Non-Europe' in Public Sector Procurement*.

Commission of the European Communities (1988d), *Research on 'The Costs of Non-Europe': Basic Findings, Vol.11, The EC Automobile Sector*.

Commission of the European Communities (1988e), *Research on 'The Costs of Non-Europe': Basic Findings, Vol.12, part A, The 'Costs of Non-Europe in the Foodstuffs Industry'*.

Commission of the European Communities (1988f), *Research on 'The Costs of Non-Europe': Basic Findings, Vol.16, The Internal Markets of North America: Fragmentation and Integration in the US and Canada*.

Council on Environmental Quality (1985), *Environmental Quality*, Sixteenth Report, Washington, DC: Government Printing Office.

ENDS Report (1988), 'Landmark EEC Court Case on Returnable Bottles Gives Boost to Environment', No.164, Sept., pp.3–4.

Gardner, D. (1991), 'Green Hopes Rise in a Grey Area', *Financial Times*, 13 May 1991.

Garrett, G. (1992) 'International Cooperation and Institutional Choice: The European Community's Internal Market', *International Organisation*, Vol.46, No.2, pp.533–60.

George, Stephen (1991), *Politics and Policy in the European Community*, 2nd ed., Oxford: Oxford University Press.

Haigh, Nigel (1989), *EEC Environmental Policy and Britain*, 2nd ed., Harlow: Longman.

HL 135 (1987), Select Committee on the European Communities, *Fourth Environmental Action Programme with Evidence*, London: HMSO.

HL 53-II (1992), Select Committee on the European Communities *Implementation and Enforcement of Environmental Legislation Volume II Evidence*, London: HMSO.

Lascelles, David (1992), 'A Mission to Make the Polluters Pay', *Financial Times*, Tuesday, 8 Jan., p.16.

Lindblom, C.E. (1959), 'The Science of Muddling Through', *Public Administration Review*, Vol.19, pp.79–85.

Macrory, R. (1991), 'European Court Shakes up Legal Basis of EEC Environmental Policy', *ENDS Report*, No.197, pp.15–16.

Majone, G. (1989), *Evidence, Argument and Persuasion in the Policy Process*, New Haven, CT. Yale University Press.

Mueller, E. (1986), *Innenwelt der Umweltpoltik*, Opladen: Westdeutscher Verlag.

National Environmental, Policy Plan: To Choose or Lose (1989), Second Chamber of the States-General, The Hague: SDU uitgeverij.

Official Journal of the European Communities C112 (1973) 'Declaration of the Council of the European Communities and the Representatives of the Governments of the Member States meeting in the Council of 22 November 1973 on the Programme of Action of the European Communities on the Environment' 20 December 1973.

Official Journal of the European Communities (1983) C 46, 17 Feb. 1983, 'Resolution on the Continuation and Implementation of a European Community Policy and Action Programme on the Environment (1982–1986)'.

Official Journal of the European Communities (1987) C 328, 7 Dec. 1987, *Fourth Action Programme on the Environment*.

Pearce, D., Markandya, A. and B. Barbier (1989), *Blueprint for a Green Economy*, London: Earthscan Publications.

Pelkmans, J. and A. Winters (1988), *Europe's Domestic Market*, London: Routledge.

Pigou, A.C. (1920), *The Economics of Welfare*, London: Macmillan.

Sabatier, P.A. (1986), 'What Can We Learn from Implementation Research?', in F.-X. Kaufmann, V. Ostrom and G. Majone (eds.), *Guidance, Control and Performance Evaluation in the Public Sector*, Berlin: De Gruyter.

Simon, H.A. (1957), *Models of Man*, New York: John Wiley & Sons.

Task-Force on the Environment and the Internal Market (1989), *1992: The Environmental Dimension*, Luxembourg: Commission of the European Communities.

Underdal, Arild (1980), 'Integrated Marine Policy: What? Why? How?' *Marine Policy*, Vol.4, No.3, pp.159–69.

Weale, A., O'Riordan, T. and L. Kramme (1991), *Controlling Pollution in the Round*, London: Anglo-German Foundation.

Weale, A. (1992), *The New Politics of Pollution*, Manchester: Manchester University Press.

World Commission on Environment and Development (1987), *Our Common Future*, Oxford: Oxford University Press.

A Sound European Environmental Policy: Challenges, Possibilities and Barriers

JAN VAN DER STRAATEN

This study focuses on EC environmental policy, and its legal recognition as part of European policy with the signing of the Single European Act. The environmental policy of the EC has its roots in traditional neo-classical economic approaches, and emphasises the concept of the negative external effect, which should be neutralised by government policies. However, it is extremely difficult, and in many cases impossible, to give a market price to the environment. Traditional neo-classical economics focus on topics such as per capita income, employment and the level of production. This implies that environmental aims are very often marginalised by vested economic interests, and using these traditional arguments the polluting industries are not the weakest among these interests. In the EC this divergence between the interests of production on the one hand, and the unpriced production factor 'natural resources' on the other hand, has not been solved till now. The solution of this problem is only possible if labour and capital no longer misuse the production factor 'natural resources', but understand, both of them, that a sound environment favours production possibilities in the future. The Single European Act contains the conceptual framework to realise this understanding.

Before the signing of the Single European Act there was, as other contributors to this volume point out, an environmental policy of the European Community; but only with the SEA did environmental protection become a legally recognised part of European policy directly related to the principal aim of the EC – namely, the integration of the economies of the European countries. The purpose of this study, therefore, is to examine the relationship between environmental and economic policies and the implications of this relationship for the establishment of a sound environmental policy. Special attention is paid in the first section to the impact of traditional economic theories in the field of economic and environmental policies; in the second section the way in which the EC decision-making process itself affects the integration of environmental issues is considered; and in the third section attention is paid to the theoretical foundation of environmental policy. The fourth section then

This contribution was written before 'Maastricht'.

demonstrates the importance of non-EC institutions for the implementation of a sound environmental policy in Europe, and the final section examines the potential that the completion of the internal market holds for environmental protection.

The Underlying Economic Theoretical Paradigms of the European Community[1]

Classical economists believed that the value of a good is determined by the quantity of labour necessary to produce it (the 'labour theory of value'). The starting point in this theory is a constant quantity and quality of nature [*Ricardo, 1823*]. Production and consumption do not have a negative effect upon the quantity and quality of natural resources (*see* among others Dietz and Van der Straaten [*1990*]).

Classical economists base themselves also, however, on the law of diminishing returns (for exceptions see Dietz and Van der Straaten [*1992*]). According to this law, the production of goods will decrease in the course of time, in spite of an increasing input of production factors. The population theories of Malthus [*1798*] and the 'steady state' of J.S. Mill [*1886*] are derived from this law of diminishing returns. In this way of thinking natural resources are the key factor in the production process. One may therefore argue that classical economists have laid the basis for the theoretical insight that production involves three factors: labour, capital and natural resources.

It can be held in general that the dominant analytical framework for economics is now neo-classical theory. The key starting point in this framework is that economic value can be found in the market, where supply and demand meet. The market price is a reflection of the costs of producing the product and is also related to the subjective value for the consumer. This implies that the value of a good is related to market prices. Marshall [*1890*] can be regarded as the founder of these theories. Neo-classical economists consider the market process to be of greater importance than classical economists generally do. This is because of changes which took place during the process of the industrial revolution, which was characterised by a totally new use of natural resources. During the industrial revolution a conversion took place from flow entities to stock entities, in the use of natural resources. As a result, an increase in the production of goods could be realised. Stock entities such as coal and iron ore became the new cornerstones of wealth and welfare.

This production, on a large scale and concentrated in place and time, needed an outflow to the world market. Naturally, economists in this period increasingly concentrated their analysis on the market process. This development also changed the way in which economists looked at the importance of natural resources. Neo-classical economists could see with their own eyes that there was an abundance of natural resources. This abundance resulted in a stream of inventions, especially in the field of physics. This technological development provided new impulses for industrial growth processes [*Marshall, 1890: 180*], which moved the production factor 'natural resources' to the background.

The rise of the market process and the development of neo-classical economic theories related to it cannot be described as an independent phenomenon. When natural resources are at stake, the changes which took place in the use of them are at least as important. The conversion to stock entities has led 'by a natural progression' to the exhaustion of these resources. Moreover the discharge of great quantities of these materials, abnormal for the environment, led to a kind of environmental disruption that was hitherto unknown to mankind. This disruption is so severe as to constitute a serious social and economic problem.

Traditional neo-classical economists did not recognise these problems, for in their period this phenomenon was hardly evident at all. The volume of stock entities was extremely large related to the use of these resources and so they were seen as inexhaustible. The disruption of ecocycles occurred only locally and on a small scale; global disruptions were not at issue. This development was driven by the dynamics of the market process, and a continuing substitution of production factors took place. As long as limits to the use of natural resources have no relevance, an increase in production is possible. This development led to the situation that economists did not discuss the problem of natural resources between 1870 and 1960. Only a few individuals issued warnings about these problems [*King, 1919; Fabricant, 1947 also Martinez-Alier and Schluepmann, 1987*]. This neglect of environmental problems was not only found in neo-classical circles. Marxists demonstrated the same limited vision as far as environmental problems were concerned [*Ullrich, 1979; Dietz and Van der Straaten, 1990*].

Within the neo-classical approach, however, there is an initiative which can help to analyse and solve the problem. Pigou developed the concept of external diseconomy and applied this to environmental problems [*Pigou, 1920*]. The negative effect is caused by the fact that market parties have a negative influence on the welfare of non-market parties. The diseconomy is called external because it is found outside the market, which is in the core of the theory. As a result of this phenomenon social cost price is not the same as private cost price and so an optimal allocation of production factors is disturbed.

According to Pigou, the solution can only be found through intervention by the state as an economic actor, directed to serving the common good. The state can realise this by making an inventory of negative external effects together with the related costs. These costs are transferred by the state to the polluting industries. By doing this, social cost price is the same as private cost price again, and an optimal allocation of production factors is restored. For many years this approach played only a theoretical role; and no attention was given to this concept until environmental problems were seen as a severe social and economic problem [*Blaug, 1978*].

It was natural that economists, when confronted with environmental problems, started to use the concept of the negative external effect. They knew the concept and at first glance it appeared that it could be used successfully. Mishan [*1967*], for instance, used this concept for the basis of his criticism of the neglect of environmental problems. In the Netherlands Hueting [*1980*] in particular, tried to use this concept for an analysis of environmental problems. This approach, however, presented a number of problems in the quantification of costs and benefits relating to environmental measures (see also Opschoor [*1974*]). These problems meant that preferences regarding a sound natural environment could not be calculated which in turn meant that the prices of goods and services which are produced at the expense of the environment are not a real reflection of the sacrificed scarcity.

The response of economists to this problem has been quite varied. The majority act as if the problem does not exist, a view which suggests that economics only deals with the interests of labour and capital. The production factor 'natural resources' is given attention only when it is bought and sold on a market. In this view economic parameters are only those elements that have a meaning in the context of the market process, such as employment, the deficit of the state, the price level, the level of production, the balance of payments, and so on. The environment and nature are, for these economists, something like the Third World, the community centre and public health. One cannot avoid doing something about them; but if the economic situation becomes worse there is only one solution: reduce the budget for these expenses. This approach is very popular in the present economic policy in many countries of Europe (see, for example, Rutten [*1989*]). In many cases this starting point has the result that national authorities protect not the environment, but their own polluting industries [*Dietz, Van der Straaten and Van der Velde 1991; Van der Straaten, 1990*].

Many environmental economists do not realise that this approach is connected with the lack of a generally accepted economic theory regarding natural resources. If an optimal point of pollution cannot be determined with the help of the price mechanism, other steering mechanisms should be developed. Finding such a steering mechanism is of great importance. If one does not have such a steering mechanism at one's disposal, no economic statements about the allocation of natural resources are possible. Goudzwaard [1970], Baumol and Oates [1988] and Daly [1972; 1977] have chosen to situate these problems in the realm of economic policy. This approach has the advantage that in economic policy every subjective starting point can be introduced without serious problems. This approach prevents the researcher from being blamed for introducing subjective elements into the economic theory itself. In this approach the theory itself remains free of values and norms.

Introducing the environment into economic policy whilst neglecting it in economic theory, leaves a huge problem unsolved. In this approach, everything in economic theory stays the way it was. From an analytical point of view, the production factor 'natural resources' will be banished from economic theory. One could defend such an approach, if there was not such a long tradition in economic theory of making a distinction between labour, capital and natural resources as independent production factors. It is possible, of course, to deviate from such a tradition and to restrict economic theory to labour and capital. In the present situation, however, with enormous environmental problems which threaten the possibilities of production in the long run, one cannot defend this approach. One cannot escape from the necessity of giving the production factor 'natural resources' the same weight as labour and capital when analysing economic problems and 'natural resources' should be integrated into economic theory. The role of nature and the environment in economic theories is of the greatest importance. Without a useful theory it is impossible for economists to have sound arguments in the field of environmental problems. An important question in economic theory is the definition of the value of economic goods; in this case it is the value of natural resources that is especially important.

These arguments and theories have had a significant influence on EC environmental policy. The main argument of the Treaty of Rome is the establishment of a common market. In traditional neo-classical theories it is axiomatic that a common market of several countries will lead to an increase in welfare. The more the market expands, the more producers are able to specialise, and this results in economies of scale. Producers are able to produce at lower cost. Consumers benefit from lower production costs, which will lead *ceteris paribus* to higher welfare. In addition, a common market leads to less need of government intervention in economic life. Government expenditure can therefore be lowered.

Arguments of this kind are often used with respect to the European Common Market. When harmonisation of the rules is under discussion, the arguments of lower expenditure for national states are also often mentioned, because there is less need for control at the boundaries of national states.

With this in view, the European Commission asked a special committee under the chairmanship of Paolo Cecchini to estimate the costs of the as yet uncompleted common market. In their report the Cecchini group calculated the economic advantages of the abolition of especially non-tariff barriers between the member states of the European Community. Table 1 contains the most important results from the Cecchini report.

When the decrease of government deficits (2.2 per cent) is used for tax reductions and governmental investments, production will increase by

TABLE 1
THE CHIEF CONCLUSIONS OF THE CECCHINI REPORT

Growth of production (in % of GNP)	4.5
Decrease of price level of consumption (in %)	6.1
Decrease of governmental deficit (in % of GNP)	2.2
Increase of employment in mln jobs	1.8
Decrease of unemployment (in % points)	1.5

Source: Cecchini et al. [1988: 151, 183].

7.5 per cent instead of the 4.5 given in Table 1. However, these optimistic calculations of the Cecchini committee have been criticised [Centre for Business Strategy, 1989 and Central Planning Bureau, 1989]. Generally speaking, the picture that the Commission presents is considered to be too optimistic. Therefore, the calculations should be seen as a possibility rather than as a real growth in the European economy. This criticism, however, does nothing to diminish the likelihood that competition in the European Market will result in a substantial increase of production.

In the Cecchini report no attention is given to the effects of a rise in production on environmental disruption. An increase of production will also create new scarcity, if we choose to incorporate the environment into economic welfare (see, for instance, Mishan [1967] and Dietz and Van der Straaten [1988]). Fresh air, fossil fuels and minerals will become more scarce as a result of the increase of production. In many cases this increased scarcity is not reflected in higher market prices, and so the increased scarcity of environmental goods will not be registered by traditional economic parameters. But the increase of production caused by the completion of the Common Market will lead to increasing environmental deterioration and increased scarcity of environmental goods.

Yet, a lack of international coordination is often mentioned as an important cause of frustration in the debate about environmental disruption. As long as countries are able to poison rivers and oceans the environmental problem is 'exported' to other countries. The completion of the European Market could, theoretically, offer an opportunity to abate international environmental disruption. It is difficult, however, to imagine that this development will be realised, as in reports like the Cecchini report, the integration of environmental protection is not envisaged

In sum, we may conclude that traditional neo-classical theory, which is dominant in mainstream economics, does not have sufficient categories to analyse and describe environmental problems. The focus placed on the market and market prices implies that environmental policy is always in a weak position when 'real' economic issues are at stake. In this situation it is extremely difficult to establish a coherent system of environmental policy including ends positing not only goals, but also the formulation of the instruments needed to reach ecological goals. It should not surprise us that it took approximately 30 years from the beginning of the establishment of the European Community for the EC to formulate explicitly – on paper – that environmental policy was a responsibility of the community. In the next section we investigate the difficulties encountered by the European Community in constructing a sound environmental policy using effective instruments.

The Decision-making Process in the EC

Roughly speaking the EC treaty envisaged decision-making by majority voting in the areas of the EC's exclusive authority. However, common standards were to be achieved by unanimity through a process of harmonisation between and among such provisions, laid down by national law, regulation or administrative action in member states, as they directly affect the establishment or functioning of the common market.

In practice the distinction between majority voting and unanimity was lost, as all decisions were made unanimously. This turned out to be an excellent procedure for not reaching any decisions at all, as compromises satisfying the six, nine, ten and later twelve national bureaucracies and the one EC bureaucracy, could be frustrated by any one of them saying no. The EC's habit of non-decisions took one of two forms: either nothing was done at all, or unyielding points of view were glossed over by vague or contradictory legal texts. Public decision-making became a paradise for private lobby activities: you only have to gain agreement in one of the 12 capitals to successfully ward off any unwanted EC regulation, or harmonisation of national standards, thus leaving the field open to different national regulations and the protectionism that may be enshrined in them.

This gave rise to an arduous process of testing whether these national standards could be allowed to infringe the free movement of goods, normally required in a common market. In order to conform, these national standards had to fulfil the requirements of Article 36, which did not preclude prohibitions or restrictions on imports, exports, or goods in transit justified on grounds of public morality, public policy or public security; the protection of health and lives of humans, animals or plants; the protection of national treasures possessing artistic, historic or archaeological value; or the protection of industrial and commercial property. In the litigation before the Court of Justice these grounds were expanded by the rule of 'reason', which stated that as long as the decision-making process was held up at EC level, it was reasonable to accept national divergence.

Another factor weakening the EC's capacity to set up an effective policy is the so-called democratic gap, pointing to the fact that contrary to West European tradition, law in the EC is not made by the representatives of the people directly but by national governments meeting in the Council of Ministers and acting on the advice of the EC Commission. This democratic gap severely hampers public debate about possible measures to be taken, as there is no really relevant parliamentary debate, and decision on EC regulations and guidelines are shrouded in the secrecy of the Council.

The European Parliament's frustration about its merely advisory capacity, and the frustration of major industries about the continued fragmentation of the common market into national markets, combined in a drive to change the treaty. The result of this process left the European Parliament somewhat short-changed: the political solution to the question of European union is not to be found in the old treaty. The advocates of the real common market appear to have carried the day, as the original goals were restated, this time under the catchword of the internal market. Majority voting was once again adhered to, and for the first time extended to the harmonisation process. The political negotiation process set up for harmonisation under article 100 (requiring unanimity) was derogated by article 100A which requires a qualified majority for the adoption of measures necessary for the internal market. Although the adherents of the completion of the internal market may have carried the day, this may not be at all permanent, as an exemption of Article 36 was built into the decision-making procedure, allowing a member state to deviate from the majority. This might make possible the differentiated integration advocated by Hey and Jahn-Böhm [1981].

The enchanced status of majority voting made the democratic gap more painful. Therefore a new cooperation procedure was written into the treaty, binding the law-making Council of Ministers to the European Parliament in a delicate procedure. The outcome of this procedure may be that a qualified majority in the Council, acting in accordance with the Commission, can give an absolute majority in the European Parliament the opportunity to force a majority decision on the Council. This comes about because amendments made by Parliament, and accepted by the Commission, can only be amended by the Council if it acts in unanimity. A lobby now needs one member state acting in accordance with the Commission and an absolute majority in Parliament, to enact the latter's wishes. In other words, a negative lobby has to be successful with either the commission, the majority in Parliament or all 12 national capitals in order to ward off an unwanted regulation or guideline.

A Sound European Environmental Policy

The conclusion previously drawn was that the calculation of social costs as a result of environmental pollution is not possible in most cases, due to the lack of a market in which environmental goods are bought and sold. This implies that the imposition of levies, which is an important instrument in neo-classical approaches, is accompanied by significant problems. There is no information about the desired level of the levies that are necessary to curb environmental pollution to the optimal pollution point, where marginal social costs of environmental pollution equal marginal social benefits. It should not surprise us that the implementation of economic instruments in European environmental policy is a rare phenomenon. Legislative procedures are the common practice.

Legislation has the advantage that authorities can be sure about the effects it will have on the level of pollution. They can, indeed, force industries to limit their emissions. Most economists argue that this situation is not optimal from an economic point of view [*Peeters, 1991*]. When, for instance, marketable emission rights are introduced, these rights will undoubtedly be used by industries which are able to reduce emission at low prices. The crucial question in reality is, however, how many permits should be given – or sold – to which industries. Until now, this problem has not been brought to a solution.

This implies that until now legislation has been the normal procedure, which gives the polluting industries the possibility to negotiate with the authorities about the maximal emission of polluting substances to be included in the permit. This puts authorities in a difficult position, since from an environmental point of view, they are interested not in the maximal level of emission, but in the level of depositions. However, there are no well-defined relations between emissions and deposits. In addition, in many cases, such as air and water pollution, the emitted substances are transported to other countries, increasing the level of the deposits abroad.

Authorities need the help of polluting industries. Without technical information about the polluting production process authorities cannot possibly formulate the complicated text the permits require. Generally speaking, the people in the polluting industries have a much better technical knowledge of the production processes than the people in the ministries responsible for the permits. This causes authorities to be in a dependent position. But there are more complications. Severe norms in environmental policy will undoubtedly lead to higher production costs. These higher costs will influence the competitive position of these industries. The latter do not hesitate to emphasise this fact, as has been the case when proposals have been made to implement an energy tax. Polluting industries can use traditional economic arguments to neutralise a sound environmental policy, and in many cases they do. From the previous discussion it becomes clear that this will leave environmental policy in a difficult position from an economic point of view. The negative effects of environmental measures on the 'economy' are given full attention by quantifying them, while the positive effects of this policy are very difficult to translate into economic benefits. Summarising, one may conclude that the weakness of dominant neo-classical economic theory to analyse and describe environmental problems gives polluting industries a strong starting position in negotiating with national or international authorities when the introduction of severe norms comes on to the agenda.

If neo-classical approaches do not take us far in solving the economic analytical problem of natural resources, we are forced to look for a more appropriate approach. In our opinion, two levels should be distinguished. In the first place, there is the problem of using increasing quantities of stock entities, as was mentioned above in the discussion of the industrial revolution. In the second place, there is the manner in which mankind uses the yields of the ecocycles. Both problems will now be discussed.

The use of natural resources takes place within the social system. The crucial point is whether or how to integrate the dynamics of the ecosystem into this social system. In neo-classical thinking this is either neglected or supposed to be realised by the dynamics of the market mechanism. However, as we have argued before these assumptions do not meet reality. As a starting point for the working of our model we shall take the notion of sustainable development, which has been propagated by the Brundtland Commission [1987] as an attempt to close the gap between economic analysis and environmental policy. This concept of sustainable development has been given full attention by many economists. The problem is how to define such a generally accepted concept (see among others Kuik and Verbruggen [1991]; Opschoor and Van der Straaten [1993]). We shall attempt to use this concept taking the possibilities of the ecosystem as a starting point for economic analysis. In this sense the model may work if a certain number of limiting conditions are fullfilled. In principle it is possible to stop the extraction of materials from the stocks and not use them in the social system. But it is impossible to accomplish this in the short run and a better aim is diminished use of these materials. The same holds true for raw materials and energy resources.

Such a change in production processes leads to a decrease in the use of ores and fossil energy resources. This change can only be realised when the recycling of fossil materials becomes common practice in production. However, energy cannot be recycled. Therefore, the only possibility is a drastic change in the direction of deriving energy from flow quantities such as sun and wind energy. This, in fact, will have an effect upon the earnings of many countries in the Third World which are largely dependent on the export of such materials as iron ore, copper and oil. In the industrialised part of the world these materials are bought and used in the production process, causing an environmental problem when these materials are emitted in the environment, since the environment cannot cope with them. The problems for the exporting countries in the Third World cannot be discussed here (see among others Opschoor and Van der Straaten [1993]).

Consequently, the total discharge of materials alien to the environment would decrease. Moreover, the exhaustion of fossil resources would be slowed down. Technological development can play a very important role in this process of conversion. Current economic instruments can be used to realise this policy. With the help of charges, subsidies, controls and demands, the desired development can be influenced by government. Subsidies should be given from collective funds to steer technological development in the direction of saving the environment.

As was shown above, traditional cost-benefit analysis cannot solve the problem of determining the optimal pollution point. The price mechanism does not give sufficient information for this purpose. Yet the determination of this point is of great importance. There is only one instrument which can be used. When charges for materials from the stocks are being assessed, the functioning of the ecosystem itself is the norm which should be applied. These norms are needed as a way of determining a level of discharge which is sustainable from an ecological point of view. They have to be established by the government or other authorities; critical loads, emission limits and extraction quotas can be used in this respect. Such an environmental policy can be realised using current economic instruments. The price mechanism can play an important role. In many cases, however, these instruments cannot solve all of the problems and physical regulation may be a necessity. The way these instruments work is completely different from the situation in traditional neo-classical theory,

FIGURE 1

GLOBAL INTERACTION BETWEEN THE SYSTEM OF PRODUCTION AND
CONSUMPTION AND THE ECOSYSTEM

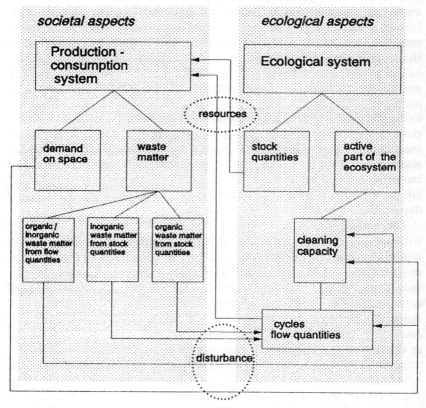

in which the negative external effect should be quantified by authorities. The government can internalise these social costs by the implementation of an environmental policy. In our model the norms originate in the ecological system with the aim of reaching a sustainable development. Prices are an instrument for realising the ecologically desired ends, which were mentioned above. Furthermore, when a certain natural resource is used, the dimensions of this resource should be considered. Dimensions are not a static entity; the resource can in some cases be regenerated [*Opschoor and Van der Straaten, 1993*].

It is precisely this integration of economic analysis and environmental policy that causes difficulties in realising a sound environmental policy. This integration is in fact the reintegration of the unpriced production factor 'natural resources' into economic theory, as has been the case with classical economic approaches. One might argue that neo-classical analysis is a theoretical system which finds its origin precisely in the neglect of unpriced production factors. Today's reality in relation to the quality and quantity of natural resources forces the theoretical economic system to integrate this factor back into economic theory and to implement a sound environmental policy based on such a theory. This is a far from easy task.

The priced production factors 'labour' and 'capital' with their firm position in neo-classical economic theory, were able to 'solve' their problems by pushing the unpriced production factor 'natural resources' to the margin of economic reality. By doing this they were able to build up powerful positions during the last century in the state and the state machinery. The result is that, generally speaking, ministers of economic affairs are not dealing with *economic* issues (including natural resources), but with *production and consumption* to the advantage of the positions of labour and capital. In this process they have brought about the present deplorable state of nature and the environment.

The threat to nature and the environment by polluting industries without any costs increased the relative competitive power of these polluting industries. If emissions are to be brought down with the help of environmental policy, one might not expect these competitive polluting industries to give up their powerful position without a struggle. On the contrary, these industries have been trying, and will keep on trying, to defend their positions by stressing the importance of their industries to employment, value added, the export position or the trade balance. All of these arguments favour the priced production functions 'labour' and 'capital' [*Van der Straaten, 1990; Dietz et al., 1991*].

Other European Initiatives

From many discussions about a European environmental policy one might get the impression that only the European Community can solve environmental problems in Europe. This is far from being the case for many environmental problems. Everything depends on the scale of the problem. In most cases environmental problems are recognised as serious when the victim is able to 'prove' that his environmental position is severely damaged by economic activities of other countries.

Indeed, in the first half of the 1970s the international activities of the Scandinavian countries, which argued that their environment was seriously affected by air pollution emitted by other countries, brought this problem onto the international agenda of the United Nations Stockholm Conference of 1972. But even then other countries were unwilling to take serious measures. They argued that first of all it should be proved that they were responsible for the bad condition of the Scandinavian lakes. Such a problem could not be solved in the context of the European Community as several of the countries involved were not members of the EC. The way out was found by the Economic Commission for Europe, which is part of the United Nations. They spent funds on massive research in the Scandinavian countries. The results of these investigations were unambiquous: air pollution was largely a transboundary pollution with very significant negative effects on the ecosystems of Scandinavia [ECE-EMEP, 1981; Drabløs and Tollan, 1980]. The sources of this pollution were mainly located in the industrialised areas of North-western Europe. It was this information that forced the European countries to take measures, which resulted in the protocols of Helsinki and Sofia, where significant reductions in the emissions of NO_x and SO_2 were agreed.

The position is the same in the case of the pollution of rivers and seas. There are, for instance, only a limited number of European countries involved in the problem of the pollution of the Rhine. These countries are negotiating over a diminution of emissions. In particular the downstream countries such as the Netherlands and Germany are in a difficult position as they have to pay the costs of purifiying Rhine water, which is used on a large scale as a source for drinking water. Their problems are illustrated by the salination of the Rhine, which is mainly caused by French industries. So far France has managed to let the Dutch authorities pay to stop this salination. However, this payment has until now had no effect. French industries continue to discharge salt into the Rhine. Incidentally, this is a perfect example of the way in which the polluter-pays-principle does not work in international situations. In this case it is the victim who has to pay to persuade the polluter to stop his pollution. Even where the victim pays, the polluter still goes on with his polluting activities.

This salt problem of the Rhine should not cast a shadow over the many positive effects of the negotiations of the countries involved in the pollution of the Rhine. Though these negotiations took a long time and were in many cases laborious, the positive effects should not be over-looked. The quality of the Rhine water is improving particularly as regards oxygen demand. The burden of heavy metals and non-degradable chemicals is still very high and poses a threat to water quality.

As regards water quality there has been an abundance of negotiations between countries on the Meuse, the Scheldt, the Baltic Sea, the Mediterranean Sea, the North Sea, and the Danube. Some of these negotiations have not had the desired effect, as in the case of the Scheldt, where the Netherlands and Belgium have been unable to improve the quality of the water. The federal structure of Belgium and the complete neglect of pollution problems in this country have until now worked as absolute barriers. The negotiations regarding the water quality of the North Sea and the Mediterranean are proceeding more satisfactorily (on paper at least). In all these cases we see that institutions and politics present the most important barriers. The victims are always in a weak position.

It is often argued that co-operation in the EC will generate new possibilities for the solution of environmental problems. In the case of conflicts about the water quality of rivers and seas it is doubtful that this will be so. The institutional barriers between adjacent countries such as Belgium and the Netherlands regarding the Scheldt and the Meuse are so great that one cannot imagine EC regulations solving these problems.

In some cases environmental problems have a global character, such as the greenhouse effect and the deterioration of the ozone layer. This implies that European institutions cannot find solutions to these problems. It is at world conferences such as that in Rio de Janeiro that these problems should be discussed. It is in fact desirable that the European Community should have a uniform standpoint at these conferences.

The Single Internal Market – 1992 and Beyond

The Single European Act will provide significantly better possibilities for the implementation of a sound environmental policy than has been possible under the Treaty of Rome. One should not overlook the fact, however, that the willingness of the European Community to implement a sound environmental policy is not the same thing as its realisation in the future. It cannot be denied that the recent formulation of the Articles regarding environmental policies is a positive step. However, we have seen that the countries of Western Europe, all of which have taken significant steps towards implementing a sound environmental policy, have not really been successful in realising these aims [*Van der Straaten, 1990; Alcamo, Shaw and Hordijk, 1990*].

The publication of the Fifth Environmental Action Plan is an issue of importance. Ryan [1991] demonstrates that this programme is an ambitious one presenting many opportunities for generating a good policy. One should not forget, however, that this is a plan on paper and nothing more. There are significant barriers and pitfalls which may hamper the implementation of such a policy.

First of all one should not forget that this Action Plan has been delayed by many months as a result of the massive obstruction organised by traditional vested interests of labour and capital in the core of the European Community. This obstruction is an example of the controversy between economic analysis and environmental policy which was discussed above. There is a potential conflict between the interests of polluting industries and the implementation of severe norms in environmental policy. Agriculture, traffic, the use of energy in general, air traffic, water pollution, acid rain and the emissions of non-degradable chemicals and heavy metals are a significant threat to the environment, of which the solution is far from realisation. The solution to these problems cannot be realised without a decrease in emissions and perhaps of production.

These threats are not evenly distributed over all countries of the European Community as is the case with emissions of polluting industries. This implies that all countries of Europe have different interests in curbing the specific emissions of certain industries. When agriculture and road traffic are subject to environmental policies Dutch farmers and haulage companies will do what they can to avoid severe norms and will certainly argue that other sectors of the economy are more significant polluters. This places the European Commission in a difficult position. In addition, it is becoming more and more clear, for instance, that certain parts of Europe are more vulnerable to air pollution than others [Hettelingh, Downing and De Smet, 1991]. In these circumstances the introduction of flexible norms relating to the buffering capacity of the ecosystem could be defended. This problem is exacerbated by the economic differences between countries in the southern part of the European Community and the northern part of it. Portugal, Spain and Greece will inevitably argue that the introduction of severe norms are important for relatively rich countries, but not in their economies, which are just begining to develop their industries.

Considerable doubts about the Action Plan emerge. The concept of shared responsibility is the general line of the plan. The result of this concept is a plea for the introduction of covenants with the polluting industries. But the experience of these covenants in European countries is disappointing in many cases. The authorities are thus the prisoner of the polluting industries. In the plan strong arguments are used for the introduction of market oriented instruments. It is not clear, however how these instruments can be introduced [*Jensma, 1991*].

It is likely that the European Community will have to face important economic problems in the near future. The re-unification of Germany will inevitably absorb a huge amount of investment, which will place Germany in a difficult competitive position. The current depression will attract a lot of energy to solve problems of unemployment and the transformation of agriculture and other industries.

One may conclude therefore that the Fifth Action Plan is a good starting point for the implementation of a sound environmental policy. However, it is not clear how this can be realised. There are significant pitfalls and barriers in the field of the integration of the unpriced production factor 'natural resources' in economic analysis.

Conclusions

From the foregoing discussion some conclusions may be drawn:

- First, in traditional neo-classical economic theory there are no useful categories for analysing environmental problems, as this theoretical framework focuses on market values where economic goods have to be priced. Environmental goods, however, in many cases do not have, a price.
- Second, this has had a significant influence on economic policies in Western countries. There has been a widely accepted opinion that economics is related to production and consumption, and to the priced production factors labour and capital. In this view the environment is something outside the economy.
- Third, this opinion is untenable when industrial societies are more and more confronted with a dramatic increase in environmental issues, which can no longer be ignored.
- Fourth, in the Single European Act, an attempt has been made to lay down a sound environmental policy. One could say that the act incorporates a framework of sufficient quality to realise this.
- Fifth, the concept of sustainable development, as introduced by the Brundtland Commission, can play a significant role in curbing pollution and the degradation of natural resources. However, the concept of sustainable development is not an easy one. The concept should be reinforced with concrete measures, an important one being a decrease in the use of stock resources, raw materials as well as energy.
- Sixth, however, one should not overlook that until now polluting

industries have been able in many cases to stress their importance for traditional economic variables such as income, employment and the level of production, which has resulted in a subsequent weakening of environmental policies.

- Seventh, the only way to neutralise these efforts can be found in the recognition by both the production factors labour and capital that a sound environment is a prerequisite for the future well-being of production and consumption. Environmental groups can play an significant role in this process.
- Finally, in many cases controversies between nations about environmental issues can be solved more easily outside the European Community. This is particularly the case when only a limited number of countries are involved in a specific topic such as the Baltic Sea, the North Sea, the river Rhine and the Mediterranean Basin.

NOTE

1. This issue is discussed in more detail by Dietz and Van der Straaten [*1991; 1992*].

REFERENCES

Alcamo, J., Shaw, R. and L. Hordijk (1990), *The Rains Model of Acidification*, Dordrecht/Boston: Kluwer Academic Publishers.

Baumol, W.J. and W.E. Oates (1988), *The Theory of Environmental Policy*, Cambridge: Cambridge University Press.

Blaug, M. (1978), *Economic Theory in Retrospect*, Cambridge: Cambridge University Press.

Cecchini, P. *et al.* (1988), *The European Challenge 1992: The Benefits of a Single Market*, Aldershot: Edward Elgar.

Central Planning Bureau (1989), *Nederland en Europa '92* (the Netherlands and Europe '92), Working Paper 28, Den Haag.

Centre for Business Strategy (1989), *1992: Myths and Realities*, London: London Business School.

Commission of the EEC (1986), 'European Act', *Bulletin of the European Communities*, Supplement 2/86.

Daly, Herman (1972), *Toward a Steady State Economy*, San Francisco, CA: Freeman.

Daly, Herman (1977), *Steady-State Economics: the Economics of Biophysical Equilibrium and Moral Growth*, San Francisco, CA: Freeman.

Dietz, F.J. and J. van der Straaten (1988), 'The Problem of Optimal Exploitation of Natural Resources: the Need for Ecological Limiting Conditions', *International Journal of Social Economics*, Vol.15, No.3–4, pp.71–9.

Dietz, F.J. and J. van der Straaten (1990), 'Economic Analyses of Environmental Problems: A Critique of Marxist Approaches', in S. Brander and O. Roloff (eds.), *Politische Oekonomie des Umweltschutzes*, Regensburg: Transfer Verlag, pp.147–71.

Dietz, F.J. and J. van der Straaten (1992), 'Rethinking Environmental Economics: Missing Links between Economic Theory and Environmental Policy', *Journal of Economic Issues*, Vol.XXVI (March 1992), pp.27–51.

Dietz, F.J., J. van der Straaten and M. van der Velde (1991), 'The European Common Market and the Environment: The Case of the Emission of NO_x by Motorcars', *Review of Political Economy*, Vol.3 (Jan.), pp.62–78.

Drabløs, D. and A. Tolland (eds.) (1980), *Ecological Impact of Acid Precipitation*, SNSF Project.

Economic Commission for Europe – EMEP (1981), *Cooperative Programme for Monitoring and Evaluation of the Long Range Transmission of Air Pollutants in Europe*, Technical Report 1/81.

Faber, M. and F. Beyer (1980), 'Eine ökonomische Analyse konstitueller Aspekte der europäischen Integration', *Jahrbuch für Sozialwissenschaft*, Vol.31, pp.213–27.

Fabricant, S. (1947), in *Studies in Income and Wealth*, Vol.10, Conference on Research in Income and Wealth, New York.

Goudzwaard, B. (1970), *Ongeprijsde Schaarste* (Unpriced Scarcity), Den Haag: W.P. van Stokkum en Zn.

Hettelingh, J.P., Downing, R.J. and P.A.M. de Smet (eds.) 1991, *Mapping Critical Loads for Europe*, Bilthoven: National Institute of Public Health and Environmental Protection.

Hey, C. and Jutta Jahns-Böhm (1989), *Ecology and the Single Market*, Freiburg: European Environmental Bureau.

Hueting, R. *New Scarcity and Economic Growth*, Amsterdam: Elsevier.

Jensma, H. (1991), 'Milieubeleid van EG zit op vele fronten vast' (The EC Environmental Policy is Confronted with Many Troubles), *NRC/Handelsblad*, 14 March 1992.

King, W.J. (1919), *The Wealth and Income of the People of the United States*, New York/London.

Kuik, O. and H. Verbruggen (eds.) (1991), *In Search of Indicators of Sustainable Development*, Boston/Dordrecht: Kluwer Academic Publishers.

Malthus, T.R. (1798), *An Essay on the Principle of Population* (1982 edition), Harmondsworth: Penguin.

Marshall, A. (1890), *Principles of Economics* (1925 edition), London: Macmillan.

Martinez-Alier, J. and K. Schlüpmann (1990), *Ecological Economics*, Oxford: Basil Blackwell.

Mill, J.S. (1886), *Principles of Political Economy*.

Mishan, E.J. (1967), *The Cost of Economic Growth*, London: Staples Press.

Opschoor, J.B. (1974), *Economische Waardering van Milieuverontreiniging* (Economic Evaluation of Environmental Pollution), Assen: Van Gorcum.

Opschoor, J.B. and J. van der Straaten (1993), 'Sustainable Development: An Institutional Approach', *Ecological Economics* (in print).

Peeters, M. (1991), 'Legal Aspects of Marketable Pollution Rights', in F.J. Dietz, F. van der Ploeg and J. van der Straaten (eds.), *Environmental Policy and the Economy*, Amsterdam: North-Holland, pp.151–65.

Pigou, A.C. (1920), *The Economics of Welfare* (1952 edition), London: Macmillan.

Ricardo, D. (1823), *The Principles of Political Economy and Taxation* (1975 edition), London: Everyman.

Rutten, F.W. (1989), 'Op weg naar voltooiing van het sociaal-economische herstel' (On the Way to the End of a Social-Economic Upsurge), *ESB* (4 januari 1989), pp.4–9.

Ryan, P. (1991), 'The European Community's Environmen Policy: Meeting the Challenges of the 90's', *European Environment*, Vol.1, Part 6 (Dec. 1991), pp.1–6.

Straaten, J. van der (1990), 'Acid Rain and the Single Internal Market: Policies from the Netherlands', *European Environment*, Vol.1, (Feb. 1991), pp.20–24.

Ullrich, O. (1979), *Weltniveau*, Berlin: Rotbuch.

World Commission on Environment and Development (1987), *Our Common Future*, Oxford: Oxford University Press.

Product-oriented Environmental Policy and Networks: Ecological Aspects of Economic Internationalisation

FRANK BOONS

Environmental policy programmes are finding a new focus in the Netherlands: increasingly programmes are developed that deal with the environmental effects of the production, consumption, and waste activities around a product rather than with the effects of separate production processes. This development, which is also occurring in other European countries, coincides with the process of internationalisation that is currently changing the face of Europe. As this latter process is to a great extent focused on economic activities, it is important to analyse the mutual influence of both developments. This analysis, which gives insight into the positive, as well as problematic aspects, is based on the example of the formulation of the EC-Directive concerning the control of chemicals, and its implementation in the Netherlands, Germany, and the UK.

Within the Dutch environmental policy field, there is a development towards product-oriented rather than process-oriented measures. Although a policy paper on this topic will be drafted by the environmental and economics ministry only at the end of 1992, products increasingly turn out to be the focal point of attention of actors dealing with environmental problems [*van den Berg, 1992*]. Apart from a number of governmental activities, the increasing attention given to products is indicated by the structural cooperation between environmentalist groups and consumer organisations.

While this development of intensifying attempts to solve ecological problems from the perspective of products evolves, a process of internationalisation is taking place. Among other consequences, this process results in increasingly international markets for products, as well as an intensification of relations between economic actors in different countries. In this paper, the relation between both developments will be analysed, and the intention is to provide an insight into the (potential) beneficial or detrimental results of an international approach towards environmental problems from the product-perspective.

One important reason why Dutch governmental organisations have taken the product orientation as a basis in the formulation of policy programmes is that such an approach corresponds with the basic economic processes of supply and demand, as well as with decision-making procedures within business. Such correspondence is seen as necessary because of the strategy of the Dutch Environmental Ministry to bring environmental problems to a solution through mutual understanding and the internalisation of responsibility of corporations. Several initiatives of (parts of) industry show that an approach to environmental problems from the product perspective is seen as interesting by them as well [*VNCI, 1989*].

The process of internationalisation, which is currently taking place, has important implications for environmental policy programmes which focus on products. At the same time, the reverse applies: environmental programmes that are adopted in one country can have substantial consequences for economic actors in other countries. An important example of such a programme is the German *Verpackungsverordnung*, which applies to all producers that bring products to the German markets. As a consequence of the intensive trade between the Netherlands and Germany, this has led to sometimes substantial changes in the operation of Dutch producers. Such changes are bound to have effects on their activities in other markets. Thus, the economic aspects of internationalisation, which are at the heart of the '1992' programme of the European Community, and the increasing attention on environmental effects of products, are intimately linked, and therefore demand analysis.

Although new as a systematic approach, policy programmes that focus on the environmental effects of individual products, or categories of products, have been formulated in a number of countries. An example is the German eco-labelling programme, called the 'Blaue Engel', which was initiated as early as 1978. Also, at the European level, there have been programmes dealing with specific categories of products. In this respect, EC regulations dealing with the control of chemicals are an interesting example. Because detailed documentation of the formulation and implementation of this policy programme is available, this case provides a good empirical basis on which an inventory can be made.[1]

In the second section below, the approach usually referred to as 'network analysis' is presented as the one most suitable for making such an inventory. After a description of the relevant features of the chemical industry in general, this approach is used in the fourth section for analysing the national and European policy processes concerning the control of chemicals. The study ends with a number of observations concerning possible problems and opportunities that arise with the use of a product-oriented perspective on environmental policies within an international context.

A Network-Approach towards a Product-Oriented Environmental Policy Programme

Product Orientation

An ecological approach based on products focuses on the environmental effects that occur during the total life-cycle of the product. This life-cycle consists of a number of phases, from the extraction of raw materials, via production and consumption of the product, to recycling, and disposal of the resulting waste. This approach differs from the traditional approach to environmental problems which focuses on the emissions that are a result of individual processes of production and consumption. The product orientation looks at different processes that are related to one product, and what is most important, looks at the interrelations between those processes. This opportunity to look at the relations between the effects that occur in different phases is seen as one of the main advantages of the product-oriented approach [*Huppes et al., 1986*].

The Network Approach

As may be expected, policy programmes that aim directly at products in the minimisation of effects of human activities on the environment trigger activities, both economic as well as political, from a number of societal actors. Thus, an analysis of the process leading toward such programmes, as well as the process in which they are implemented, should take this multi-actor character into account.

In a special issue of the *Journal of Political Research* [*1992*], which deals with policy networks, the definition of Hanf [*1978: 12*] is taken as a starting point. This definition points out that the term 'network' 'merely denotes, in a suggestive manner, the fact that policy making includes a large number of public and private actors from different levels and functional areas of government and society'. Similarly Laumann and Knoke [*1987: 5*] define policy programmes as the 'product of complex interactions among government and nongovernment organisations, each seeking to influence the collectively binding decisions that have consequences for their interest'. This definition will form the starting point for the description of the 'network' approach used here.

First of all, this definition is not limited to regulations formulated by governmental bodies. Although they are an important part of it, the term 'collectively binding decisions' also refers to policy programmes that are developed and/or enforced by non-governmental actors. Thus, the definition explicitly refers to non-governmental actors as relevant parties in the policy process. Although governmental activities are an important ingredient in the development of policies, they are not the only actors to be considered. Instead of seeing the activities of interested actors as peripheral to those of government, it should be recognised that they can play a substantial, if not central, role in the solutions society provides towards environmental problems. Second, the definition refers to organisations instead of persons. Although interactions of course take place between individuals, it is reasonable to assume that they represent the interests of the organisation of which they are a member; in fact, this membership is a necessary condition for joining the interactions that take place in the policy process. However, individuals can play an important role, as their personal relations can interact with the relations that exist between the organisations they represent.

Defined most simply, the network-approach focuses on the relations between a number of actors. Such relations emerge as a result of the mutual dependency between those actors. When speaking of policy programmes, dependency is a result of the following, general situation.

(1) Every policy programme formulated by government affects a number of societal actors. Consequently, they attempt to influence the content of the programme. Empirical studies have shown that these attempts cannot be ignored in the analysis of policy formulation.

(2) Governmental institutions depend on non-governmental organisations, because they possess information that is necessary to formulate policy. Furthermore, their commitment is often necessary to ensure a successful implementation of these programme. Studies of private interest government [*Jacek, 1990*] show the importance of this phenomenon.

Thus, the actors who have an interest in a policy programme are to a certain extent dependent on each other in achieving a certain policy outcome. This dependency is the basis for relations between actors; in one way or another they have to take each other's decisions and actions into account in order to achieve their preferred outcome. Thus, for a specific policy problem, a network of relations between involved actors can be distinguished.[2]

A central assumption of the approach outlined here is that the characteristics of a network partially determine the activities of the included actors [*Kickert and van Vught, 1984*]; they open up certain possibilities, while at the same time closing down other lines of activities. Thus, to the extent to which these characteristics influence the strategies of actors, they determine the policy process, as well as its outcome, because they are the results of those strategies.

Four features of networks are relevant in determining the strategies of actors.

Distribution of power: As a result of differences in the distribution of resources, the actors that are included in the network are not equally dependent on each other. This results in differences in the power that actors has over other actors – that is, the extent to which actors can push their own preferred outcome when other actors prefer other outcomes. Thus, the distribution of power is a first important network feature in explaining policy outcomes.

Exchange of information: A second important characteristic is the way in which information is distributed and exchanged within the network. To be able to influence the actions of other actors, 'timely and trustworthy information' is essential [*Laumann and Knoke, 1987: Chapter 7*]. Disseminating such information is an important means of exerting influence over other actors. Furthermore, the exchange of information is almost always an essential part of the implementation of policy programmes. Thus, controlling the (exchange of) information relevant to the policy programme is an important power source in both the formulation and implementation phase of the policy process.

Division of interests: Third, it should be clear that the interests of actors involved in the interactions concerning a policy programme can diverge. Basing himself on these interests, which can be specifically related to the topic of the programme, but also be more general (for instance preventing governmental intervention in its activities), each actor employs a strategy in order to attain its preferred policy outcome. When describing the network, it is important to consider whether the division of interests of the actors involved can be characterised as polarised or consensual.

Rules of the game: Next to these structural features, the third feature relevant to explaining policy outcomes is of a more 'cultural' nature. In every network, certain 'rules of the game' can be identified. These rules are either the unintended result of continuous interaction between a group of actors, or the result of formal processes of institutionalisation.

Owing to the interdependency between actors to arrive at an agreed solution, it will be common for actors to employ a strategy. Such a strategy will consist first of all of the interests of the actor. As the features of the network determine to a certain extent the outcome of the policy process, an actor can also employ a strategy which aims at altering these features in such a way as to make sure that they lead to the outcome they prefer. For instance, a strategy of forming a coalition with other actors is essentially a strategy directed at changing the power structure of the network.

Embeddedness

Basing themselves on the concepts that are central to the network approach, political scientists have developed, through the description and analysis of political processes, a number of different types of networks that differ on important points. Recently, there have been new attempts to provide a classification for these different types [*Jordan and Schubert, 1992; Rhodes and Marsh, 1992*]. For the purpose of this paper, the network approach is seen as an analytical tool with which certain elements of institutional patterns within society, and their characteristics in as far as they determine policy processes, can be identified. Thus, rather than using one of the classifications that have been proposed, it is enough to emphasise the importance of differences in durability and scope of a network. This last characteristic can best be approached through the concept of 'embeddedness' [*Granovetter, 1985*]. This term indicates the different ways in which actors, their interactions, and the processes they initiate, are embedded.

First, several actors will be members of other policy networks. Governmental agencies which are confronted with sectoral organisations on an issue in the environmental policy field meet the same organisations on other issues in this field, or in other policy fields such as industrial policy. Also, the actors which form the national environmental policy network usually meet one another in the international network as well. This linkage of actors over different networks is important because the strategies employed by actors within a certain network, as well as their interests, can be influenced by their position and interests in another network. A simple example would be the fact that a sectoral-organisation will not join a coalition with a governmental agency even if their interests are to a great extent congruent, because they are in conflict in another policy network. A second form of embeddedness concerns personal relations between network actors. As Useem [*1991*] has pointed out, relations between persons from different organisations within a network can have an important influence on the policy process, and on the way in which coalitions are formed. Finally, when dealing with policy programmes directed at industry, events and processes within the economic sphere of society are relevant. This form of embeddedness has two dimensions. First, the interests and strategies of corporations and the organisations that represent them are intimately linked to their economic strategies. The economic position of a corporation determines to a large extent its possibilities in the political network. Also, governmental actors are constrained in their choices and actions by characteristics of the economic system. Although political scientists disagree over the way in which this takes place, it is clear that the choices and strategies of governmental agencies within policy networks are influenced by economic factors.

In sum, an analysis of the policy process on a certain issue and its outcome, requires the identification of the power relations, means of information exchange, and rules of the game of the network of actors who have an interest in this issue. Secondly, the interests and strategies of these actors must be identified. Finally, the embeddedness of the interactions between the involved actors within personal networks, other policy networks, and the economic system, must be taken into account. With these concepts, it is possible to analyse the policy networks that emerged as a result of the issue of the control of chemicals.

The Chemical Industry in Europe

In the preceding section, it was stated that policy networks are embedded in economic structures and processes. When dealing with policy programmes that deal with products, this fact is particularly, very important. This section describes the chemical industry, the sector which was affected by policies aimed at the control of chemicals. Special attention will be given to the sector's associational system.

The chemical industry consists of corporations whose principal activities are to transform materials chemically into different substances, giving them new chemical and physical properties' [*European Communities, 1990: 8–4*]. This industrial sector is important within the economies of the UK, the FRG and the Netherlands, as well as within the EC economy. For instance, in the EC it is the third manufacturing industry, responsible for 10 percent of the total value added in 1988 [*European Communities, 1990: 8–11*]. The sector is fully international, which is indicated by the large percentage of production being exported throughout the world as well as the high number of multinational companies in the sector. Finally, the sector is highly concentrated; mainly as a result of the fact that its activities are both capital intensive and research intensive.

These characteristics are important elements in understanding the strategies of actors representing the chemical industry. In the FRG, the so-called 'three sisters' (Hoechst, BASF, Bayer) are the leading companies in this branch of industry; in the UK, ICI is the predominant company; while in the Netherlands, AKZO, Shell, and DSM dominate this sector.

Chemical Interest Representation Associations

The chemical industry has been relatively successful in building a well established structure of interest representation. This appears to be the result of the relatively small number of corporations involved, the relatively strong personal relations between managers from different corporations, and the fact that the interests of these companies are relatively homogeneous because they are confronted with similar economic environments.

The structure of national interest associations concerned with the chemical industry is very similar in countries such as the UK, the FRG, and the Netherlands. Members of these associations are individual corporations, as well as a small number of sub-sector organisations. In all countries, one association represents the entire chemical industry. Every association has a board, consisting of representatives of the leading national firms. This board decides, among other things, on the position of the sector towards policy issues. Decisions are prepared by task forces, working groups, and so on, which are constituted by corporate experts and members of the staff of the association, which is relatively small. Because of the increase in attention given to environmental problems, all associations have at least one permanent group dealing with these issues.

Although similar to a great extent, the form and activities of the associations in the three countries differ with the political structure and policy style of a country. Thus, the German association, the *Verband der Chemischen Industrie* (VCI), differs from that in the Netherlands and the UK in being constituted of eight *Landesverbände*, parallel to the federal system of government. While the VCI deals with interest representation at the federal level, the Landesverbände organise the political lobby in the Länder. This is especially relevant on environmental issues, as the Länder have important responsibilities on these matters.

Another difference concerns the strength of the structure provided by the association. In the United Kingdom, the interest representation is not confined to the Chemical Industries Association (CIA), because government 'places a considerable emphasis on building direct relations with individual companies to complement contacts through industry associations' [*Paterson et al., 1988: 106*]. This is partially the result of the fact that government has been dissatisfied with the effectiveness of many trade associations [*Paterson et al., 1988: 64*]. Thus, all large corporations have government relations divisions, which provide information for, and coordinate interest representation by, corporate officials. In contrast, in Germany interest representation seems to be structured very tightly. The VCI places great emphasis on coordinating all activities concerning the representation of interests. Thus, government relations divisions such as those in British corporations are absent in the FRG. This seems to be the result of a strong awareness that individual activities could undermine the representativeness, and thus the effectiveness, of the VCI [*Paterson et al., 1988: 104*]. The Dutch association, the *Vereniging van de Nederlandse Chemische Industrie* (VNCI) is in this respect similar to the VCI.

At the European level, the most important organisation representing the interests of chemical industry is CEFIC, the *Conseil européen des fédérations de l'industries chimique*. Members of this organisation, which was founded in 1972, are the national interest associations of European (EC as well as non-EC members) countries. Since 1985, it has been possible for large corporations to join CEFIC directly, by becoming members of ACAM, the Assembly of Corporate Associate Members. ACAM is an advisory board to the Committee of Directors of CEFIC, which consists of the directors of the national associations. Arriving at a common position is not always easy as a result of this structure. First, national associations sometimes differ in their perspective towards certain problems, as the activities of the corporations in their country vary. Moreover, differences in opinion can arise between non-EC members and national associations from EC member states, as CEFIC is primarily directed at influencing EC policy. However, some common position is usually possible. That CEFIC is valued as a representative organisation by its members is indicated by the high rate of participation from corporate experts in CEFIC working groups and task forces. Such participation is essential, because the staff of CEFIC is relatively small.

In sum, the chemical industry can be characterised, in the words of Atkinson and Coleman [*1989: 53*], as a highly mobilised sector. By this, they mean an industrial sector whose associational system is characterised by among other things, a horizontal division of labour; a high density (a high percentage of firms within the sector is represented by the association); considerable in-house capacity for the generation of information, both technical and political; associations can bind their members to agreements which they negotiate with the state. These characteristics play an important role in the strategy of the chemical industry in national as well as international policy processes, as will become clear in the case described in the next section.

The Control of Chemicals

Until the mid-1970s, governmental programmes directed at the control of chemicals were confined to substances with specific applications such as food additives and pharmaceuticals. Control over other substances was left to individual corporations. In response to several incidents in Japan concerning health effects of chemicals, governments started initiatives to fill this legislative gap. Moreover, the possibilities for the control of these substances increased with improvements in testing methods.

The control of chemicals basically consists of notifying government about the properties of new substances. Using this information, governmental institutions assess the effects of the substance on the environment and on humans and regulate the introduction of the substance if they think it is necessary. An important aspect of such control systems is whether notification must take place before marketing the new substance (pre-marketing notification), or before producing it (pre-manufacturing notification).

The International Initiation of Control Programme

In 1975, the French government notified the EC of its intention to regulate the marketing of new chemicals. Because this initiative would interfere with the international trade of chemicals, the European Commission found it necessary to develop a response. It did so by announcing the preparation of an Amendment to a Directive of 1967 (EC67/458, 27.6.67).

The formal process leading to an amendment of an EC Directive starts with the preparation of a Commission proposal by the appropriate Directorate General, the administrative body of the EC. Usually, intensive consultation of experts from organised interest groups and national administrations takes place, especially on technical issues. Clearly, a policy programme aimed at regulating new chemical substances deals with complex technological expertise which of course was not available at the responsible EC Directorate. Given the potential economic impact of such a programme, it is easy to see why the organised interest groups of the chemical industry, as they are described in the previous section, were consulted during this process.

After the Commission's approval, the proposal is sent to the Council of Ministers, which is constituted of the national ministers responsible for the issue; also, the European Parliament and the Economic and Social Committee can state their position on the proposal. Before the Council decides, the proposal is discussed within the member states. Thus, due to its embeddedness within the general EC framework, within the rules of the game, as well as within the relations between a number of actors, the network concerned with the control of chemicals and its associated processes evolved along these lines.

Furthermore, it is important to note that most of the actors at the European level are representatives of national governments and industry associations. Consequently, there is a high interdependence between national political processes and the formulation of policy on the EC level. In turn, this provides a strong push towards an EC policy process that is largely determined by national interests and the strategies of national actors.

After the Commission's announcement, the German chemical industry attempted to persuade CEFIC to try to stop the Commission from developing legislation. CEFIC, however, decided to support the EC-proposal. The VCI then successfully formed a coalition with the German government, which brought its objections to the attention of the Commission. This provides a clear example of the way in which national relations influence the strategies of actors in the international network. It also shows that, although international relations are well developed within the chemical industry, these relations do not automatically lead to the adoption of a common position by the European sector as a whole. Also, this is an example of a strategy directed at changing the power structure under which an issue is discussed. Both actors employ a strategy directed at handling the issue at the EC level, because they expect less influence from environmentalists and the public on this level than in their national network.

When analysing the EC control network, related developments in other parts of the world are important. In this context, the enactment of the Toxic Substances Control Act (TSCA) in the United States in 1976 was a significant external influence. Apart from domestically produced substances, the TSCA also applied to substances imported from abroad. Because of their exports to the US, European – and especially German – firms were thus anxious to influence this regulation. Officials of European governments were also eager to influence the US initiative, because they 'were not consulted prior to the enactment of a statute having such potential significance for international trade in chemicals' [Brickman et al., 1985: 276]. Because both national governments and the chemical industry were aware of the fact that a common European position on this issue would enhance their bargaining position towards the United States, they became advocates of regulation, by the EC.

Apart from this international incentive, the harmonisation of the control of chemicals was stimulated by national interests. Most important, the German chemical industry preferred harmonised regulation over different national notification schemes because of their substantial export to EC countries. They also preferred the issue to be settled in àn international environment, because then trade arguments would dominate the discussion. In their national political system, they could expect political pressure from environmental groups [*Brickman et al., 1985: 277*]. Thus, the support of the German industry, as well as of government, for EC regulation was part of a strategy aimed at getting the issue discussed in a network with characteristics favourable to its own interests. This strategy proved to be successful; although essentially an ecological and worker-protection issue, it was placed on the agenda primarily because of trade arguments which dominated the discussion.

As a result of the initial German opposition, as well as of the limited resources of the EC administration, the Commission abstained from a central, EC-wide control system, and proposed a notification system in which companies would test new substances and notify the results to their national governments, which would then decide whether measures against the new substance would be necessary [*Paterson et al., 1988: 299–300*]. Despite the agreement over the necessity of a control system, intensive bargaining took place between the member states. This was caused by differences in opinion over the specific form of a notification system. The conflict concentrated on two issues: 'the extent of exemptions from testing requirements and the degree of flexibility allowed to national authorities in adapting testing requirements to individual chemical substances or classes of substances' [*Brickman et al., 1985: 278*]. The differences in the position of Britain, Germany and the Netherlands towards these issues shows how national policy styles influence actions of national actors within the European network.

Preferring informal, flexible standards, the British opted for a system that would not specify rigid testing requirements; moreover, they wanted to exempt all substances that would be marketed in quantities less than one ton from such requirements. In contrast, the Germans wanted a system that would link amounts of substances marketed to specific testing requirements (the so-called *Stufenplan*), starting at quantities of 100 kilogrammes. The reason for this position was that the German government wanted to force other countries to take the same measures as themselves. If autonomy was allowed for, they would certainly go further than other member states, thus weakening the position of their chemical industry. For the same reason, the German chemical industry supported the Stufenplan [*Brickman et al., 1985: 278–9*].

Such a detailed system was also supported by the Dutch government. However, they wanted a notification period of 60 days, because the proposed 30 days would be too short to assess fully the data on the substance. This position was a result of the earlier experience of the Dutch government with information exchange between government and industry [*Boons, 1991*]. The position of the Netherlands differed from that of other countries on yet another point. The Dutch Environmental Ministry was in favour of a stricter system than was proposed by the European Commission, and several Dutch political parties supported this position. The Dutch chemical industry, as well as the Economics Ministry, opposed such a system, but they did not push this too far because, if the Dutch position was reflected in the Directive, it would apply to competitors in other EC countries as well.

In 1979, some agreement was necessary because of the imminent implementation of American and French legislation. The resulting compromise, which led to the acceptance of the sixth Amendment in September 1979 (EC 79/831), contained a Stufenplan, which started at one ton, and left considerable autonomy in testing requirements. To accommodate the Netherlands, the notification period was set at 45 days. In addition, the European Commission made it clear that it would be possible for the Dutch government to develop legislation that would go further than the Amendment [*Boons, 1991*]. This indicates that the Amendment left considerable room for national differences in notification procedures of new chemical substances.

The Formulation of the Dutch Control Programme

As a number of studies on the implementation of EC directives have shown, reaching agreement at the EC level does not imply that national policy programmes will be similar. Both in Britain and in Germany, policy programmes which intended to implement the sixth Amendment were in fact very similar to that Amendment. In the Netherlands, however, a law was developed that differed on important points. Below, a description of the Dutch formulation process is given, together with some comparative notes from both other countries.

In all three countries, the basic policy formulation network consisted of the ministry responsible for the implementation of the EC directive, the economics ministry, parliament, and the national chemical interest association. However, the positions of these actors in the network differed significantly. First, all three countries had different ministries responsible for installing a control programme. In the Netherlands, the Environmental Ministry was responsible, while in the UK, the Health and Safety Commission, was responsible. In general, in all three countries the relation between the governmental agency involved and the chemical industry association was characterised by intensive consultation, based on the mutual dependency of both actors. Yet, there are differences in the business–government relations in the formulation of environmental policy.

In Germany, consultation on environmental policy is institutionalised in the environmental programme of 1971, and it is referred to as the *Kooperations-Prinzip* [*Bennet, 1989: 101*]. In contrast, consultation in the UK seems to be much more informal; the distance between government and business is much less than in Germany. As for the Dutch situation, consultation took place, but there was an absence of a consultative tradition as in the other two countries. This is indicated by the recurring statement of the VNCI that they were not sure whether government would be able to assure confidentiality of submitted data.

Another difference lies in the position of the Economics Ministry within the network. In Britain, until 1988, a 'sponsorship division' of the DTI was directed at assessing the impact of governmental programmes on the chemical industry, and subsequently defending the interests of this sector. In Germany, such a division does not exist, but the Economics Ministry is generally seen within industry as an advocate of the interests of industry. This is shown by the coalition between this ministry and the VCI in transferring the responsibility of the control of chemicals to the Ministry of Youth, Family and Health. Thus, in both countries, the chemical industry had an actor within the governmental system that looked after its interests, and provided direct access to the policy process. In the Netherlands, a chemical unit exists within the ministry, but it had little political power. This is indicated by the fact that the VNCI sees lobbying via this unit as a last resort, only to be used when all other possibilities are exhausted. An important reason for its limited power in the network is that this ministry was preoccupied with developing programmes for industrial sectors that were in trouble. Thus, the Chemical Department was poorly-staffed.

Finally, the position of parliament deserves attention. In Germany as well as the Netherlands, parliament was involved in the formulation process, because the control of chemicals was to be laid down in law. But as we will see, parliament played an important role in the Dutch network, while in Germany its role was limited. As the legal basis for a control system already existed in Britain, the British parliament played only a minor role in the process.

We can now turn to the interests of the actors within the national policy formulation networks. In the Netherlands, the Environmental Ministry was in favour of a system that would go further than was possible in the EC. First, it wanted a pre-manufacturing-notification instead of the pre-marketing system that the EC directive demanded. Furthermore, it proposed to bring intermediate products within the scope of the system. It was argued that this was necessary to achieve effective protection of humans and the environment. Secondly, the Ministry found that control of chemicals was too important to leave the discussion over new substances to governmental and corporate experts. Thus, it proposed a public notification procedure, in which interested parties could participate. Furthermore, this procedure would result in a ministerial announcement that would state the policy towards the substance under consideration.

It is important to note that parliament supported this position, thus giving the ministry a political mandate to formulate a stricter system. Apart from ideological arguments, this position seems to be linked to the fact that the issue of controlling new chemicals was exceptional because EC policy was formulated before national legislation became a matter of discussion. Normally, the Netherlands is ahead of EC policy, which means that parliament can exert more influence on the position of government within the EC. Furthermore, the Ministry of Social Affairs was in favour of such a system. This ministry, which entered the network on an *ad hoc* basis, was developing new legislation on worker protection, and was in favour of a pre-manufacturing notification because it would produce information that could be used in this programme.

The position met with strong opposition from industry and the Economics Ministry. As corporations would be forced to notify substances, including intermediate products, before manufacturing, they would have to do it much earlier than their foreign competitors. Also, they would face much higher costs, because they would have to notify products that their competitors would not have to notify. As to the public notification procedure, the VNCI argued that this would destroy innovation, because other corporations would have access to valuable information about new products. Although the Environmental Ministry stated that it would be possible to claim confidentiality for certain data, industry doubted if this confidentiality would be honoured.

The Dutch formulation process developed as follows. Between 1978 and 1981, some negotiations between the Environmental Ministry and industry took place. In addition, notwithstanding their conflicting positions, both actors started a pilot project, in order to find out what would be the practical consequences of a notification system. In 1981, a draft of the Law on Hazardous Substances (WMS) was presented to parliament. Although the VNCI succeeded in making some adjustments to the initial proposal, the elements that were their main concern remained. That the Environmental Ministry was able to force through its own position was first of all a result of the political mandate given by parliament. Further-more, in order to prevent both the Environmental and the Social Affairs Ministries from instituting their own notification systems, it was decided that a combination of both systems would be more effective. Finally, the weak position of the Economics Ministry contributed to the success of the Environmental Ministry.

In September 1983, the Environmental Ministry presented a substan-tially revised draft. The reason for this revision was that the Economics Ministry succeeded in getting the WMS subject to a deregulation pro-gramme. This meant that industry had another opportunity to remove less desired elements from the draft. During the consultation that took place during this process, industry succeeded in removing the public notification procedure from the WMS. In addition, several tests were removed from the notification, which substantially reduced the costs for corporations. However, the elements to which the VNCI had most objections, and which were the most important to the Ministry (that is the pre-manufacturing notification and the intermediate products policy), remained in the draft. In addition, the revised draft continued to leave industry with uncertainty over the confidentiality of submitted data.

Prior to the discussion of the WMS in parliament, the VNCI, as well as several individual companies, made their position clear to members of parliament. Due to this lobbying, an evaluation of the system was included in the WMS. Apart from this success, the law passed without substantive revisions.

Implementation of National Control Programme

Contrary to the differences in the policy networks directed at the for-mulation of control programmes, the implementation networks in all three countries are broadly similar. They consist of the ministry respon-sible for the control of chemicals, individual corporations, and a number of research institutes, which are governmental in Germany and the UK, and partially non-governmental in the Netherlands.

Thus, these networks are characterised by close co-operation between governmental and corporate experts, with little interference from other actors such as environmentalist groups. Although in the Netherlands the public has access to information which is not available in other countries, this possibility is hardly ever used. As all the information on which government assesses its position towards a notified substance is obtained from corporations, they have an advantageous position in relation to government. Moreover, the resources (finances, staff, knowledge) of corporations exceed those of the participating governmental organisa-tions.

Discussion

When the case described in the previous section is considered, there can be little doubt about the existence of an international policy network concerning the *formulation* of the EC policy programme on the control of chemicals. For a substantial period, there existed a pattern of relations between a number of actors which had an interest in this programme. And although environmentalist groups certainly played a role in getting the issue of chemicals control on national agendas, at the EC level, the central positions within the network were occupied by governmental officials and business representatives.

Within this network, an important problem is the quality of decision-making. As has already been noted, decision-making on control of chemicals took place within the general rules of the EC framework. With respect to decision procedures, the general rule before the Single European Act was adopted in 1986 was that directives dealing with environmental issues were based on one of Articles 100 and 235. These articles are essentially aimed at arriving at a Common Market, and decisions within the Council of Ministers must be taken unanimously. With decisions that have to be taken unanimously, the problem is often not *whether* a certain programme should be established, but rather what *form* such a programme should have. Here the interaction between decision-making rules and national interests becomes important. National governments in general are in favour of European legislation, but only if it is designed according to their specific policy style. Interaction with this combination of situational and preferential characteristics is referred to in game theory as the 'battle of the sexes', and is known to be characterised by difficult, compromise-generating negotiations [*Elster, 1983*]. Usually, as in the case study described above, pressure of time is the incentive to reach such compromises. As will be clear, policy programmes that are produced in this way can hardly be expected to be the optimal solution to a particular problem.

Since the Single European Act, some decisions no longer require unanimity. Although this eliminates some problems, it gives rise to other problems, because it becomes a matter of discussion which decision-making procedure should be used on a certain issue. Again, this choice can give rise to difficult negotiations, which influence the outcome significantly.

The same problem arises on a more basic level – that is, when the choice is being made of which issues will be dealt with on the European level. Here, the distinction between the necessity of international measures and the 'decision' to formulate those measures is important.

Ideally, these decisions should be congruent with current knowledge on the nature of environmental problems, and the level on which a solution should be formulated. However, this knowledge is not always unanimous. Taken together with institutional factors, and the diverging interests of the actors that form the international policy network, this means that the decision to search for an international solution is not automatically related to the nature of the problem under discussion.

A second aspect concerning the quality of decision-making is the involvement of interested parties. This is to a large extent based on the distribution of information relevant to policy issues. When regulations concern the chemical industry, this information is almost always highly technical and complicated. Furthermore, as this information is often related to the development of new processes or products it is often confidential. Combined with the limited capacity of EC institutions to acquire this kind of information, it is necessary for them to consult the chemical industry to obtain the necessary data.

Although their position is not as strong as that of business, environmentalist groups have relatively good access to the environmental DG as well. Again because of its limited capacity, DG XI uses the knowledge and support of those groups in order to strengthen its position towards the more powerful DGs [*Lowe and Goyder, 1983*]. This dependency is indicated by the financial support the EC gives to the European Environmental Bureau, the European representative of national environmentalist groups. However, due to the effective associational system that has been built by the chemical industry, their penetration into national as well as international policy processes is more effective. For instance, an indication of the effectiveness of the coordination provided by CEFIC is the fact that EC institutions such as DG III and DG XI value the expertise of this organisation; CEFIC is often involved in the formulation of EC-policy relevant to the chemical industry.

Apart from the quality of decision-making, an important point is the extent to which an international policy network generates international policy programmes. As far as the EC is concerned, the character of directives is important. As they only state the goal that must be achieved, and not the means, they leave room for substantial autonomy in formulating national regulations. The implementation of the sixth Amendment shows that this can result in national policies which differ on important points. In addition, it should be noted that, with few exceptions, the actors that form the international network are in fact national actors. Representatives of national governmental agencies, national business associations, and so on are the persons that interact. Moreover, the EC policy process is mixed with policy processes that occur at the national level. Thus, as the emergence of an international policy network is not accompanied by a decrease in the significance of national networks, the policy network at the EC level can become an arena in which national conflicts are fought out, instead of being a basis for the development of international programmes.

A second point serves as an additional qualification. This concerns the interests that have dominated the international policy process. From the outset, the reason for the Commission taking the initiative for the sixth Amendment was related to the problem of trade barriers. Although it is not surprising, given the history of the European Community and the goals which it has set itself, it is important to note that a policy programme aiming at minimising ecological and human health effects of chemical substances is determined almost exclusively by trade considerations. This bias of the EC towards economic integration within the general EC framework is indicated by the fact that a separate DG for environmental affairs was established only a few years ago.

As a result of this emphasis on trade, joint strategies between national governments and the corresponding industry association can occur, because both place the interest of their national industry sector at least as high in their priorities as formulating international regulations. Indeed, the strategy of the German government and the VCI is an example of this process. The same argument goes for the policy processes in the national networks. An exception is the Dutch network, in which parliament insisted on a system in which products are notified before production, thus leading to a system which is stricter than that in other European countries.

Thus, it can be concluded that, with the institutional framework that is presently shaping international policy processes, there is no guarantee that truly international policy programmes will be generated.

The relative importance of national versus international networks is also relevant for the role of multinational corporations. There are indications that managers of chemical corporations are currently facing the question of whether to centralise their environmental strategy. This choice depends, among other things, on the way in which the European policy network will develop. If environmental policy in Europe continues to be determined by national institutions, relations and interests, chemical corporations will adapt to the resulting complex of diverging regulatory systems by decentralising their strategy. Although difficult to predict in detail, this will no doubt pose additional barriers to the development of an international network that produces an international policy programme.

A last consideration deals specifically with the product-orientation which forms the basis of the sixth Amendment, and which can be expected to gain importance within environmental policy programmes. In this respect, the position of corporations is important. When corporations increasingly aim at producing environmentally friendly products, this means that the environmental strategy will become part of the competitive process. This poses a threat to the previously stable political coalitions and common positions taken by corporations in political discussions concerning environmental problems. In the Netherlands, several examples of this destabilisation can be mentioned, of which the phosphate-detergent issue is the most illustrative. During a long and at certain moments heated discussion, industry, environmentalist groups, and government discussed the elimination of phosphates from detergents, because of the contribution of this substance to the eutrophication of the surface water in the Netherlands. In this process, detergent producers formed a stable coalition, which was represented by the Dutch association of detergent producers (NVZ). This organisation made two successive agreements with the Dutch government. After that, one of the producers succeeded in developing a phosphate-free detergent, which was introduced in an intensive marketing campaign, directed at the ecological aspects of this product.

This commercial strategy broke down the coalition between detergent producers, which resulted in the elimination of detergents containing phosphates, as the producers were forced, due to the success of the phosphate-free detergent, to follow the same line.

This example calls for a review of the effect of commercialisation of corporate environmental strategies on industry coalitions. On the one hand, it can result in the breaking down of coalitions that are purely defensive and directed at preserving the *status quo*. This can result in outcomes that are preferable from an ecological perspective. Such an outcome, however, requires several additional conditions to be met. The most important of these is that corporate strategies that aim at gaining a competitive edge by responding to environmentally based consumer demands must use reliable information about the problem under consideration. As consumer demands are based on the problem as defined within the public discussion, this condition is by no means always fulfilled.

On the other hand, these coalitions should not be seen as always barring solutions that are preferable from an ecological perspective. Often, the arguments of corporations are valuable, because they are based on information about production processes that are not available to other actors in the political system. This is indicated by the oft-employed consultative strategy of governmental agencies. Furthermore, these coalitions are also used by governments to obtain support and legitimation for their programmes, which is necessary for their implementation. Thus, the effects of the commercialisation of corporate environmental strategies can be preferable from an ecological perspective, but it can also produce difficulties which are detrimental to optimal policy outcomes.

A last remark concerns the *probability* that commercialisation of the environmental strategy of individual corporations will result in destabilising intercorporate coalitions. Apart from national differences in this structure, it seems likely that this effect will be limited to problems that provide commercial incentives to individual corporations, and will not directly influence co-operation concerning problems that pose threats to the sector as a whole. Due to its 'global village' character, it can be expected that in such cases the chemical industry will continue to coordinate its political activities on a national and international level. At least on these issues, the chemical industry will be able to maintain its tradition of (inter-)national co-operation.

NOTES

1. The European policy process concerning this programme has been described by Brickman (1985) and Paterson (1988). They also provide accounts on the roles of national actors from Germany and the United Kingdom. The data on the Dutch situation, as well as the involvement of Dutch actors within the EC-network, have been collected by the author.
2. For a discussion on defining the boundaries of networks, see Laumann *et al.* [*1983*].

REFERENCES

Atkinson, M.M., and W.D. Coleman (1989), 'Strong States and Weak States: Sectoral Policy Networks in Advanced Capitalist Economies', *British Journal of Political Science*, Vol.19, No.1, pp.47–67.
Bennet, G. (1989), *The Internal Market and Environmental Policy in the Federal Republic of Germany and the Netherlands*, The Hague: DOP.
Berg, A.V. van den (1992), 'Milieurecht voor stoffen en produkten', *Tijdschrift voor Milieu en Recht*, No.4.
Boons, F. (1991), 'Environmental Policy and Chemical Industry in Europe: Conflict Cooperation and Commercialization', paper presented at the ECPR joint Workshops on 22–28 March 1991.
Brickman, R., Jasanoff, S. and T. Ilgen (1985), *Controlling Chemicals – The Politics of Regulation in Europe and the United States*, Ithaca, NY and London: Cornell University Press.
Elster, J. (1983), *Explaining Technical Change*, Cambridge: Cambridge University Press.
Granovetter, M. (1985), 'Economic Action and Social Structure: The Problem of Embeddedness', *American Journal of Sociology*, Vol.91, No.3, pp.481–510.
Hanf, K. (1978), *Interorganizational Policy Making*, London: Sage.

Huppes, G., van den Berg, M., de Groot, W., van Koten, M. and D. Schmidt (1986), *Potenties van produktbeleid*, CML mededelingen nr. 26, Leiden: CML.

Jacek, H.J. (1990), 'Private Interest Governments as Solutions to Global and Regional Problems: The Example of the Contemporary Chemical Industry', paper presented at the ISA World Congress of Sociology, July 1990.

Jordan, G. and K. Schubert, (1992), 'A Preliminary Ordering of Policy Network Labels', *European Journal of Political Research*, Vol.21, Nos.1–2, pp.7–28.

Kickert J.M., and F.A. van Vught (1984), 'Beleidsnetwerken en maatschappelijke sturing', in A.J. Bekke and U. Rosenthal (eds.), *Netwerken rond het openbaar bestuur*, Alphen a/d Rijn: Samson.

Laumann, E.O. and D. Knoke (1987), *The Organizational State – Social Choice in National Policy Domains*, Madison, WI: University of Wisconsin Press.

Laumann, E.O., Marsden, P.V. and D. Prensky (1983), 'The Boundary Specification Problem in Network Analysis', in R.S. Burt and M.J. Minor (eds.), *Applied Network Analysis – A Methodological Introduction*, London: Sage Publications, pp.18–34.

Lowe, P. and Goyder, J. (1983), *Environmental Groups in Politics*, London: George Allen & Unwin.

Paterson, W., Grant, W. and C. Whitston (1988), *Government and the Chemical Industry – A Comparative Study of Britain and West Germany*, Oxford: Clarendon Press.

Rhodes, R.A.W. and D. Marsh (1992), 'New Directions in the Study of policy networks', *European Journal of Political Research*, Vol.21, Nos.1–2, pp.181–205.

Useem, M. (1991), 'Business and politics in the United States and the United Kingdom', in S. Zukin and P. Dimaggio, *Structures of Capital – The Social Organization of the Economy*, New York: Cambridge University Press, pp.261–91.

VNCI (1989), *Op weg naar integraal kringloopbeheer*, VNCI-brochure 1989 No.7, Leidschendam: VNCI.

PART II: PROCESSES

Environmental Groups and the EC: Challenges and Opportunities

SONIA MAZEY and JEREMY RICHARDSON

Even though the basic 'rules of the game' may be familiar to lobbyists at the national level, the EC policy process is in many ways unique. Its multi-national, neo-federal nature, the openness of decision-making to lobbying, and the considerable weight of national politico-administrative elites within the process create a rather unstable and multi-dimensional environment to which all pressure groups must adapt.

Environmental groups have at least three fundamental strengths in the context of this complex policy process – a capacity to build European-level coalitions in the form of Euro-groups and umbrella organisations via the creation of cross-national Euro-level networks; an ability to contribute to European integration in the manner predicted by neo-functionalist theory; and an ability to set the political agenda in the environmental sector. In contrast, they have several fundamental weaknesses – they may be too dependent upon DG X1 and on the European Parliament; they may lack the resources or the will to participate within the policy process intensively from the initiation phase right through to implementation; other competing interests are becoming more effective in their mobilisation around the environmental issue; the environmentalists may also be in a degree of competition with each other; and their lobbying styles may limit their long-term capacity to influence policies.

Lobbying and Policy-Making in the EC: Some Special Characteristics

Whilst the environmental sector exhibits some special characteristics – not least of which is the currently very high political salience of environmental and green issues and the almost unique cross-sectoral nature of the environmental issue – groups lobbying in this sector face the same range of opportunity structures as other groups in the EC. Indeed, we argue elsewhere [*Mazey and Richardson, 1993a, 1993b, 1992c*] that the fundamental rules of the game for lobbyists at the European level are

This study is part of a project on lobbying in the EC funded by the ESRC. The authors wish to thank David Judge and Laura Cram for their comments on an earlier draft, and the many Commission officials and environmental groups and firms who agreed to be interviewed.

much the same as at the national level. Although politics in Brussels is not yet akin to the 'village life' which is thought to exist, say, in Whitehall in Britain, there are nevertheless some basic cultural norms that are not so dissimilar to those of more tightly integrated and unified national bureaucracies.

Thus, the successful groups are those that exhibit the usual professional characteristics – namely resources, advance intelligence, good contacts with bureaucrats and politicians, and above all an ability to provide policy-makers with sound information and advice. Reputations for expertise, reliability, and trust are key resources in lobbying in Brussels as elsewhere. A respondent from DG XI, for example, stressed the need for groups to be 'responsible' – by which was meant a willingness to be involved in the policy-making process without publicity. This means that lobbying *styles* may be as important as the content and objectives of the lobbying itself. The way that business is conducted will affect policy outcomes, as it plays a significant part in shaping the perceptions of participants and, therefore, their willingness to listen to each other, and to make concessions during the processing of issues. As another respondent remarked to us, there was a marked difference in the degree of professionalism of groups that approached the Commission and hence in the weight that was attached to their views. As we will suggest in the next section, perceptions may be especially relevant to a consideration of the politics of the environment in the EC, as the three main groups of interests – bureaucrats, environmentalists, and industrialists – have particular perceptions of each other which may affect their effectiveness in the policy-making process.

Even though the 'basic rules of the game' may be familiar, however, the EC policy process is in many ways unique. Its multi-national, neo-federal nature, the openness of decision-making to lobbying, and the considerable weight of national politico-administrative elites within the process, create a rather unstable and multi-dimensional environment to which all pressure groups must adapt if they are to achieve their objectives.

A major problem for all groups in the EC policy process is the comparative instability and unpredictability of the agenda setting process. In the UK, to take what may be an extreme example, significant policy change is usually preceded by a rather slow and well-known process, in which the 'affected interests' are given early warning of the possibility of policy change. Moreover, once the policy process is underway, it is unusual for there to be abrupt changes once basic agreement within the 'policy community' has been achieved [*Richardson and Jordan, 1979; Jordan and Richardson, 1987*]. The existence of these well-defined policy communities at the national level (especially in the Northern European democracies) is possibly the greatest contrast between national and EC policy-making at present. The European Commission is not yet sufficiently mature as an organisation for it to have developed widespread 'standard operating procedures' for processing policy issues. Of particular relevance to the lobbying strategies of groups trying to influence the EC is the fact that the Commission is still in the process of developing its consultation and co-ordination procedures. (For a discussion of the early development of the Commission see Mazey [1992].)

As two DG XI officers described the process to us, it can still appear 'far too haphazard' and something of a 'free for all ... [leaving] the door open for any groups wishing to contact Commission officers, rather than a selective grouping'. Yet there is an apparent contradiction in this characterisation of the consultation process, possibly explained by the fact that the Commission is an 'adolescent bureaucracy'. Thus a mixed style of consultation appears to exist. For example, there is some evidence that something like standard operating procedures are emerging in some sectors. Thus, in social policy there is a quite developed framework for negotiation and consultation, and in the environmental sector itself there are now plans to set up an official environmental forum (see conclusion below). There may now be sufficient examples of institutionalised and regularised consultation to suggest at least the existence of a 'procedural ambition' on the part of Commission officials to achieve a more stable (though possibly informal) set of policy actor relationships. Arp [1991: 14] cites the example of car emission regulations which are translated into the language of engineers and discussed as technical questions. These discussions are chanelled through The Motor Vehicle Emissions Group composed of Commission officials, national experts, the car industry, and consumer and environmental organisations Similarly, the issue of how to respond in practice to the EC's international treaty obligations regarding the depletion of the ozone layer was processed with the advice and participation of a group of industry representatives which the Commission convened.

In contrast to most national policy-making systems, policy-making power in the EC is dispersed and there are several informal policy initiators. Though the Commission announces its own legislative programme at the beginning of each year, other more pressing items may be added as a result of European Summit decisions. In addition, every national government uses its six month presidency of the Council of Ministers (during which period it also chairs and sets the agenda of all Council working groups) to push favoured projects to the front of the agenda (for example, the promotion of the 'social dimension' of the internal market by the French government) whilst MEPs, individual commissioners, ambitious ministers and interest groups all seek to push the Commission in certain directions. The multiplicity of 'opportunity structures' for groups is often perceived to be an advantage by all groups, but particularly by those denied access to national policy-makers. Yet this permeability of the system is also a disadvantage to groups. With few exceptions (agriculture may be the only one) no one set of groups – and certainly no individual group – can rely on *exclusive* access.

Thus, the process is best described as policy-making through loose, open, and extended issue networks, rather than through well defined, stable, and exclusive policy communities. Participation in the policy process is unpredictable, and policy ideas may appear suddenly and from little known sources. In practice, therefore, keeping track of EC policy initiatives is a major undertaking for groups, many of which lack sufficient resources to perform this task on their own. Our own research to-date suggests that the need to monitor EC policy developments is now widely acknowledged by national lobbies and is often cited as an important factor in their decision to form and join Euro-groups, however ineffective those groups might be. For example, one British company told us that it joined virtually every relevant trade association, at both the national and European level, as part of its information gathering system and in order to demonstrate to its peers that it was a good corporate citizen within the various industrial sectors in which it operated. In practice it often did not rely on the relevant Euro-group and preferred to lobby Brussels directly itself.

A second reason for the uncertain agenda is the existence of different national political agendas, which in turn leads to a degree of competitive agenda-setting within the EC itself. Again, our industrial contacts have suggested to us that this is their main weakness – an inability to influence, let alone control, the agenda setting process within Brussels and Strasbourg. This produces a *reactive* style of lobbying. More often than not, firms and industries are conducting rearguard or fire-brigade campaigns in response to agendas set by others – often by the environmentalists. While many Community issues are common across national boundaries, others are country specific; in other cases there are cross-national variations in the position of common issues or differing ideological stances, or both. Environmental policy is an example of the differing emphases found in EC states and of the EC's own agenda being pushed along by certain enthusiastic actors. For example, domestic 'green' pressure in West Germany played a part in encouraging its government to take the initiative in pressing for limits on car exhaust emissions, as did the interests of the German car industry. In the event, the issue soon became more complicated than a simple conflict between environmentalists and polluters [*Jordan and McLaughlin, 1993*]. The controversy, in 1991/92 over possible EC controls on packaging is also a case of a national agenda impinging on the EC's agenda. The German 'Packaging Decree', implemented in January 1992, placed responsibility upon manufacturers and distributors to the German market for the collection and disposal of all packaging materials, with further restrictions coming into force in April 1992 and January 1993. The German interest in the issue had a knock-on effect at the EC level, where a draft Directive on Packaging was being prepared. Fear that something like the German legislation would be introduced at the EC level caused consternation in the European packaging industry. For example, a representative of the Euro-federation – The Industry Council for Packaging and the Environment (INCPEN) – commented on the German proposals as follows: 'Never mind the Nimby factor (Not in My Back Yard), they seem to be suffering from the Banana syndrome – Build Absolutely Nothing Anywhere Near Anyone.' (*The Independent, 10 September 1991*). Significantly perhaps, INCPEN is a relatively new and predominately British actor at EC Level.

This particular example is illustrative of another general phenomenon of relevance to any discussion of environmental politics in the EC – namely that national action in the environmental field can soon be caught up in broader questions relating to the Single Market. There is an increasing fear that environmental action at the national level can be used as back door trade restrictions or to give special market advantages to firms that are launching new products or that have perfected a particular innovation [*Sargent, 1993*] The environmental field may be especially rich in cases of a close link between innovation and regulation and we must, therefore, be cautious in portraying the politics of the environment as a straightforward conflict between two blocks of interests groups – polluters and environmentalists. We suspect that, as the sector becomes more stable (in the sense that competing interests, and interested bureaucrats, may all tend to seek stability of processes and structures) we may see the emergence of rather unusual and complex coalitions of interests around particular policy problems. For example, the exhaust emissions issue was not a simple case of polluters versus environmentalists because of the different anti-emission technologies being developed by different car manufacturers, who soon came into conflict with each other over the preferred solution to the problem.

As suggested above, stability and predictability have certainly not yet arrived – if only because the basic formal processes of EC policy-making (and *implementation* mechanisms) are still in a state of flux. Also in the environmental sector, the legal competence of the Commission is relatively new. In that sense, all players are involved in a game in which the goal posts are bound to move. Yet, as Majone suggests, in the 20 years from 1967 to 1987 almost 200 directives, regulations and decisions were introduced by the Commission. This is despite the fact that environmental protection is not even mentioned in the Treaty of Rome and that the Commission's authority in this area was not recognised until the passage of the Single European Act (SEA). Moreover, as he notes, the rate of growth of environmental regulation appears to have been largely unaffected by 'the political vicissitudes, political crises, and recurrent waves of Europessimism of the 1970s and early 1980s' [*Majone, 1989: 165*]. Thus, environmental policy-making is now relatively well developed and in some cases the appropriate 'constituencies' of interests have been organised and mobilised and to some degree integrated into the policy process. More recently, the possibility of a 'partnership' between the interested parties has been emerging as an important concept presenting the opportunity to produce a greater degree of stability and predictability than described by the officers cited above (see conclusion below).

In fact, very little detailed research has been done on the subject of how groups generally have responded to the shift in policy-making power away from national capitals to Brussels, although much research is now under way. It is very clear, however, that the nature of the interface between the EC and interest groups generally is in a state of flux and is recognised by the Commission and the Parliament as a problem to be addressed. It is also clear that the constant shift in power to Brussels has resulted in increased pressures upon national groups to co-ordinate their lobbying activities through the European Federations. This trend has been encouraged by European Commission officials who are currently trying to rationalise the growing problem of group consultation and who have an official preference for dealing with Euro-groups. Preliminary findings suggest, however, that many European Federations (especially industrial sectoral federations) are beset by internal cleavages along national, ideological, organisational and policy lines [*Collie, 1993*].

Moreover, the European community, despite its growing importance, is not a sovereign state. Legislative power is shared between national member states and the Community. In consequence, groups must maintain existing national lobbying strategies whilst developing new strategies in response to the growing legislative competence of the EC. They must do this in a way which does not undermine existing relationships at the national level. Thus, 'playing the Brussels card' against a national administration may work on any given issue, but it may have serious long-term consequences in undermining relationships at the national level which have taken a very long time to build. This is especially relevant to environmental groups, many of which have worked hard over many years to achieve the respectability and consultative status at the national level which industrial associations have traditionally enjoyed.

A further problem for groups is that they have to contend with the fact that within the European Commission, policy-making is highly compartmentalised with little horizontal co-ordination between different Directorates-General which have a shared interest in an issue. Despite the fact that the Commission is a collegiate body, there is nevertheless a risk that once a legislative proposal has become the property of a particular DG and the particular constellation of interests surrounding it, other groups may find it difficult to be consulted effectively. Conflicting policy proposals relating to the same issue can emerge from different parts of the Commission. In order to avoid being taken by surprise, groups must be able to monitor and respond to policy developments in more than one DG. For environmental groups, for example, this task is rendered more difficult by the high turnover of people employed by the Commission on temporary contracts and the considerable variation in the internal organisation, culture and working methods (including consultation procedures) of different DGs, and different divisions within the same DG.

Another important feature of the Commission is its small size. Despite the popular image (especially in Britain!) of the Commission as a bloated bureaucracy, it is in fact very small when compared with national administrations. If we take an environmental example, there are approximately 15 staff in DG XI concerned with the control of chemicals yet in the US the Environmental Protection Agency has over 500 staff. The small size of the Commission has two important consequences for lobbying – it leaves the Commission very dependent upon outside sources (both pressure groups and national administrations) for expertise and information and it leaves the Commission very weak in terms of the oversight of EC directives once they have been incorporated into national legislation. (The European Court is, of course, also involved in the oversight of implementation and the Commission is involved in cases which come before the Court).

The Commission's aspiration is to be able to deal with Euro-groups which are at the same time *representative* and *expert*. In practice Commission officials regularly depart from this procedural ambition and consult not only national groups but individual firms. There is also a tendency to bypass representative structures altogether, as for example in the establishment of the Industrial Round Table in 1983. This horizontal Euro-Grouping brings together the heads of the leading European companies and multinationals. Significantly, membership of the ERT is by invitation only. (It currently consists of approximately 44 members drawn from individual companies and is chaired by Wisse Dekker from Philips, with Vice-Chairmen from Siemens and La Compagnie Lyonnaise des Eaux-Dumez.) Similar groupings include the European Information Technology Round Table created in the late 1970s at the initiative of the Commission and the Association for the Monetary Union of Europe, established in 1987. Those companies denied access to these groupings are under further pressure to join forces with their EC counterparts in the various Euro-groupings. Commission attempts to 'rationalise' the process of interest intermediation may mean that the EC policy-making process becomes corporatist in nature in those areas which have hitherto been more pluralist. The corporatist ambitions of the Commission are widely acknowledged. The key issue, however, is the extent to which the deregulatory thrust of the Single Market Programme, the internal characteristics of key interest groupings and the EC decision-making structures will permit such a development [*Gorges, 1991; Rhodes, 1990*]. In the case of the environment, there are very specific problems with the SEA. As Huelshoff and Pfeiffer [*1991: 145*] argue, 'the ambiguity of the SEA and the opposition of some member states to higher environmental standards have led to market goals being put before environmental goals in the EC'.

Since all legislative proposals are drafted by the Commission, it tends to be the focus of EC lobbying. Of particular importance in this respect are the 1,000 or so advisory groups and consultative committees some of which can play an important role in the initial drafting of EC proposals as well as being involved in the implementation of policy. Not surprisingly, membership of these groups is highly valued by groups. Since the adoption of the SEA, the European Parliament has also become a more important focus of lobbying activities and if the Maastricht Treaty is adopted, it looks set to increase further its role in environmental policy. However, within the EC the final decision on all policies is taken by *national* officials and politicians in the Council of Ministers. Groups at this stage must rely principally upon the negotiating skills and support of national civil servants and government ministers. Thus, somewhat paradoxically, the growing importance of EC legislation may sometimes reinforce the dependency which exists at the national level between groups and 'their' ministers. The degree of co-operation between groups and national administrations in this respect varies considerably, both between countries and between groups – not all of which enjoy the same degree of political legitimacy. In the environmental sector, groups at the national level are often in conflict with their own national administrations and hence see the EC as an alternative arena in which to excercise influence.

Finally, any assessment of the techniques of Euro-lobbying must examine the use of the courts by groups. The European Court of Justice, which is responsible for interpreting and enforcing EC law, is of crucial and increasing importance for EC lobbyists concerned with *implementation* of EC law. Since the 1970s, environmental organisations and women's groups especially, have used the Court (whose appellate powers resemble those of the US Supreme Court) as a means of forcing recalcitrant national governments to implement EC legislation concerning, for example, the quality of drinking water and equal treatment between working men and women (on the latter see Mazey [*1988*]). Under Articles 169 and 170 of the EEC Treaty the Court rules on whether member states have failed to uphold their Treaty obligations. Actions may be brought by the European Commission or by other member states. More generally, the principle of direct effect means that individuals and groups can rely upon EC law in national courts.

Environmental Groups in the EC: A Preliminary Analysis

If we set the ambitions and activities of environmental groups in the context of the characteristics of EC policy-making, as described in the first section, how might the groups be rated in terms of their likely efficacy as lobbyists? What are their strengths and weaknesses?

It appears that environmental groups have at least three fundamental strengths in the context of the EC at present[1] (although as we shall argue, these advantages may be eroded over time). They are in no particular order of priority:

(1) a capacity to build European level coalitions in the form of Euro-groups, umbrella organisations, or through the creation of cross-national Euro-level networks;

(2) through these coalitions, an ability to contribute to European integration in the manner predicted by neo-functionalist theory and hence, in a manner likely to be attractive to the Commission;

(3) an ability to set the political agenda in the environmental sector and to structure the content of issues in ways which place other interests at a disadvantage. In contrast, environmental groups may have certain fundamental weaknesses;

(4) these groups may be too dependent upon good relations with one part of the Commission, namely DG XI, and upon the European Parliament;

(5) they may lack the resources or will to participate within the policy process *intensively* from the initiation phase right through to policy decision and beyond, up to implementation;

(6) other interests are becoming more effective in their mobilisation around the environmental issue, presenting much more competition for the attention and consideration of policy-makers;

(7) notwithstanding (1) above, the environmentalists may be subjected to some of the competitive and entrepreneurial tendencies to which all pressure groups are subject, and this may ultimately limit the effectiveness of their coalition-building capacities;

(8) their lobbying style may limit their capacity to influence policy-making, yet if it changes, they may face problems in maintaining support within their own constituencies.

We shall deal with these strengths and weaknesses in turn, although it should be emphasised that they are, of course, interrelated.

All researchers have emphasised the weakness of Euro-groups, essentially because these groups are usually composed of very diverse interests, often in fierce competition with each other in the market place. The Euro-federation representing the chemical manufacturers is usually cited as one of the few really successful Euro-federations. This alleged success has much to do with the fact that CEFIC is dominated by a few large manufacturers within European and worldwide interests and that the structure of the European Chemical Industry does not vary as much as, say, the financial services sector in Europe [*Knight et al., 1993*]. The most common criticism of Euro-federations representing industry is that they are understaffed [*Collie, 1993*] and that in so far as they have anything to say, it is characterised by the label 'lowest common denominator' – that is, the internal divisions are such that their policy statements are more like peace treaties designed to keep the Federations together, than well argued technical proposals on which EC officials can act. Thus many, if not most, peak and sectoral associations representing industry are not highly regarded, are under-resourced with small (but increasing) staffing, and subject to unwitting undermining by the actions of the Commission itself – namely by the Commission regularly consulting individual firms and national organisations. Moreover, it is often the case that these federations are often not staffed by people who have a long-term future in their own industries, in that it is relatively common for them to be staffed

by personnel who are nearing retirement. Thus, it appears that few companies see sending their young or middle managers to Euro-federations
as part of a programme of long-term career development.

In contrast, environmental groups appear to have a *prima facie* advantage in that they are not inherently competing with each other for market
share, in the sense that, for example, European car-makers are. Purely
local environmental and civic groups may engage in the equivalent of
market behaviour when they adopt the NIMBY principle, but there is no
evidence that national environmental and Euro-environmental groups
have been tempted by those tactics. Indeed, a good deal of the effort of
European level groups is directed to influencing the EC (and its associated industries) *not* to exploit Third World countries, for example,
either by exporting its pollution problems or by adopting aid policies
which lead to non-sustainable development. Thus, the World Wide
Fund for Nature (WWF) has argued that development policies both
within the EC (regional, social, and agricultural guidance funds) together
with its aid programmes for Central and Eastern Europe (PHARE), the
African-Caribbean countries (ACP), Asian and Latin American
countries (ALA), and Mediterranian countries '... must be placed on a
new sustainable footing ... plans, programmes and projects must demonstrate through quantitative and qualitative assessments how the stock of
natural resource capital will be maintained or increased' [*WWF, 1991:
11*].

Following the EC's increasing involvement in international affairs (the
EC is currently involved in the negotiation of over 20 international
treaties), environmental groups and other Non Governmental Organisations (NGOs) are present in large numbers whenever and wherever
international negotiations take place and are of increasing influence in
these negotiations, albeit that they are not *directly* involved in them.
There is also, of course, a widespread and genuine recognition within the
environmental movement that problems are cross-national and worldwide and that there is little point in trying to redistribute environmental
costs between one country and another through the lobbying process.
Few *industries* are capable of taking a co-ordinated industry-wide European – let alone a worldwide-view – of their long-term interests (for
example, in such industries as telecommunications, the concept of
national champions dies hard). The big conflicts of interest which arise
within European industry (and between European industry and the
Americans and Japanese) generally do not arise between environmental
groups. They have different interests and emphasise different issues, but
they are essentially on the same side fighting the same cause and have a
common interest in better environmental regulations. There is not the

kind of competition to use regulatory regimes to gain comparative advantage in which industrial and commercial interests are engaged.

This relative lack of conflict of interest enables environmental groups – and other NGOs [*Harvey, 1993*] – to construct large networks of interests which link Euro-level organisations and national level organisations. These are *potentially* powerful if they can be managed successfully. The European Environmental Bureau (EEB) is one example of such a network, consisting of over 120 NGOs in the environmental field. It was founded 16 years ago, in part because the Commission (particularly DG XI) needed an NGO movement as a counterweight to the industrial lobby. Consequently, the EEB receives significant amounts of the EC funding to hold seminars (for example, on eco-labelling) and round tables on specific issues, although opinions on EEB's actual policy impact differ considerably. The mobilisation and management of these networks (there is a proliferation of them) is a problematic task, but they represent a considerable resource – both in political and expertise terms – if they can be made to work, and there are few if any permanent equivalents on the industrial and commercial side.

The networks do also possess the potential predicted for groups by the neo-functional theorists such as Haas [*1958*], who suggested that groups would play a central role in European integration. They would turn to supranational means when this course appears profitable to their members. He argued that this process of group formation would be purely *tactical* as organised employer interests in a pluralistic setting outgrew the nation state [*Haas, 1958: 354*]. This lack of 'ideological cohesion' which he saw in industrial and commercial interests is not however, as we have argued, really a problem within the environmental movement, which is much more often able to express a genuinely European view. This is, of course, attractive to the Commission which is particularly anxious to see all lobbying presented in European terms. (All commercial lobbying firms advise their commercial clients to present arguments in European and not national terms, for example.) In this sense, the environmentalists have reached a much more advanced stage in the Europeanisation of lobbying and have already adopted the ideals of European integration. They are much more integrated in their behaviour than are the groups with whom they normally compete, and do not find the adoption of a European perspective nearly as problematic as industrial and commercial groups (for an example see Knight *et al.* [*1993*]).

The ability of environmental groups to set the political agenda is perceived by the industrialists to whom we have spoken as perhaps the greatest current asset of the environmentalists. Indeed, one leading European environmental campaigner told us that he saw his organisation as very much at the 'ideas level' and rather less involved in the very specific technical details of policies. Indeed, he argued that his organisation has eschewed the 'expertise' approach. It saw itself as dealing in the currency of ideas and in creating the conditions under which the level of detail could then be decided. The strategy appeared to be to place issues on the agenda and to define the issues sufficiently clearly so that technical detail could safely be left to others. We might qualify this view by suggesting that the environmentalists are in fact rather effective in translating scientific findings of a complex kind into more generally comprehensible political issues (for example, global warming, or heavy metal pollution) to which policy-makers and other interests have to respond. Indeed, environmental groups might be said to be one of the key links in modern society between science and politics, often being responsible for some kind of 'megaphone' effect transmitting scientific ideas from the private world of professional science into the world of public policy. The fact that many of the groups have especially good links with the European Parliament also lends support to the thesis that agenda setting is their forte; in so far as the Parliament has influence, it is better at raising issues than in processing them. The downside of this power on the part of groups is that it may be heavily dependent on what Gregory [1971] termed the 'halo effect' of the environmental issue. Currently (as in the 1970s) the environment is high on the political agenda and all interests are inclined to take it seriously. But if the environment were again to enter the downward sector of the Downsian issue attention cycle [Downs, 1972], the environmentalists might find greater difficulty in exercising what Schattschneider terms the supreme exercise of political power – determining what politics is actually about [Schattschneider, 1960].

Turning now to the possible weaknesses of the environmental movement at the EC level, perhaps the most obvious is their relative dependence on DG XI. Indeed, one Commission official suggested to us that the task force which preceded the formation of DG XI was originally so weak that it sought the support of the NGOs and mobilised and supported them in order to defend itself. He believed that without NGO support DG XI might have died in its early years. This suggests that the Directorate is possibly an example of a phenomenon described by Downs as being common to all bureaucracies – namely that in the early stages of their life, they deliberately cultivate external clients who then come to depend upon them and will defend them in times of crisis faced by the agency [Downs, 1967]. It is certainly the case that the NGO movement generally (including environmental groups) receives financial support from the Commission (directly or via various contracts) and it can be argued that as a result, there is an unhealthy degree of dependency (indeed one Commission official described some of the environmental groups as having been 'tamed'; however, groups like Greenpeace deliberately avoid Commission funding, and WWF has set a limit of between 10 and 15 per cent on funding from public agencies). Gradually, the environmentalists are gaining more access to other Directorates General – quite successfully on some specific issues – but most environmental respondents reported what we would see as 'skewed' access to the Commission, with much better access to DG XI than elsewhere. Some (rival) interests see this ready access as 'agency capture' by the environmentalists and argue that it is extremely difficult to represent an alternative (industrial) view to most of DG XI. They therefore seek representation at levels higher than the Service level and attempt to mobilise other Directorates General to fight their corner on environmental issues. Of much more importance to the environmentalists is the fact that so many other Directorates General are responsible for policies which have major environmental implications. This means that the task of lobbying the Commission is that much more difficult (say compared with that for interests in the IT field) and demands vast resources if the 'environmental waterfront' (in lobbying terms) is to be covered properly. Even in those areas where the environmentalists have especially good contacts, Commission officials have the ability to 'close' the issue without much difficulty, unless the group can mobilise pressure in the European Parliament. There is no doubt, however, that there is a degree of 'greening' of the Commission as a whole, reflecting European wide pressure on all national governments and parliaments to pay greater attention to environmental issues.

The question of *resources* and its impact on the efficacy of environmental groups is quite difficult to assess. The European level environmental groups may seem quite well resourced when compared with sectoral business associations at the European level. For example, Greenpeace has 12 full-time staff in its European office compared with a typical sectoral federation such as The European Association of Textile Polyolefirms (EATP) which has only four staff yet represents 60 members drawn from 15 European countries [*Peckstadt et al., 1992*], or indeed with a peak business association such as UNICE [*Collie, 1993*]. Moreover, Greenpeace claims to have access to over 1,200 environmental and scientific experts worldwide and feels able to compete with industrial groups in terms of specialist advice, as well as in the more political arena for which it is best known through its publicity seeking activities. Our own interviews with officials within DG XI also suggest that environmental groups (and indeed the NGO movement generally in other fields such as poverty, housing and health) are rather well regarded by many (though not all) officials for their groups' expertise in environmental matters. Groups like World Wildlife Fund for Nature (WWF) can also claim considerable field expertise and have a degree of legitimacy from their direct involvement in the *implementation* process. Thus, WWF currently spends 19.5 million ECUs per year on conservation work in Europe. By no means all of the work is in Western Europe as WWF has recognised the growing importance of environmental problems in Eastern Europe, for example, and is involved at a very practical level in developing schemes for better environmental management of resources [*WWF, 1991*]. It is not simply an advisory group, raising issues and helping to define the agenda, but it also has the resources (a limited proportion of which, unlike Greenpeace, came from the EC) both to devise and implement practical solutions. This is particularly important in certain areas of the EC where local administrations may not be the best agents for service delivery – for example, in Spain. In these contexts, WWF can actively devise and deliver field projects.

Groups such as WWF, Greenpeace, and FoE can also mobilise the resources of their *national* organisations to lobby individual national administrations, thus influencing deliberations in the Council of Ministers. Yet, there still remains a doubt concerning the group's ability to stay with an issue from A to Z of the EC policy process. Two important rules of lobbying in Brussels are that groups need to get in *early* – when the issue is but a gleam in an official's eye [*Hull, 1992*] and to *stay* with the issue at every stage throughout the whole process. Our interviewees suggest that the environmentalists do not really have the capacity to stay with the detail of an issue through its life cycle in the policy process. (Thus, the view cited above, to the effect that agenda setting may be sufficient, is a high risk strategy; the devil may be in the details!) Alternatively, they may not have the deep-seated *interest* that, say, a company whose very survival is threatened by EC legislation would have. Sargent's [*1993*] study of trade associations points out that firms are often reluctant to commit resources to a trade association (at either the national or the European level) but are more willing to set up specific, *ad hoc*, well resourced organisations, on issues that are of special significance to them. It is, therefore, misleading to compare the resourcing of environmental groups with equivalent Euro- and national trade associations. Firms both devote resources to *ad hoc*, one issue, organisations and do a lot of direct lobbying with Commission officials and MEPs. Our evidence suggests that in those areas of environmental policy where industry has a really keen and vital interest, the resources mobilised are very considerable indeed and usually far outweigh those of any of the environmental groups. This is because, although industrial Euro-associations have very small staffs, they are able to call upon both the personnel and the expertise of their member firms.

In fact, key firms are probably the first port of call for some EC officials wanting particular types of data and information. The firm's national and Euro-association will be 'consulted' but often only after prior 'testing' of problems and ideas at the level of the firm. A related weakness for environmental groups, in terms of resources, is that – as one environmental group official put it to us – 'we can't follow *every* issue of relevance to the environment – they are too many – and we have to choose on which of the many issues we can concentrate our resources.' One consequence of this is that there appears to be a degree of 'product specialisation' (itself an advantage in terms of expertise) by the main Euro-level environmental groups, which may be leaving significant tracts of 'environmental policy space' to the lobbying activities of industrial and commercial groups (IT policy and R & D policy may be examples). Thus, Greenpeace has a strategy of concentrating in four areas of campaigning – ocean ecology; toxics; nuclear; and atmosphere and energy, and WWF is especially interested in the EC Structural Fund's relationship between trade and the environment, and in the Common Agricultural Policy.

Perhaps the greatest long-term threat to the influence of environmental groups is that other interests are becoming much more active in this sector. Essentially, industrial interests are now taking the environmental issue much more seriously and are beginning to devote the lobbying resources needed if their voice is to become more effective and if they are to become less 'reactive' in their lobbying styles. There is increasing pressure on DG XI, for example, to talk to industrial interests. Also, the industrial interests can be expected to defend their existing relationships with other DGs as the environmentalists try to expand their sphere of influence. Moreover, we should not underestimate the capacity of industry to take on board the environmental issue at the company level, partly in response to their perception of public pressure and in part out of purely commercial self interest. As one participant put it to us, he had not come across very many environmental issues that really were life and death to a particular company or industry. He was surprised how often legislation was originally opposed because it would be 'the end of the industry', only for the industry to absorb the extra costs (or pass them on to its consumers) with relative ease once the legislation was in place.

Thus, 'delay' rather than 'stop' may well be the slogan more appropriate to industrial lobbying in the environmental sector, with the more sophisticated industrial actors being aware that being pro-active (pre-emptive strikes) may be the best lobbying stategy of all. Whether or not this is true, there is little doubt that industrial interests are becoming much more active in presenting technical and well researched arguments when faced with challenges, and in actually *anticipating* possible challenges. Nor should it be assumed that industrial interests necessarily seek to obstruct the introduction of EC environmental legislation. Within the internal market, a competitive advantage accrues to environmentally progressive companies. This may gradually improve the bad public image of industrialists and enable them to engage in political dialogue more effectively. Also, they may be more willing to enter into a direct dialogue with the environmental interests, forcing the latter to rethink their own lobbying strategies, too.

Finally, we may speculate that, in practice, the environmental sector is not quite as 'uncompetitive' as we have earlier suggested. There is broad ideological agreement and generally an absence of conflicts over policy – yet in one sense there is a degree of competition within the environmental sector. True, there is much collaboration and co-ordination at the European level – for example the main Euro-level organisations have regular meetings every four to six weeks in order to exchange information and ideas. Similarly, as we have suggested, there is a degree of 'product specialisation' or 'niche marketing' – to use two commercial analogies. Yet it is also possible to characterise the leaders of environmental groups – and of other NGOs – simply as essentially entrepreneurs who wish to expand the influence of their organisations just as firms wish to expand their markets – and whose own success to some degree depends on their organisation's achieving some special status in the policy process. They may also be in competition for members and financial support and need to demonstrate 'action' and success' (not always synonymous) to their members as well as to the broader policy network as a whole. This is especially true at the national level, where the organisational representation of the environmental issue may well be beyond saturation point in some of the Northern democracies. However, it is not at all certain that there is a total absence of competition at the European level or that some organisations might not be squeezed by a degree of over-representation of interests at the European level.

Conclusion: Lobbying Styles and Long-Term Success

By way of brief conclusion we now turn to the difficult concept of 'lobbying styles', as this does still present a problem to the environmentalists. The sometimes confrontational styles of environmental groups – and the increased use of legal actions (see below) – may be perpetuating an image which at least some of the groups might wish to shed. For example, one environmental respondent told us that his organisation was working hard to create a rather different image because some EC officials saw environmentalists as obstructionist, anti-growth and heavily reliant on the use of the media to attack both decision-makers and companies alike. His ambition was to emphasise a new perspective, which was to engage in a political and economic discussion in those policy areas hitherto regarded as more centrally economic than environmental. (Significantly one official, dealing with this group, commented to us that he had indeed found the group considerably more useful and better informed of late.)

If our underlying assumption is correct – namely that the Commission will gradually seek to establish a more regularised and structured form of group participation in the policy process (whether by the establishment of policy communities or even corporatist structures, or by structures that are peculiarly European, remains to be seen) – then this will present a serious challenge to the environmentalists. This is because confrontational and challenging styles of lobbying may well be incompatible with the unwritten rules of the game implied by the policy community model or its variants. Essentially, policy communities are about the private management of public business [*Richardson and Jordan, 1979*]. However, the nature of the EC policy process, with increased use of the Court and an increased role for the Parliament, may mean that it will be difficult to confine the processing of issues within the bounds of well defined policy communities. Whether resort to more public and openly conflictual arenas of decision-making is conducive to the development of stable long-term relationships between decision-makers and groups is, however, open to doubt.

A particular problem may arise because of the increase in 'whistleblowing' by environmental groups who now play an important role in warning the Commission of implementation failure at the national level. Thus the number of complaints by individual citizens (often encouraged by pressure groups) and the number of legal actions by groups themselves is showing a rapid increase. For example a number of British groups, including the UK branch of FoE, have been involved in complaining to the Commission about the British government's handling of various road schemes – notably the M11 link road and the East London river crossing – resulting in Carlo Ripa di Meana's challenging the UK government in October 1991.

In the short run, national groups are gaining considerable benefit from this type of activity and the Commission seems anxious to maintain this unofficial monitoring function by groups, as it is increasingly conscious of the 'implementation gap'. Yet it does risk placing the groups in what at the national level would be regarded as the 'outsider group' category and this process may be counter-productive in terms of their developing a more co-operative dialogue with national governments (still of central importance in the implementation of environmental policy, despite the growth of EC influence). It may also affect the perception that Commission officials have of the Euro-level environmental groups. The temptations of demonstrable success now – of considerable importance in maintaining membership support and media coverage – may be at the price of a more fundamental influence in the policy process in the long-run. The trade-off may be between maintaining a high public profile through an action-oriented approach to lobbying, and sacrificing a chance of long-term influence in the *processing* of issues.

The toughest test so far for the environmentalists is the Commission's proposal to set up an environmental forum, under the fifth Environmental Action Programme. The proposed advisory forum is designed to enable a dialogue with the social partners (by which is meant the 'interested parties' in the environmental sector) who will play an influential role in Community policy-making. This is a reflection of the Commission's desire to shift the pattern away from regulatory instruments towards the promotion of what it calls collective responsibility. If this ambition is achieved, the two competing interests will have been incorporated into the policy process as joint partners – with all the constraints and responsibilities that that entails.

NOTE

1. For the purposes of this study the term 'environmentalists' is used to describe individuals or groups whose primary objective is the introduction of policies beneficial to the environment. In contrast to firms and industrial federations which may promote environmentally friendly products, environmentalists have no direct material interest in EC environmental policy.

REFERENCES

Arp, Henning (1991), 'European Community Environmental Policy: What to Learn From the Case of Car Emission Regulation?', Paper presented to Conference on European Integration and Environmental Policy, Woudschoten, Netherlands, 29–30 Nov 1991.

Collie, Lynn (1992), 'Business Lobbying in the EC: The Union of Industrial Employers' Confederations of Europe', in Mazey and Richardson [*1992c*].

Downs, A. (1967), *Inside Bureaucracy*, Boston, MA; Little, Brown.

Downs, A. (1972), 'Up and Down with Ecology – the "Issue Attention Cycle"', *The Public Interest*, Vol.28, pp.38–50.

Gorges, M.J. (1991), 'Euro-Capitalism? The System of Interest Intermediation in the European Community', Paper delivered to the Annual Meeting of the American Political Science Association, Washington, DC, 29 Aug.–1 Sept 1991.

Gregory, R. (1971), *The Price of Amenity*, London: Macmillan.

Hass, Ernst B. (1958), *The Uniting of Europe: Political, Social and Economic Forces* Stanford, CA: Stanford University Press.

Harvey, Brian, (1992), 'European Lobbying: The Experience of Voluntary Organisations', in Mazey and Richardson [1993b].

Huelshoff, Michael G. and Thomas Pfeiffer (1991), 'Environmental Policy in the EC: Neo-functionalist Sovereignty Transfer or Neo-realist Gatekeeping', *International Journal*. Vol.47, No.1, pp.136–58.

Hull, Robert (1992), 'Lobbying in Brussels: A View from Within', in Mazey and Richardson [*1993b*].

Jordan, A.G. and J.J. Richardson (1987), *British Politics and the Policy Process*, London: Allen & Unwin.

Jordan, A.G., and A.M. McLaughlin (1992), 'The Rationality of Lobbying in Europe: Why are Euro-Groups So Numerous And So Weak: Some Evidence from the Car Industry', in Mazey and Richardson [*1993b*].

Knight, Jeffrey, Mazey, Sonia and Jeremy Richardson (1993), 'Groups and the Process of European Integration: The Work of the Federation of Stock Exchanges in the European Community', in Mazey and Richardson [*1993b*].

Majone, G. (1989), 'Regulating Europe: Problems and Prospects'. *Jarbuch zur Staats – und Verwaltungswissenschaft*, Baden-Baden.

Mazey, Sonia (1988), 'European Community Action on Behalf of Women: The Limits of Legislation, *Journal of Common Market Studies*, Vol.27,' No.1, pp.63–84.

Mazey, Sonia (1992), 'The Administration of the High Authority 1955–56: Development of a Supranatural Bureaucracy?', in R. Morgan and V. Wright. *The Early Principles and Practice of the EC (European Yearbook of the History of Administration)*.

Mazey, Sonia P. and Jeremy J. Richardson (1992), 'British Pressure Groups in the European Community: The Challenge of Brussels', *Parliamentary Affairs*, Vol.45, No.1, pp.92–127.

Mazey, Sonia P. and Jeremy J. Richardson (1993a), 'Interest Groups in the European Community', in J.J. Richardson (ed.), *Pressure Groups*, Oxford: Oxford University Press.

Mazey, Sonia P. and Jeremy J. Richardson (eds.) (1993b), *Lobbying in the EC*, Oxford: Oxford University Press.

Peckstadt, Jean-Pierre, Mazey, Sonia P. and Jeremy J. Richardson (1992), 'Defending and Promoting a Sectoral Interest Within the European Community: The Case of the Textile Polyolefins Industry', in Mazey and Richardson [*1993b*].

Rhodes, M. (1990), 'The Social Dimension of the Single European Market: National vs. Transnational Regulation', *European Journal of Political Research*, Dec.

Richardson, J.J. and A.G. Jordan (1979), *Governing Under Pressure*, Oxford: Martin Robertson.

Sargent, Jane (1993), 'The Corporate Benefits of Lobbying: The British Case and its Relevance to the EC', in Mazey and Richardson [*1993b*].

Schattschneider, E.E. (1960), *The Semi-Sovereign People: A Realist's View of Democracy in America*, New York: Holt, Reinhart & Winston.

WWF (1991), *Focus in WWF in Europe*, Brussels.

The Green Voter in the 1989 European Elections

MARK N. FRANKLIN and WOLFGANG RÜDIG

Green parties achieved a major breakthrough in the 1989 European elections. Who voted green in these elections? This first comprehensive comparative analysis of the green voter in Europe reveals, that, as expected, green voting is more common among the young, well-educated, and middle class, and green voters also tend to be left-wing, post-materialist and concerned about the environment and arms limitation. But these stereotypical attributes of greenness closely apply to the German and Dutch Greens only: green voters in other countries comply far less, if at all, with this socio-demographic profile. The one pervasive predictor is environmental concern, which is dominant in Britain, France, Belgium and Ireland. It is rather less important in Germany and the Netherlands where post-materialism and a left-wing orientation are more prevalent instead. The basis of green voting is thus rather less narrow than previously thought. The sharper delineation of support for the German Greens has contributed to a relatively stable green vote in the past, but the potential for attracting other sectors of the electorate are clearly very limited. Green parties in most other countries appear to be able to attract votes from a wider spectrum of the population but the commitment of these voters is likely to be far more volatile.

The European elections of 1989 provided a major boost for the green movement. Virtually all over Europe green parties made gains, even in some countries which had previously not been noted for their enthusiasm for such parties. The most surprising result was recorded in Britain where the previously hardly known Green Party polled a staggering 14.9 per cent of the vote, the highest ever share that a green party has achieved in nation-wide elections anywhere in the world. The French Greens who previously had also looked like a rather weak party with poor electoral prospects provided the second surprise, polling 10.6 per cent. While the

The authors are grateful to Lynn Bennie, John Curtice, Michael Marsh, Tom Mackie and an anonymous referee of *Environmental Politics* for their helpful comments on previous versions of this study. Naturally, all remaining faults are their responsibility alone.

British Greens were prevented by their majority voting electoral system from sending any member to the European parliament, the French achieved a major breakthrough and got nine MEPs elected. Green parties generally did well in other European countries, too [*Curtice, 1989; Niedermayer, 1989; Mackie, 1990*].

At the same time, it is noteworthy that the German Greens failed to improve significantly on their previous results. *Die Grünen* merely confirmed the results of the previous general election. Similarly, the Dutch 'Rainbow' list, which claimed the green mantle in the Netherlands, failed to make any significant breakthrough.

The results of the 1989 European elections raise a number of important questions about the character and future of green politics in Europe. First, who are all the new green voters, and what are the chances of their voting green again in future elections? European elections are regarded as 'second order elections' [*Reif, 1984*] in which voters are more inclined to vote for small parties because the result in their view does not really matter. However, in the past, green parties have quite successfully used European elections as a spring-board to national respectability: interpretations of early successes of Belgian and German green parties in European elections in terms of protest votes were confounded by the subsequent firm establishment of these parties in their respective national party systems [*Curtice, 1989: 218*]. The question is thus whether green parties in Britain and France (and also in some other countries) can repeat this pattern. Conversely, does the disappointing result for the German Greens augur badly for their long-term future? To answer this question, we will not only look at those who actually voted green in 1989 but also at those who expressed a potential to vote green in the future.

The second key question we would like to explore concerns the nature of green politics generally. There are many shades of green, and the various European green parties are not necessarily of the same green tint. The German Greens and the Dutch Rainbow parties have long been regarded as 'New Left' groupings which do not exclusively or even primarily define their identity in ecological terms, pursuing instead a broader agenda of issues including economic deprivation, racism, and a host of other radical causes [*Rüdig, 1985*]. The French and British green parties, on the other hand, are generally seen as more narrowly 'ecological' parties. The European election result suggests that the left-wing green parties were not doing very well, in contrast to their more 'ecological' counterparts in Britain and France.

On the other hand, while there is evidence on the existence of these differences in terms of the genesis of parties and their programmes, do these differences actually filter through to the voters? In other words, do 'ecological' and 'left' green parties really have different political constituencies? And, if so, what implications does this have for the stability of green voting preferences?

These questions have important political and theoretical implications. Green parties have been seen by some writers as the representatives of a new cleavage which, potentially, gives them the chance to establish themselves firmly in the party system. On the other hand, green parties could be seen as a more ephemeral phenomenon. With an increasing dealignment of the electorate from big parties and party politics in general, the old certainties and stabilities are gone. Party choice has become volatile, and any party, even the Greens, can suddenly benefit from this volatility [*Franklin, Mackie, Valen et al., 1992*]. However, any such electoral gains could disappear as quickly as they appeared [*Franklin, 1985*]. The key question is whether the break-up of old party systems has indeed led to a volatile situation where party choice is essentially unpredictable and (almost) anything is possible, or whether the old certainties are in the process of being replaced by new ones, including the formation of a new green constituency which identifies with green parties and votes for them on a regular basis.

These questions will be explored in this article with the help of the results of the 1989 European Elections Study.[1] Green voting behaviour has been studied before, but there has never been a truly comparative analysis involving any large number of European countries. The data from the 1989 European Elections Study now give us the first proper chance to compare green voters in different countries systematically.

First, we will look at some of the theories that have underpinned research on green voting behaviour so far. We will then present and analyse our own data, leading to a discussion of the likely future course of green politics in Europe.

Theories of Green Politics

The rise of green parties in the 1980s has recently led to a burgeoning literature on green politics, espousing a variety of theoretical approaches to its explanation [*Lowe and Rüdig, 1986; Kitschelt 1988a; 1989; Kitschelt and Hellemans, 1990; Müller-Rommel, 1989a; 1989b; Rüdig, 1990*]. The strengths and drawbacks of the various theories are linked to the particular focus of their explanatory endeavours.

A number of these theories were developed out of the specifically German situation. For example, Bürklin [*1984; 1987*] and Alber [*1985;*

1989] have argued that green politics is essentially a function of the blocked mobility of a new class of unemployed academics: green supporters are young and highly educated, but they are not part of mainstream economic activity. Rather they are marginalised and excluded. This has several important implications: support for green parties is likely to melt away once the specific historical conditions which have brought green politics about (an educational revolution combined with a baby boom and a stagnation of the tertiary sector) disappear or are addressed by the established parties.

If we follow this approach, what would we expect the green voter in Europe to look like? He or she should be predominantly young, highly educated, and without regular employment – students and unemployed could be expected to support the greens particularly strongly. Even before we can test this relatively simple hypothesis, it looks unlikely that the rather sudden rise of the greens in Britain and France could be explained by Bürklin's and Alber's theories: there was no rise in graduate unemployment at that time in these countries, and other factors must have been at work to cause this sudden electoral upsurge of the greens.

What other theories could fill this gap? Apart from the possibility of treating green votes in 1989 as protest votes, we should note that one of Bürklin's sharpest critics has been Herbert Kitschelt [*1988b*] who has put forward a comprehensive theory of the emergence of what he terms 'left-libertarian' parties. Kitschelt [*1988a; 1989*] argues that these 'left-libertarian' parties are the outcome of certain structural developments: they form a response to growth-oriented, bureaucratic and anti-democratic political structures. They are 'left-libertarian' because they combine a commitment to individual autonomy and public participation with a programme of social justice and economic redistribution. They open up a new cleavage and are not ephemeral protest parties likely to disappear quickly. Kitschelt applies this model to explain the international differences in the strength of green parties: countries with a low per capita income, low growth rate, underdeveloped welfare state provisions, a low degree of labour corporatism, a high strike rate and without major socialist or communist party participation in government are unlikely to develop significant left-libertarian parties, and vice versa.

The model seemed to work reasonably well before 1989, but the 1989 results have shown the emergence of major green parties in countries which do not show the right combination of macro-sociological factors, particularly France and the UK. There are two possibilities: either the model of left-libertarian parties is faulty, or the parties which have emerged in France and the United Kingdom are different from green parties elsewhere. Indeed, given Kitschelt's definition of 'left-libertarianism' as containing a major commitment to redistribution, the programme of the British and French Greens as 'ecological' rather than 'red-green' parties may well warrant their exclusion from the category of 'left-libertarianism'. We would expect the factors propelling the success of green parties in France and the UK to be rather different from most other green parties in Europe, particularly in West Germany and Belgium. And this would shed serious doubt on the applicability of Kitschelt's theory of 'left-libertarianism' to the phenomenon of green parties generally.

Kitschelt's analytical focus is very much on the macro-level, on the different development of national parties. At the level of individual green voters, the theory that also suggests that green parties are the result of a more fundamental structural change is the well-known theory of post-materialism. The basic tenets of that theory have been spelled out often enough and need not be repeated here. The theory of post-materialist value change [*Inglehart 1977; 1990*] has been the dominant source of reference for many studies of green voting behaviour. Preference for post-materialist values has been shown in a number of studies to be linked to voting for green parties [*Lowe and Rüdig, 1986; Müller-Rommel, 1989b; Poguntke, 1993*]. Again, we can test this theory with our data.

What has been less clear in previous work is the relative importance of post-materialism is comparison with other variables. Post-materialism is associated with high levels of education and has a negative relation to age, due to differences in generational experiences; but how much of the variance in (in our case) green voting could be explained by age and education alone, and how much is left to be explained by post-materialism once other (often causally prior) effects have been taken into account?

Furthermore, one of the main criticisms of post-materialism has been that it does not really measure value change but simply changes in attitudes on particular issues [*Clarke and Dutt, 1991*]. Given that all green parties have a dominant concern for 'the environment', irrespective of their different view on the traditional social questions of redistribution of wealth and social justice [*Rüdig, 1990*], will an attitude-related index with more specific concern for issues which are of key importance to green ideology (the environment, nuclear energy, arms limitations, and so on) not be equally or more successful as a predictor of green voting? Alternatively, if green parties are predominantly 'left-libertarian' in their outlook, will the voter's placement on a traditional left–right scale not be an equally good predictor of green voting as their espousal or otherwise of post-material values?

We now have a number of hypotheses on the likely shape of the 'green voter' and we can proceed to test these hypotheses with data from the 1989 European election study.

Data

The survey from which our data derive was carried out over a four-week period, starting on 20 June 1989, in all EC countries. Because the share of green votes for Spain, Greece, and Luxemburg is too small to be interpreted, we will concentrate in this paper on the data for Britain (excluding Northern Ireland), West Germany, France, Belgium, Italy, Netherlands, and Ireland.

Turning to individual countries, green votes in Belgium include both votes for *AGALEV* and *ECOLA*. For France, the corresponding figures include only votes for *Les Verts*. Votes for some smaller groups, for example one list concerned with animal rights, were not included. Equally in West Germany, the figures only refer to *Die Grünen*, and votes for smaller ecological parties such as the ÖDP were not included. No similar problem arose for Ireland and Britain since there is only one Green Party in each of these countries. However, the Irish Greens only had candidates in two out of four constituencies. For our analysis of actual green voting, we have excluded inhabitants of these regions who were unable to vote for a green candidate.[2] In Italy, two major green formations, *Verdi Europa* (Greens Europe) and *Verdi Arcobaleno* (Rainbow Greens) took part in the elections. There were only 15 voters for the more left-wing Rainbow group in the sample, and this did not provide a basis upon which to compare them with the more 'ecological' Greens. Therefore it was decided to put these voters together into one category. An even more complicated situation arose in the Netherlands. There, the 'ecological' Green Party did not take part in the elections, but a group called *Regenboog* (Rainbow), formed by parties of the so-called Small Left (Radical Party, Pacifist-Socialist Party, Evangelical People's Party, and the Communist Party) did participate. After the European elections, these parties decided also to join forces for the national elections and formed a new party called Green-Left. The rival 'ecological' Green Party polled very few votes in these elections, but Green-Left managed to establish itself and is now increasingly recognised by other European green parties as a 'green party'. Any reference to the Dutch 'Greens' thus refers only to the Rainbow group that took part in the European elections.

Table 1 provides a list of votes cast for green parties (as defined above) in the seven countries with which we are concerned, and compares these official statistics with the proportion voting green as recalled by respondents to our surveys. In the final column of the table we also present a figure for 'potential' green voting, which deserves somewhat more explication.

In addition to asking respondents to recall how they voted in the recent European parliamentary election, voters were also asked, for each party contesting the election, to state how likely they thought it was that they would vote for that party in national elections at any future time. Respondents were presented with a scale of 1 to 10 which labeled 1 as 'not at all probable' and 10 as 'very probable'. In our analysis we rescaled this variable into a probability ranging from 0 (no chance of a green vote) to 1 (every likelihood of a green vote at some time), or sometimes from 0 to 100 in order to facilitate comparisons with percentage green voters.

TABLE 1

GREEN VOTES

Country	Votes Cast for Greens in EE 1989[a]	Recalled to have voted Green in EE 1989[b]		Potential Green Voting[c]	Claimed to have voted in EE 1989	Actual turnout
	%	n	%	%	%	%
France	10.6	77	13.3	55.7	55.6	47.3
Great Britain	14.9	81	15.7	42.0	54.3	36.6
Germany	8.4	86	9.7	40.3	73.8	61.6
Italy	6.2	73	8.5	43.3	85.0	74.4
Netherlands	7.0	53	8.5	-	64.4	47.1
Belgium	13.9	118	14.0	51.1	82.0	83.1
Ireland	3.8	25	3.3[d]	46.2	73.9	66.5

(N = 7224)

a. *Source*: Mackie [*1990*].
b. Excluding non-voters.
c. Average probability of voting green in national elections at any future time.
d. 4.6% in the constituencies contested.

Respondents not giving any probability rating for green parties were excluded. All references to potential green voters also exclude the Netherlands where this particular question did not refer to the voting potential for a green party but only to the three 'Small Left' parties which eventually formed a green party. As there may be a major difference between the potential Small Left vote and the potential green vote, we feel that we cannot deduce anything about the potential votes for the new Green-Left party from the aggregation of potential votes for its Small Left predecessors.

The share of green voters in our sample was generally slightly higher than the share of votes in the European elections. This discrepancy is not necessarily due to sampling bias. The recall of previous voting choices is influenced by a range of factors which have a distorting effect. In particular, many respondents may not want to admit that they did not vote in the European elections. As shown in Table 1, the share of respondents claiming to have voted in the 1989 European election is substantially higher than the actual turnout, with the exception of Belgium where a compulsory voting system leads to unusually high turnouts. In manufacturing a response to the voting question that follows, they are likely to mention the more popular parties rather than the less popular ones. Green parties had certainly attracted unprecedented attention in June 1989, and their good showing in the election may be reflected in these responses given shortly after the election.

Results

The various theories that have hitherto been employed to explain green politics suggest a number of bivariate relationships between green voting and various socio-demographic and other variables. We will first explore whether or not our data confirm the various expectations before we conduct a multivariate analysis to explore the relative predictive qualities of these variables more closely. As the comparative analysis of green voting is still in its early development, we also thought it would be valuable simply to document the relationships at a bivariate level for the information of an academic and non-academic readership. We start with a number of socio-demographic variables and then turn to political attitudes and related variables.

Sex

Surveys of attitudes on nuclear energy and nuclear weapons regularly find women to be more concerned about these issues than men [*Young, 1990*]. We could thus expect that women are more inclined to vote green than men. Our data provide some support for this assertion. Women are slightly more likely to vote green than men, but the relationship is very weak, both for actual green voting ($r=.037$, $p\leqslant0.01$) and for potential green voting ($r=.050$, $p\leqslant0.001$). The only country where there is a more sizeable relationship between potential green voting and sex is Germany (r=.096, p≤0.001) but this is still a rather weak, even if statistically significant, relationship.

Age

Theories of green politics uniformly predict that it is young people who are attracted to green parties. There are some subtle differences, however, between these theories in terms of the exact age group which is thought to be likely to vote green. An approach focusing on political generations may predict that it is those socialised in the 1960s who will provide the backbone of green politics, supplemented by the followers of the 'new' social movements of the late 1970s and 1980s. Other theories would predict that those socialised during the period of post-war affluence as a whole and benefitting from the 'educational revolution' would be the most likely to vote green since, first, a major proportion of the group in question still stands outside the pressures of industrial society, being still in full-time education or without regular employment,

TABLE 2

GREEN VOTING ACCORDING TO AGE[a])

COUNTRY	TOTAL	AGE GROUP					r^b
		18–24	25–34	35–44	45–59	60 and over	
France	13.3	21.7	19.2	19.4	10.3	5.2	-.177***
GB	15.7	25.7	24.4	19.2	13.0	8.9	-.165***
Germany	9.7	20.3	16.5	8.8	3.9	1.7	-.230***
Italy	8.5	21.8	12.6	8.8	3.3	1.8	-.230***
Netherl.	8.5	18.3	16.5	6.8	4.1	2.5	-.205***
Belgium	14.0	21.0	20.2	18.4	8.2	5.0	-.180***
Ireland	4.6	13.8	4.1	4.4	2.2	3.7	-.103***.
Total	10.6	20.3	16.0	12.0	6.0	4.2	-.178***

a. Cell entries are average percentage voting green and, in the last column, correlations (Pearson's r) between green voting and age.
  Level of statistical significance:
  *** p≤0.001
b. Equivalent to Phi when computed for a 2×2 contingency table.

and secondly, this group has not (yet) had the opportunity to be socialised into the habit of voting for any particular party.

The results shown in Tables 2 and 3 indicate that younger voters are indeed more likely to vote green than older voters, though there are some potentially interesting differences between countries. In all countries, it is the 18–24 age group that has most green voters.[3] Green voters are most

TABLE 3
POTENTIAL GREEN VOTING ACCORDING TO AGE[a])

| COUNTRY | TOTAL | AGE GROUP | | | | | r[b) |
		15–24	25–34	35–44	45–59	60 and over	
France	55.7	58.2	63.1	56.6	53.1	46.6	-.163***
GB	42.0	52.7	45.3	42.1	38.9	35.0	-.199***
Germany	40.3	54.8	53.0	39.9	28.6	25.0	-.386***
Italy	43.3	57.5	50.1	43.5	37.1	29.2	-.303***
Belgium	51.0	58.2	58.6	56.4	45.1	38.2	-.230***
Ireland	46.2	52.3	49.0	50.3	44.9	32.0	-.186***
Total	46.2	55.6	53.4	47.8	40.2	34.6	-.248***

a. Cell entries are averages of the percentage probability for green voting and, in the last column, correlations (Pearson's r) between potential green voting and age.
  Level of statistical significance:
  *** $p \leq 0.001$
b. Equivalent to Phi when computed for a 2×2 contingency table.

evenly distributed among the age groups in Britain. Considering that 1960s student movement activists must now be in their forties, it is noticeable that the share of green voting of that age group is reasonably high in France, Belgium and also Britain. But in the rest of the countries, including Germany, Italy and the Netherlands, which all had very strong student and other protest movements in the 1960s, green voting falls back quite sharply in the 34 to 44 age groups in comparison with the younger generations. The preponderance of the 18–34 group generally sheds doubt on the thesis that green voters are heavily influenced by their socialisation in social movements. This may be so for green party activists [*Kitschelt, 1989; Kitschelt and Hellemans, 1990; Rüdig et al., 1991a*] but this does not appear to play a major role in voting behaviour. The fact that it is mainly the very young voters who are attracted to the greens provides support for the party socialisation thesis. For green parties this does, however, introduce a level of uncertainty: their electoral fortune appears closely tied to their ability to appeal to new, young voters. The data on the age distribution does suggest that green parties find it more difficult to keep the support of these voters once they become older.

Looking at potential green voting, the 15 to 24 age group displays the highest potential except in France and Belgium. The potentials recede with advancing age, particularly so in Germany and Italy.

TABLE 4
EDUCATION AND GREEN VOTING[a])

COUNTRY	Education[b)] Actual Green Voters	Potential Green Voters
France	.192***	.083**
GB	.196***	.165***
Germany	.232***	.252***
Italy	.220***	.224***
Netherlnds	.220***	–
Belgium	.174***	.258***
Ireland	.086*	.169***.
TOTAL	.192***	.210***

a. Cell entries are correlations (Pearson's r) between green voting (and potential green voting) and education.
  Level of statistical significance:
  * p≤0.005   ** p≤0.01   *** p≤0.001
b. Education: Age completed education, four categories: 1) 15 or younger, 2) 16–17, 3) 18–20, 4) 21 or older.

In summary, there is a fairly strong relationship between green voting and age. The data suggest important differences, though, in the reliance of green parties on new voters. The data on potential green voting gives us a strong indication that it is particularly in Germany that the appeal of the greens is restricted to the younger age groups while this is rather less the case in France and also in Britain.

Education

All theories of green politics predict that a high level of education is related to green voting. In Table 4, the correlation coefficients between education and actual and potential voting are presented. Education levels were measured in terms of the age when the respondent left education, with four categories: less than 15, between 16 and 17, between 18 and 20, and 21 or older. For actual and potential green voting, there is a statistically significant relationship in all countries. The figures do suggest interesting differences. In some countries, in particular Germany Italy, actual and potential green voting are more or less equally strongly related to education. In Belgium and Ireland, the relationship is far stronger for potential voting. The reverse is true for France and Britain, suggesting that in these countries, the greens are appealing to a somewhat broader spectrum of the electorate, at least as far as their education levels are concerned.

Looking at the green vote in Great Britain and France, we thus find some evidence which would suggest that the green vote in these countries is not as tightly defined by age and education as, for example, in Germany.

Occupation

According to one theory of green voting, green voters should come from a particular section of the population whose educational achievements have not been rewarded with a matching position and influence in society. The Greens could thus be expected to be the party of 'frustrated academic plebeians' [*Alber, 1989: 205*]. An alternative explanation which has already found widespread empirical support in studies of social movement activists, at least in Britain [*Rüdig et al., 1991b*], predicts that the Greens should have a particularly fruitful recruiting ground in a particular sector of the middle classes: non-commercial and human services (education, health, alternative economy, and so on) as well as from other groups standing outside mainstream economic activity, such as those still in full-time education.

Our data are not ideally suited for testing the theory that greens come from a particular section of the middle class because we cannot identify those in 'caring' professions. The closest we could get to this group is to look at public sector employees. The data allow us to make a more comprehensive assessment of the role of more broadly defined occupational profiles, such as students and unemployed.

Table 5 shows a number of broad occupational categories and their inclination to vote green. Overall, manual workers are slightly less likely to vote green, professional and other middle class occupations are somewhat more likely to vote green. But the difference is not large and in some countries, respondents with a 'working class' occupation show a greater likelihood to vote green than those with 'middle class' occupations. The group which is consistently rather hostile to the greens is retired people, perhaps not surprisingly if we consider our previous findings on the influence of age. Students on the other hand figure very strongly as a group attracted to green politics all over Europe, but particularly in Germany and Italy. There are some interesting differences as far as the unemployed are concerned: they figure strongly among actual green voters in West Germany and the Netherlands but otherwise they do not play any significant role. This ties in well with the more left-wing orientation of the Dutch and West German greens, emphasising social justice and welfare issues in their programmes. Overall, the eta values demonstrate that occupation as defined in these terms does have a sizeable effect particularly in Germany.

Is the high proportion of green votes from German unemployed and students a confirmation of the Bürklin/Alber thesis of green politics as the outcome of the frustrations of the academically unemployed? We need to analyse the effect of being in full-time education or unemployment in a multivariate context before we can say anything with any confidence, but a look at percentage differences already demonstrates clearly that such an interpretation would mainly apply to the German and Dutch cases.

A look at the influence of public sector employment on actual and potential green voting did not elicit any strong relationships, not suprisingly as this group would also include groups with an anticipated low probability of voting green, such as members of the security forces or employees of nationalised energy industries. For all countries together, we found small positive correlations between public sector employment and actual ($r=.075$, $p\leqslant0.001$) and potential green voting ($r=.070$, $p\leqslant0.001$). The only country where public sector employment had a more noticeable positive effect was Belgium with coefficients of $r=.151$ and $r=.160$ ($p\leqslant0.001$) for actual and potential green voters, respectively.

Social Integration

An individual's occupation is certainly one of the most important indicators of his or her standing in society. But there are many others that could also be of importance for a theory that sees green support predominantly coming from temporarily marginalised sectors of society. In his analysis of the German green voter published in 1987, Bürklin constructs a cumulative 'social integration index' which is intended to capture this section of the population. This index is based on five

TABLE 5
OCCUPATION AND GREEN VOTING (IN %)

Occupation of Respondent

Country	Total	Working Class	Middle Class	Retired	Housewife	Student	Unemployed	Eta
France A	13.3	19.8	16.6	6.0	11.5	24.0	8.3	.171
P	55.7	61.2	59.0	46.9	53.6	56.4	54.2	.171
GB A	15.6	15.0	23.8	8.1	8.3	38.5	20.0	.223
P	42.0	44.1	42.7	34.4	37.6	59.0	47.6	.209
Germany A	9.7	6.7	10.8	2.1	5.3	31.9	29.4	.267
P	40.3	41.0	40.3	26.1	36.1	65.6	44.6	.313
Italy A	7.2	8.1	8.4	3.5	4.8	35.0	7.9	.270
P	43.3	44.3	45.0	30.1	40.6	60.7	46.7	.261
NL A	8.5	6.4	11.4	1.8	4.7	24.5	25.0	.248
Belgium A	14.0	15.5	16.6	5.4	13.0	23.8	13.1	.139
P	51.0	54.1	54.8	36.6	49.1	60.0	54.3	.232
Ireland A	4.6	4.5	5.6	4.8	3.6	9.1	4.0	.052
P	46.2	45.4	45.2	41.8	42.6	57.2	49.3	.138
Total* A	10.6	10.8	12.7	4.5	6.8	27.9	12.9	.179
P	46.2	47.9	46.8	35.7	42.8	59.8	50.4	.204
n	4846	1042	1387	911	938	290	233	

* Figures do not add up because other categories (don't knows, etc.) have been excluded from the table.
A: Actual green voters (1989)
P: Potential green voters (Mean potential, scale 100 to 1)
n: Total number of cases for actual green voting, the number of cases for potential green voting varies slightly.

variables: marital status, source of income, number of children, church attendance and housing status. A person who is not in full-time occupation and lives off unearned income, is unmarried, has no children, does not own a house, and does not go to church, is considered most marginal and is allocated a '0' in the index, a person in exactly the opposite position is considered highly integrated and is allocated a '5', with the rest of the cases being allocated values between 1 and 4. Bürklin finds that this social integration index is a fairly good predictor of green voting. Together with a second index based on personal attitudes to wealth creation and career values, Bürklin is able to explain about 20 per cent of the variance on green voting [*Bürklin, 1987*].

While we cannot fully replicate Bürklin's analysis because of the absence of comparable attitude variables in our dataset, we can test whether the social integration index proposed by Bürklin is able to add to our explanation. We constructed such an index, following Bürklin's model exactly. To compare with Bürklin's social integration index, we also constructed a dummy variable based on occupational status in which those outside mainstream economic activity, namely students and the unemployed, are pitted against the rest of the population.

Is lack of social integration, as conceived by Bürklin, related to green voting? The bivariate relationships as detailed in Table 6 suggest two things: first, the role of 'social marginality' as a predictor of green voting is essentially limited to Germany and, second, the index does not produce significantly higher correlation coefficients than the occupational marginality variable, with the exception of Germany. On the contrary, occupational marginality has a slighly higher predictive capacity (outside Germany) than social marginality.

Such a comparison is, necessarily, rather crude if compared with multivariate analysis. It remains to be seen, for example, whether any of these variables still play a role once we control for age and education levels. Bürklin's marginality index, however, does not have any broad international appeal: it fits the German situation quite well, but social marginality defined in these terms clearly is largely unrelated to actual and potential voting in other European countries.

Overall, we have tested a number of hypotheses on the relationship between green voting (actual and potential) and various socio-economic background variables. The trend we could establish is a very clear one: these variables play quite a major role for green voting in Germany, but have far less importance elsewhere. We will have to analyse how the total predictive qualities of all socio-economic variables taken together in a multivariate analysis compares with this preliminary assessment.

Before we go on to such an analysis, we first have to look at a number of other variables that could be important. As we have seen, few theories of green politics rely on socio-economic variables alone. The dominant notion, as proposed by Inglehart and others, predicts a convergence of left-wing attitudes and post-material values. Alternatively, Rüdig [*1990*] has argued that these theories completely neglect the dominant concern of green parties with the environment. Thus, the question is what, if any, influence left-right orientation, post-materialist values and environmental concern and consciousness respectively have on green voting.

TABLE 6

OCCUPATIONAL AND SOCIAL MARGINALITY AND GREEN VOTING[A)]

COUNTRY	Occupational Marginality[b)] Actual Green Voters	Potential Green Voters	Social Integration[c)] Actual Green Voters	Potential Green Voters
France	.027n.s.	.001n.s.	-.044n.s.	-.037n.s.
GB .	.084*	.159***	-.042n.s.	-.102**
Germany	.238***	.248***	-.237***	-.301***
Italy .	.206***	.184***	-.117***	-.112***
Netherlands	.212***	-	-.149***	-
Belgium	.054n.s.	.092**	-.096**	-.078*
Ireland	.006n.s.	.119***.	-.042n.s.	.030n.s.
TOTAL	.119***	.142***	-.123***	-.124***

a) Cell entries are correlations (Pearson's r) between green voting (and potential green voting) and measures of occupational and social marginality.
  Level of statistical significance:
   * $p \leqslant 0.05$ ** $p \leqslant 0.01$ *** $p \leqslant 0.001$ n.s. = not significant
b) Students and Unemployed vs. rest of population (dummy variable)
c) Bürklin's Social Integration Index, cumulative index of five dummy variables: marital status, number of children, church attendance, housing status, occupation.

Left–Right Placement

In some countries, green parties are clearly placed on the left of the political spectrum, and such parties define themselves as part of 'the left'. Thus we would expect some relationship between left–right self placement and green voting in Germany and the Netherlands. In other countries, however, green parties deny any association with 'the left'. Do their actual and potential voters share this political world view? As can be seen from Tables 7 and 8, green voting is associated with a more left than average self-placement everywhere, the only exception being Italy.

The most left-wing green voters are found in the Netherlands. This is not particularly surprising, since 'Rainbow' is a group which consists of Small Left parties (rather than independent greens). Britain and Ireland have the most right-wing green electorate. Even here green voters fall to the left of an electorate that is particularly right-wing in comparison with the average scores found in other countries.

Overall, the expectation that the German and Dutch greens are further to the left than other green parties is confirmed by the data on the

TABLE 7

AVERAGE PLACEMENT OF ACTUAL AND POTENTIAL GREEN VOTERS ON
LEFT RIGHT SCALE (1 – FAR LEFT TO 10 – FAR RIGHT)

Country	Average L-R Score (entire electorate)	Green Voters L-R Score	Diff.	Potential Green Voters L-R Scorea)	Diff.
Belgium	5.4	4.6	-0.8	5.2	-0.2
France	5.1	4.3	-0.8	4.4	-0.7
GB	5.7	5.3	-0.4	5.1	-0.6
Germany	5.3	4.2	-1.1	4.1	-1.2
Italy	4.5	4.2	-0.3	4.3	-0.2
NL	5.2	3.2	-2.0	-	-
Ireland	6.4	5.1	-1.3	5.9	-0.5

a) Average L–R score of those scoring 7 or higher on the 1–10 probability scale for voting green in the future.

TABLE 8

LEFT–RIGHT ORIENTATION AND GREEN VOTING[a]

COUNTRY	Left-Right Orientation[b]	
	Actual Green Voters	Potential Green Voters
France	-.130**	-.235***
Britain	-.073n.s.	-.199***
Germany	-.189***	-.427***
Italy	-.036n.s.	-.32n.s.
Netherlands	-.275***	-
Belgium	-.140***	-.005n.s.
Ireland	-.131**	-.222***
TOTAL	-.143***	-.188***

a. Cell entries are correlations (Pearson's r) between green voting (and potential green voting) and self-placement on a left–right scale..
    Level of statistical significance:
 * p≤0.05   ** p≤0.01   *** p≤0.001   n.s. = not significant
b. Left–right scale from 1 (left) to 10 (right)

left–right orientation of their actual and potential supporters. While German and Dutch greens clearly are positioned more to the left of the political spectrum, differences between the self placement of greens and that of the general population are often not very great elsewhere.

Remarkably, the differences between actual and potential green voters are not very substantial either. Only in Belgium and Ireland do potential green voters appear to be slightly more right-wing. In all other countries, the differences between actual and potential voters are fairly minute. Somewhat surprisingly, this is also the case for Britain and France. Obviously, there is no untapped potential that is defined in left–right terms for these parties.

Post-materialism

Turning to post-materialism, we would expect a fairly substantial relationship between green voting and a preference for post-materialist values, given the importance of this approach in the literature. We can find a relationship in all countries between potential green voting and post-material values. In the case of actual green voting, however, the relationship is rather weak in most countries, with the exception of Germany and the Netherlands (see Table 9).

Again, the major pattern we already identified for socio-economic variables repeats itself. For actual votes, there are fairly strong relationships between post-materialism and green voting in Germany and the Netherlands. For potential voters, the strongest correlation is again found for German potential greens. This time, however, Britain is not far behind while the correlation is weakest in France. For the other countries, the correlation is not strong even for potential voters. Again, we have to emphasise that the real test of the predictive capabilities of post-materialism requires a multivariate analysis (see below).

Environmental Concern

Are green parties a political manifestation of a new 'post-materialist' or 'left-libertarian' cleavage or are they, as Rüdig [1990] argues, the expression of a new 'ecological' cleavage which is based on a structural conflict about the environment? Arguably, it is difficult if not impossible to come to a final conclusion about the nature of green parties on the basis of an analysis of the attitudes of green voters. But, undoubtedly, the 'ecological cleavage' hypothesis would have little currency if we could find no relationship whatsoever between environmental concern and green voting. Equally, this hypothesis would be difficult to sustain if the influence of environmental concern would be superseded by any other 'single issue' concern.

We are restrained in our analysis of these factors by the variables we have available in the dataset of a survey which was not specially designed to test this type of hypothesis. The only suitable variable available to us at the time of writing this contribution concerns the importance of individual political issues. Respondents were asked to list the three most important political issues in order of importance. Environmental pollution was one such issue. We would thus expect that greens would consider

TABLE 9
POST-MATERIALISM AND GREEN VOTING[a]

COUNTRY	Post-materialism[b] Actual Green Voters	Potential Green Voters
France	.154***	.098**
Britain	.089*.	.249***
Germany	.239***	.334***
Italy	.034n.s.	.116***
Netherlands	.262***	–
Belgium	.071*	.138***
Ireland	.080*	.165***
TOTAL	.132***	.175***

a. Cell entries correlations (Pearson's r) between green voting (and potential green voting) and post-materialism.
  Level of statistical significance:
  * p≤0.05   *** p≤0.001   n.s. = not significant
b. Post-materialism: measures by standard four item battery, three categories: 1) Materialists, 2) Mixed, 3) Post-materialists.

the environment to be an important political issue, and that we would find a correlation between the importance of environmental pollution as a political issue and green voting (actual and potential).

Table 10 shows that for green voting across Europe, there are fairly strong correlationships between actual and potential green voting and the importance of the environment as a political issue.

The minimal hypothesis about the relationship between environmental concern and green voting is thus confirmed. Looking at other issues, we cannot find any similarly convincing relationship. Other issues for which we have data include unemployment, European integration and agricultural surpluses, none of which showed consistently significant relationships. Arms limitation was of some importance, with correlations in the region of 0.1, as was the importance of stable prices, which had a negative relationship with green voting of about the same magnitude.

In the ideal case, we would have liked to explore the relationship

TABLE 10
ENVIRONMENTAL CONCERN AND GREEN VOTING[a]

	Importance of Environmental Pollution as a political issue[b]	
COUNTRY	Actual Green Voters	Potential Green Voters
France	-.303***	-.288***.
GB	-.230***	-.288***
Germany	-.218***	-.243***
Italy	-.163***	-.183***
Netherlands	-.164***	-
Belgium	-.182***	-.262***
Ireland	-.195***	-.229***.
Total	-.189***	-.200***

a. Cell entries are correlations (Pearson's r) between green voting (and potential green voting) and the perceived importance of the environment as a political issue.
   Level of statistical significance:
   * $p \leq 0.05$ *** $p \geq 0.001$
b. Importance of the Environment as a Political Issue: Four Categories, 1) Most important, 2) Second most important, 3) Third most important, 4) Not mentioned.

between other environmental issues, for example concern over nuclear energy, or global warming, and green voting. But on the basis of the slim database we have, we can say that green voters all over Europe are strongly concerned about the environment. Green voting does not appear to be an aimless protest.

As expected, British and French greens are more concerned about 'the environment' than, say, their Dutch and German counterparts, but the difference between the coefficients is not that great. Significantly, post-materialism and left–right orientation feature more strongly at the bivariate level in the latter two countries. From these comparisons, we could form the expectation that environmental concern would be overshadowed by post-materialism and left–right orientation in the case of 'red-green' parties with the opposite being the case for 'green-green' parties. Multivariate analysis (see below) will enable us to make an assessment of which is more important when the other is taken into account, and it is to this that we now turn.

A Multivariate Approach to Explaining Green Voting

All of the analyses presented so far have been bivariate in nature. We have looked at relationships between a number of variables and green voting, but we have taken the independent variables one at a time. Such a procedure lends itself to in-depth discussion of the possible reasons for observed findings, but needs all the time to bear in mind the possibility that the findings might be quite different when other variables are simultaneously taken into account. For example, education and age are closely related. Bivariate analysis shows both of them to be important correlates of green voting, but does education add anything to our ability to explain green voting once age has been taken into account?

To conduct a multivariate analysis in a way which would allow us to compare our results between countries, we first selected all variables that had shown some promise at bivariate levels, and transformed them into dummy variables in each case.[4] Among the socio-demographic variables, education, occupation sector, being a student or unemployed, age, and sex were found to be useful in this context. For attitudinal variables, left–right orientation, post-materialism, and the importance of environmental pollution and arms limitation were included. Any other variables mentioned in previous parts did not add to our model in any significant way and were excluded.

Tables 11a and 11b show the results of two different multiple regression

TABLE 11a
EXPLAINING GREEN VOTES CAST IN THE EUROPEAN ELECTIONS
(AVERAGED OVER ALL COUNTRIES)

PREDICTOR	A	B	
Well-educated	.10	.07	
Public & service sectors	.04	.04	
Students & unemployed	.06	.06	
Young	.07	.05	
Female	.03	.04	
Variance explained a)	5.4%		(socio-demographic variables only)
Left-wing		.06	
Postmaterial		.06	
Environment		.08	
Arms limitation		.03	
Variance explained a)		9.1%	(includes attitudes and issue preferences)

a) r^2 adjusted.

TABLE 11b
EXPLAINING GREEN VOTES CAST IN THE EUROPEAN
ELECTIONS, BY COUNTRY

PREDICTOR	France A	France B	Britain A	Britain B	Germany A	Germany B	Italy A	Italy B	Netherl A	Netherl B	Belgium A	Belgium B	Ireland A	Ireland B
Well-educated	.09	-	.11	-	.13	.09	.06	.06	.10	.07	-	-	.07	-
Public & service sectors	-	-	-	-	-	-	.06	.06	-	-	.11	.09	.06	-
Students & unemployed	-	-	-	-	.12	.13	.12	.11	.12	.14	-	-	-	-
Young	.10	.08	.10	.10	.08	-	.07	.06	.06	-	.12	.11	-	-
Female	-	-	-	-	.06	.06	-	-	.05	.05	-	-	-	-
Variance explained a)	3.7%		2.9%		10.3%		7.2%		8.4%		5.5%		1.7%	
Left-wing		-		-		.08		-		.11		.09		.08
Postmaterial		.11		-		.10		-		.12		-		-
Environment		.30		.19		.08		.08		.06		.10		.13
Arms limitation		-		-		.06		-		.05		.08		-
Variance explained a)		13.2%		6.8%		16.1%		8.3%		19.0%		8.9%		5.2%

a) r^2 adjusted.

analyses (labelled A and B) for each of the countries in which any significant amount of green voting took place, and overall for all of these countries taken together. Tables 12a and 12b do the same for potential green voting. The coefficients given in the body of each table (except those relating to variance explained) are the unstandardised regression coefficients *b* and give the effect of each variable on the probability of green voting or on potential green voting. Thus, in the overall analysis A in Table 11a, those with more than an average level of education are seen to be ten per cent more likely to vote green than those with less than an average level of education.[5] Most of the independent variables similarly index the effects of having more or less than an average score on the predictor concerned, though sector and sex are of course dichotomies and yield effects based on whether respondents have some particular characteristic or not. All coefficients shown in these tables are significant at the $p \leqslant 0.05$ level or better.[6]

The two analyses reported in these tables are distinguished according to whether attitudinal variables are included. The 'A' analysis in each case focuses upon socio-demographic characteristics, while the 'B' analysis in each case shows the consequence of introducing attitudinal variables in addition.

The first important finding to emerge from these tables is the fact that socio-demographic characteristics have relatively little role to play in determining who will vote green and who will not. Education, employment sector, age and sex and being a student or unemployed all add to variance explained but together they explain only 5.4 per cent of variance in green voting over Europe as a whole, and no more than 10.3 per cent in any country.

What is the most important of these socio-demographic characteristics? Age and education figure most strongly. As the younger generations usually enjoy a higher level of formal education, one could expect that education is only related to green voting through age [*Alber, 1989: 205*]. However, our analysis does not provide much support for this thesis. In many cases, both age and education make a contribution, even if the other variable is in the regression equation. Overall, this means that higher educational achievements are a good predictor of green voting, independent of age. Of the other socio-demographic characteristics that play some role, public sector employment is a fairly good predictor in Belgium, but also plays a role in Italy and Ireland. Students and unemployed figure quite strongly in Germany, Italy, the Netherlands, and Belgium, while female green voting is only a factor in Germany and the Netherlands.

However, if we turn to potential green voting, the picture changes

TABLE 12a
EXPLAINING POTENTIAL GREEN VOTES IN NATIONAL ELECTIONS
(AVERAGED OVER ALL COUNTRIES)

PREDICTOR	A	B	
Well-educated	.08	.05	
Public & service sectors	.05	.04	
Students & unemployed	.05	.05	
Young	.11	.08	
Female	.04	.05	
Variance explained[a]	7.2%		(socio-demographic variables only)
Left-wing		.07	
Postmaterial		.09	
Environment		.08	
Arms limitation		.03	
Variance explained[a]		11.6%	(includes attitudes and issue preferences)

a) r^2 adjusted.

TABLE 12b
EXPLAINING POTENTIAL GREEN VOTES IN NATIONAL ELECTIONS, BY COUNTRY

PREDICTOR	France		Britain		Germany		Italy		Belgium		Ireland	
	A	B	A	B	A	B	A	B	A	B	A	B
Well-educated	-	-	.06	-	.10	-	.09	.09	.10	.08	.16	.14
Public & service sectors	.06	-	-	-	.04	-	-	-	.12	.09	-	.06
Students & unemployed	-	-.05	.09	.07	.10	.09	-	-	-	-	-	-
Young	.10	.09	.07	.06	.19	.15	.15	.14	.11	.10	.05	-
Female	-	.04	-	-	.06	.06	-	-	.06	.05	-	-
Variance explained[a]	3.3%		4.2%		18.3%		8.7%		7.9%		4.1%	
Left-wing	.09		-		.19		-		-		.11	
Postmaterial	-		.14		.15		-		-		.10	
Environment	.23		.15		.04		.06		.18		.17	
Arms limitation	-		-		.05		-		-		-	
Variance explained[a]	11.6%		13.0%		34.2%		9.1%		13.9%		8.5%	

a) r^2 adjusted.

somewhat. The overall predictive capacity of these variables is still rather low at 7.2 per cent of variance explained. But if we look at individual countries, we find a major difference between Germany on the one hand where 18.3 per cent of potential green voting is explained by these variables and countries such as France, Britain and Ireland where the variance explained is 4.2 per cent at best. Here we do have a very significant finding: socio-demographic background variables explain quite a considerable amount of the potential for green voting in Germany which is limited to certain strata of the population, while no similar definition, or limitation, of green potentials can be found in other countries.

Turning to attitudinal effects, we find that, overall, they are rather more pervasive. When their effects are taken into account, variance explained increases substantially everywhere except in Italy; and, in Germany, the inclusion of attitudes in our attempt to explain potential green voting yields an astonishing 34.2 per cent of variance explained; a statistic that would be impressive in most social science contexts.

The overall analysis of actual and potential voting confirms that left-wing orientation, post-materialist values and the importance of the environment as a political issue all make an independent contribution to the explanation of the potential green vote. Their relative importance, for all countries together, is very similar. However, the relative importance of these three variables does vary not insignificantly from country to country.[7]

First, it is worthwhile noting that there is only one variable, the importance of the environment as a political issue, that is associated with actual and potential green voting in all countries. There are important differences, however, in its relative importance. For actual green voting, the importance of the environment as an issue is clearly the dominant variable in France, Britain, and Ireland. In Italy and Belgium it is more important that other attitude variables. In Germany and the Netherlands, however, there is still a statistically significant relationship to green voting, but its predictive value is more limited in comparison with both socio-demographic variables as well as left-wing orientation and post-materialism. Turning to potential green voting, we still find that pro-environmental attitudes are a very strong predictor in France, Britain, Belgium, and Ireland, with a slightly more marginal role in Italy. In Germany, it also figures as a significant predictor but is clearly overtaken in importance by left-wing orientation and post-materialism.

As we saw in the bivariate analysis, this does not mean that German (and Dutch) green voters do not think that the environment is important: it is because in Germany and the Netherlands, pro-environmental attitudes are so prevalent that they have relatively little explanatory power on their own.[8] We can thus conclude that environmental concern is an important, independent predictor of actual and potential green voting, even if we control for socio-demographic variables as well as post-materialism and left-wing orientation.

If we look at the other attitude variables, we find that left-wing orientation and post-materialism are important variables, but that their predictive capabilities are rather more limited. They figure very strongly in Germany, particularly for potential green voting, with the importance of the environment as an issue coming a rather poor third together with arms limitation. For actual voting, the cases of Germany and the Netherlands look remarkably similar, in both cases left-wing orientation and post-materialism are the most important attitude variables. In other countries, the role of post-materialism is rather limited. It is quite a good predictor of potential green voting in Britain and a fairly good one in Ireland, but elsewhere, it does not add anything or very little to the variance explained once socio-demographic variables, environmental concern and left-wing orientation are taken account of.

What we have established is that actual and potential green voting across Europe is related to environmental concern, as measured here by the importance given to the environment as a political issue, even if post-materialism and left-wing orientation are in the equation. Furthermore, while there are substantial differences in the relative importance of post-materialism and left-wing attitudes amongst various green parties, environmental concern is always present as a determinant of green voting.

Conclusions

With very few exceptions, theories of green politics have hitherto been tested only on the basis of empirical data taken from individual countries, and many theoretical constructs clearly reflect particular national experiences. Our data on green voting in the European elections of 1989 provide us with a first opportunity to test the wide range of hypotheses that have emerged from this theoretical literature.

First, our results show that theories of green politics have probably overestimated the role of a range of socio-demographic variables. It is true that overall we do find support for the thesis that highly educated young voters employed in the public sector or outside full-time employment are more likely to vote green than others; but overall, socio-demographic variables only explain 5.4 per cent and 7.2 per cent of the variance in actual and potential green voting, respectively – a clear indication that green voting is somewhat less clearly defined than previously thought.

However, what we do find is that these variables are rather more important for the explanation of German and Dutch green voting in 1989 and future potential green voting in Germany. One possible conclusion which could be drawn from this is that the German greens are more than other green parties tied to particular social strata of the population, especially the young and marginal. The age distribution of its voters clearly suggests that their future depends on their continued ability to attract first-time voters. To that extent, we can confirm some of Bürklin's previous findings. Whether this profile of actual and potential German green voters does or does not bode well for the stability of the green vote is a different question. There is some evidence, discussed elsewhere [Rüdig and Franklin, 1992], to suggest a rather stronger attachment of green voters in Germany to their party than in other countries. In other words, other green parties broadly appeal to a wider section of the population but they are not necessarily in a better position to mobilise a higher share of the popular vote in national elections.

Secondly, looking at the profile of green voters in terms of left–right placement, post-materialism, and the importance of environmental issues, we found that all of these factors, independently, contribute significantly to an explanation of actual and potential green voting. Environmental concern was clearly the single variable that had the broadest appeal across all countries. The influence of post-materialism and left-wing orientation was more patchy, but in some cases, in particular in Germany and the Netherlands, these variables were far stronger predictors than environmental concern.

Again, what we find is that the dominant theories of green politics (such as Inglehart's theory of post-materialist value change and Kitschelt's theory of 'left-libertarian parties') do receive support from our analysis of German and Dutch green voters. They do not receive much support from the analysis of the green voters of other countries, however.

Again, the difference between Germany and the Netherlands and the other countries does appear to reflect a genuine difference in social reality: German and Dutch green voters have more definable characteristics both in terms of their socio-demographic profile and their values and attitudes than green voters of other countries. This finding suggests that stability may be a characteristic of German and Dutch green voting while other green parties have to contend with more flexible, but also more volatile green electorates. In other words, German and Dutch green electorates are fairly narrow with both parties having difficulty appealing to a broader section of the electorate. By contrast, green parties in Britain, France, Italy, Belgium and Ireland appeal to a broader section of the population, the potential green vote in all these countries is higher than in Germany. But this greater appeal tends to be enjoyed at the expense of a higher volatility of actual green voting.

However, we have to end with a note of caution on the validity of this interpretation. First, any consideration of stability has to take into account other factors, such as the attachment of green voters to green parties, an analysis beyond the scope of this particular paper [*Rüdig and Franklin, 1992*]. The Belgian experience and perhaps also recent French electoral results suggest that the German/Dutch model of left-green parties is not the only route to building a fairly stable green electorate. Second, it is obvious from the literature that the various theories of green politics we discussed were developed by closely analysing the German Greens. Not much attention was paid to green parties elsewhere. Both the theoretical approaches and the empirical means for analysing green votes were developed in the context of German developments and may be biased as a result. In fact, our analysis provides strong evidence that the theories that have dominated the academic literature on green politics are applicable mainly to the German Greens or other green parties elsewhere which follow the model of the German Greens closely. It was the German Greens who first brought the phenomenon of green parties to worldwide attention but it is clearly mistaken to assume that green parties in other countries share their characteristics. A 'general' theory of green politics based on the German experience is bound to fail in the explanation of the phenomenon of green politics as a whole.

One implication of our analysis is that it is probably misleading to talk about a 'European' green voter as somebody with specific characteristics. The variability of our findings from country to country does suggest that differences between countries may be more pronounced that hitherto assumed. What is necessary, therefore, is to look more closely at countries other than Germany. The fact that we cannot explain actual and potential voting in these countries as well as in Germany may well be a distinctive characteristic of green voting in these countries, but it cannot be excluded that green voting and its determinants do not fit the German-derived concepts that so far have been used to analyse green voting.

NOTES

1. The European Elections Study 1989 (EES'89) is a joint effort of Western European social scientists to take advantage of the elections for the European Parliament (EP) held simultaniously in all European Community (EC) countries in June 1989, in order to engage in cross-nationally comparative electoral research. The study was designed and

organised by a core group of researchers consisting of Roland Cayrol (University of Paris), Cees van der Eijk (University of Amsterdam), Mark Franklin (formerly at the University of Strathclyde, now at the University of Houston), Manfred Kuechler (Hunter College, City University of New York), Renato Mannheimer (University of Genova) and Hermann Schmitt (University of Mannheim) who co-ordinated the efforts of this group. The study consisted of three independent cross-sectional surveys that were conducted in each member country of the EC before and immediately after the EP elections. The questionnaires, which were administered in the language of each country, constituted one part of the European Omnibus Surveys which also contained the regular Eurobarometer (EB) surveys of the Commission of the EC. With the kind permission of the director of EB surveys, we have been able to derive from the EB data a number of variables such as demographic and background characteristics to employ in conjunction with our own questions. The relevant EB surveys were No.30 (fall 1988), No.31 (spring 1989) and No.31 A (summer 1989, immediately after the European elections). Each of these waves involved interviews with some 12,500 respondents divided into independent national samples of about 1000 respondents each. This number was lower for Luxembourg (about 300 cases) and higher for the United Kindom where an additional sample of 300 cases was drawn from the Northern Irish population. In the present paper we focus upon data collected by means of the third (post-election) wave of interviews. Funding to support the first two waves was obtained from a consortium made up of European mass media and other institutions; funding for the third wave, which is the major data source employed in the present paper, was provided largely by a grant from the British Economic and Social Research Council. The data will be deposited at the ESRC Data Archive at the University of Essex, the ICPSR at the University of Michigan, and other data archives, and released into the public domain in 1992

2. Unfortunately, the data on the regional distribution of respondents do not match the definition of constituencies exactly. While we have tried to match them as best as we can, it is inevitable that we may have excluded some respondents who did have the opportunity to vote for a green candidate and included some who did not.

3. In the analysis of actual green voting, respondents who were less than 18 years old and thus were not able to vote in the 1989 European elections were excluded from the analysis. For potential green voting, also 15 to 17-year-old respondents were included.

4. Our dataset consists of a number of separate national datasets. Therefore, we cannot use standardised regression coeffients (beta) as a basis for comparisons between countries as these are standardised in relation to each national dataset. Therefore, we are using unstandardised regression coefficients, b. In order to compare the regression coefficients relating to different datasets, we can only do so if all independent variables are constructed as dummies.

5. In the case of potential green voting, the dependent variable is interval-level, recording the probability of a green vote as reported by each respondent on a scale of 0–1. In the case of actual green voting, the dependent variable is a dichotomy, recording whether the respondent voted green (1) or not (0). A dummy variable of this kind is badly skewed when the number of voters is small (as in this case), and will yield coefficients that may contain some bias. In this article, our main focus is upon the relative magnitude of effects, which will all be similarly biassed and thus remain comparable, and upon variance explained in each analysis, which is not subject to the same kind of bias.

6. If no coefficient is shown, this does not necessarily mean that this variable is unrelated to green voting but only that this variable does not add significantly to the variance explained once the variables for which coefficients are shown are in the regression equation.

7. For a previous analysis of the relative importance of left-wing orientation and post-materialism for the support of 'new politics' parties, see Müller-Rommel 1990.

8. In Germany, only 38.6 per cent did not mention the environment as one of the three most important issues. This is only topped by the Netherlands with 25.1 per cent. The least environmentally concerned are the Irish with 81.2 per cent, followed by the French (76.3 per cent), the British (67.8), the Italians (52.5) and the Belgians (47.4).

REFERENCES

Alber, J. (1985), 'Modernisierung, neue Spannungslinien und die politischen Chancen der Grünen', *Politische Vierteljahresschrift*, Vol.26, pp.211–26.

Alber, J. (1989), 'Modernization, Cleavage Structures, and the Rise of Green Parties and Lists in Europe', in F. Müller-Rommel (ed.), *New Politics in Western Europe: The Rise and Success of Green Parties and Alternative Lists*, Boulder, CO: Westview Press, pp.195–210.

Bürklin, W.P. (1987), 'Governing Left Parties Frustrating the Radical Non-established Left: The Rise and Inevitable Decline of the Greens', *European Sociological Review*, Vol.3, pp.109–26.

Bürklin, W.P. (1984). *Grüne Politik*, Opladen: Westdeutscher Verlag.

Clarke, H.D. and N. Dutt (1991), 'Measuring Value Change in Western Industrialised Societies: The Impact of Unemployment', *American Political Science Review*, Vol.85, pp.905–20.

Curtice, J. (1989), 'The 1989 European Election: Protest or Green Tide?', *Electoral Studies*, Vol.8, pp.217–230.

Franklin, M. (1985), *The Decline of Class Voting in Britain*, Oxford: Oxford University Press.

Franklin, M., Mackie, T., Valen, H. *et al.* (1992), Electoral Change: *Responses to Evolving Social and Attitudinal Structures in Western Countries*, Cambridge: Cambridge University Press.

Inglehart, R. (1977), *The Silent Revolution: Changing Values and Political Styles among Western Publics*, Princeton, NJ: Princeton University Press.

Inglehart, R. (1990), *Culture Shift in Advanced Industrial Society*, Princeton, NJ: Princeton University Press.

Kitschelt, H. (1988a), 'Left-libertarian Parties: Explaining Innovation in Competitive Party Systems', *World Politics*, Vol.40, pp.194–234.

Kitschelt, H. (1988b), 'The Life Expectancy of Left-libertarian Parties: Does Structural Transformation or Economic Decline Explain Green Party Innovation? A Response to Wilhelm P. Bürklin', *European Sociological Review*, Vol.4, pp.155–160.

Kitschelt, H. (1989), *The Logics of Party Formation: Ecological Politics in Belgium and West Germany*, Ithaca, NY: Cornell University Press.

Kitschelt, H. and S. Hellemans (1990) *Beyond the European Left: Ideology and Action in the Belgian Ecology Parties*, Durham, N.C: Duke University Press.

Lowe, P.D. and W. Rüdig (1986) 'Political Ecology and the Social Sciences: The State of the Art', *British Journal of Political Science*, Vol.16, pp.513–50.

Mackie, T.T. (ed.) (1990), *Europe Votes 3: European Parliamentary Election Results 1989*, Aldershot: Dartmouth.

Müller-Rommel, F. (ed.) (1989a), *New Politics in Western Europe: The Rise and Success of Green Parties and Alternative Lists*, Boulder, CO: Westview Press.

Müller-Rommel, F. (1989b) 'The German Greens in the 19980s: Short-term Cyclical Protest or Indicator of Transformation?' *Political Studies*, Vol.37, pp.114–22.

Müller-Rommel, F. (1990), 'New Political Movements and "New Politics" Parties in Western Europe', in R.J. Dalton and M. Kuechler (eds), *Challenging the Political Order: New Social and Political Movements in Western Democracies*, Cambridge: Polity Press, pp.209–31.

Niedermayer, O. (1989), 'Die Europawahlen 1989: Eine international vergleichende Analyse', *Zeitschrift für Parlamentsfragen*, Vol.20, pp.469–87.

Poguntke, T. (1993), *Alternative Politics: The German Green Party*, Edinburgh: Edinburgh University Press.

Reif, K. (1984), 'National Electoral Cycles and European Elections 1979 and 1984', *Electoral Studies*, Vol.3, pp.244–55.

Rüdig, W. (1985), 'The Greens in Europe: Ecological Parties and the European Elections of 1984', *Parliamentary Affairs*, Vol.38, pp.56–72.

Rüdig, W. (1990), *Explaining Green Party Development: Reflections on a Theoretical*

Framework, Strathclyde Papers in Government and Politics, No.71, Glasgow: Department of Government, University of Strathclyde.

Rüdig, W. and M.N. Franklin (1992), 'Green Prospects: The Future of Green Parties in Britain, France and Germany', in W. Rüdig (ed.), *Green Politics Two*, Edinburgh: Edinburgh University Press, pp.37–58.

Rüdig, W., Bennie, L.G. and M.N. Franklin (1991a), *Green Party Members: A Profile*, Glasgow: Delta Publications.

Rüdig, W., Mitchell, J., Lowe, P.D. and J. Chapman (1991b). 'Social Movements and the Social Sciences in Britain', in D. Rucht (ed.), *Research on Social Movements: The State of the Art in Western Europe and the US*, Frankfurt: Campus/Boulder, CO: Westview, pp.121–48.

Young, K. (1990), 'Living under Threat', in R. Jowell, S. Witherspoon and L. Brook, (eds.), *British Social Attitudes: The 7th Report*, Aldershot: Gower, pp.77–108.

The German Greens and the European Community: Dilemmas of a Movement-Party

ELIZABETH BOMBERG

Focusing on the years 1979–89, this contribution examines the *Europapolitik* (policies and politics towards Europe) of the German Green party. It argues that as a 'movement-party' – part social movement, part political party – the German Greens have faced peculiar challenges and opportunities in the European Community. In particular, their European policy has been defined by a conflict between the demands of their grassroots supporters and the imperatives of traditional party politics. By analysing the Greens' alternative goals and strategies in Europe, this study demonstrates the contradictions inherent in the Greens' *Europapolitik*. It concludes by applying the lessons from the Greens' 1979–89 experience to the current Green group in the European Parliament.

The role of the European Community (EC) in environmental policy-making is expanding rapidly. In the process, the profile and influence of green movements and parties on the European stage also have increased. Working mostly through the European Parliament (EP), these green actors offer a 'green critique' of many EC policies and practices. The growing visibility of these green critics points to the need to understand their European goals and strategies.

Focusing on the period from 1979–89, this article examines the *Europapolitik* (policies and politics towards Europe) of one such actor, the German Green party. This article suggests that as a 'movement-party' – part social movement, part political party – the German Greens have faced peculiar challenges and opportunities in the European Community. In particular, their European policy has been defined by a conflict between the demands of their grassroots supporters and the imperatives of traditional party politics.

This study begins by applying the theoretical model of 'movement-

Fieldwork for this study was funded by the Council of European Studies and the UC Berkeley Center for German and European Studies. The author wishes to thank John Peterson for his critical comments on earlier drafts.

parties' to the German Greens. The second section examines the Greens' alternative conceptions of Europe and their goal of a new European 'community'. By analysing the German Greens' electoral strategies during European Parliament campaigns, the third section demonstrates that the Greens' European activities have been marked in practice by the conflict between movement and party imperatives. The fourth section takes an inside look at the unique mandate of the Germans sent to represent the Greens on the European level from 1984–1989. This green group could not withstand the growing tensions and contradictions inherent in movement-party existence. The fifth section shows that its collapse was the logical outcome of the Greens' movement-party dilemma. The conclusion draws lessons from the 1979–89 experience and applies them to the current green group in the European Parliament.

The German Greens as Movement-Party

The relationship between extra-parliamentary movements – focused on environmental, peace, and women's issues – and established parties is explored in a growing body of literature on 'movement-parties'. Writers such as von Beyme [1982; 1984], Frankland [1989], Lenk [1983], Raschke [1988], and Zeuner [1985] view movement-parties as political actors which are part social movement, part parliamentary party.

Parties and movements each enjoy certain advantages when pursuing political goals. The strength of a party lies in its institutional cohesion – in its access to the state and in its ability to work within established systems to effect change. Social movements enjoy different advantages. As organisations concerned with spontaneous action and change, the strength of social movements lies in their links to the grassroots and their much more fluid relationship with the wider masses [Raschke, 1988: 9].

Movement-parties seek the strengths of both movement and party, whilst avoiding the disadvantages of each. However, movement-parties may end up being torn between the two poles of organisational styles and types. Whilst they typically feel compelled to follow tendencies of organisational centralisation in parliament, they also desire the de-centralisation stressed by the social movements. They therefore drift between reformism and radicalism, often unable to survive the 'parliamentary embrace' [Smith, 1984: 93] or avoid the accommodation, incrementalism, and compromise which comes from membership in traditional party systems [von Beyme, 1982].

Indeed, most literature on movement-parties suggests an inevitable slide towards the 'parliamentarisation' of movement-parties. This means that movement-parties submit to the normalising forces of an established parliamentary system [*Frankland, 1989*]. According to this model, movements are routinised by institutional and parliamentary imperatives [*Lenk, 1983*]. Once in parliament, a movement-party begins to place increasingly more emphasis on parliamentary bargaining, compromise becomes more acceptable, and the party itself becomes more preoccupied with maximising votes [*Zeuner, 1985*].

Ultimately, parties 'suck the energy' out of the social movements, absorb their creative juices and thence weaken them [*Narr, 1982*]. The success of an official party thus signals the 'end product of an institutionalisation of a social movement' [*Lenk, 1983*]. In support of this thesis, von Beyme [*1984: 373–4*] shows that over the last century, nearly all movement-parties have been caught in the undertow of parliamentary government and have ended up compromising and accommodating to the imperatives of traditional parliamentary politics.

On forming a national party in 1980, the founders of the German Greens were determined to exploit the opportunities of electoral and parliamentary politics without being parliamentarised or falling into the traps of professionalisation and detachment of party from people. Eschewing the formal structures of established parties, the Green party sought to form a political movement in which anyone could participate and which would not produce 'functionaries and professional politicians on one side and a passive herd of uninvolved followers on the other' [*Kolinsky, 1984: 24*].

To ensure this, a number of internal rules and regulations were agreed. First, the Greens insisted on a policy of mid-term rotation of political and party posts. They believed rotation of posts would preclude the development of an entrenched, professional political elite. The concentration of power was further discouraged by segregating party positions from positions in assemblies or parliaments. The Greens also insisted that paid party employees could not hold party office. Finally, the Greens enforced the notion of *Basisdemokratie* or grassroots democracy. Party meetings at all levels were open to members and minorities were guaranteed a voice. *Basisdemokratie* also implied a consensual decision-making procedure which would allow 'the thorough venting of the issues at all levels' [*Frankland, 1989: 391–2*].

Through these measures the Greens sought to create an 'anti-party party' [*Kelly, 1980*]. They wanted to be a political party which won enough votes to enter parliaments at all levels where it could serve as a voice of opposition on such key issues as ecology, equality, and peace. At the same time the Greens sought to remain a core component of broader extra-parliamentary movements which acted on the same key issues outside parliaments. Indeed, they hoped to become the spearhead of these movements. The Greens, in short, wanted to serve as parliamentary opposition and extra-parliamentary opposition simultaneously [*Kolinsky, 1987*].

The Greens' movement-party goals and strategies were fraught with difficulties and contradictions. In their effort to translate new forms of participation and new themes into parliamentary politics, the Greens adopted several diverse issues and competing ideologies. Acting as a movement-party also meant a more pronounced need for a loose, flexible form of political organisation. Yet some of the rules intended to hamper organisational rigidity produced a rigidity of their own. For example, the practice of rotation prevented several experienced and knowledgeable office holders from serving their party in office. In the end, the practice became unworkable and was formally abandoned in 1986.

Moreover, the lack of defined functions and organisational channels meant that individual 'personalities' and those especially skilful in handling meetings were able to gain considerable influence at all levels. Within the party, personal disputes were also disruptive. Individuals emerged as spokespersons for the party, often without official backing and thus contradicting one another.

The challenges and contradictions described above were particularly evident in the European realm. The tug-of-war and internecine battling between the two poles of parliament and movement helps explain much of the Greens' policy towards Europe. More specifically, these movement-party tensions are visible in both the content and practice of Green *Europapolitik*.

Green Conceptions of Europe

As a movement-party the Greens present a vision of Europe significantly different from those of established parties and actors in Europe. Criticising the existing formal structures of Europe and the European Community, Green conceptions stress the dangers of centralisation, bureaucratisation, and overwhelming state power [*Heuglin, 1986*].

According to the Greens, the current structures of the EC and European integration violate the four key Green principles of *decentralisation*, *grassroots democracy*, *ecological sustainability*, and *non-violence*. By contrast, the Green alternative to the EC, a 'Europe of the Regions' (EoR), would embody each of these principles.

The concept of *decentralisation* features most prominently in the EoR. The Greens argue that industrialised states are overbureaucratised and hierarchical in structure. They oppose tendencies in industrial nations towards centralisation, which thwart the initiative of citizens. Alternatively, the Greens advocate a decentralisation and simplification of administrative units. In their party platform the Greens assert that: 'though we all undoubtedly live in one world, it would be quite contrary to the principles of an ecological policy if we were to try and solve all problems uniformly and through centralisation' [*die Grünen, 1980: 24–5*].

Greens argue that the modern nation-state is inherently dangerous because its centralised power 'is inevitably used for economic competition, large scale exploitation and massive wars' [*Spretnak and Capra, 1986: 48*].[1] By contrast, the Greens' vision of Europe is consciously decentralised. Under an EoR arrangement, nation-states would be replaced by smaller administrative areas or regions. Europe would not be administered from a central power. Instead, power would be distributed throughout a confederation of manageable regions which are 'historically developed, self-determined but intertwined' [*die Grünen, 1984a: 38; 1989b: 11*].

The second element comprising the EoR is the Greens' related emphasis on *grassroots control* and participation. Precisely because Europe is so large, argue the Greens, more emphasis on community representation and grassroots input is imperative. The Greens charge that the increasing centralisation and 'bureaucratisation' of Europe – 'on display in EC headquarters Brussels' – has betrayed any sense of grassroots control: 'For what actually developed in Brussels – far away from the people and their regions – was an inflated bureaucracy, costly, incomprehensible and unchecked by any kind of democratic control' [*die Grünen, 1984b: 6*].

Instead, the Greens emphasise the alternative, grassroots character of their conception of Europe. Green party co-founder Petra Kelly explains: 'We seek an ecological, decentralised, self-administered, civil Europe of the regions . . . Long live Europe from below!' (quoted in Stuth [*1984: 64*]).

Ecological sustainability makes up the third plank of the Greens' EoR conception. Essentially, ecological sustainability is based on the belief that 'our finite Earth places limits on industrial growth' and consumerism [*Dobson, 1990: 73*]. The emphasis on sustainability points to the critical roles of ecology and environmental protection in green thinking. The Greens' position on the EC's Common Agriculture Policy (CAP) offers a specific illustration. From the Greens' perspective, current agricultural practices in Europe are unsustainable and unacceptable. Intensive chemical-based farming pollutes water-ways, encourages erosion, and upsets ecological balances through intensive pest control [*Dobson, 1990: 120*]. Or, as expressed more vehemently by the Greens:

> After 30 years of CAP the results are disastrous ... The use of
> nitrogen fertilizers has increased fivefold and the use of pesticides
> threefold since CAP was introduced ... (The CAP) destroys eco-
> logically sound ways of farming, decentralised distribution systems
> and healthy food [*die Grünen, 1989c: 8–9*].

In contrast, the Greens argue, citizens in a Europe of the Regions would
promote ecological sustainability by seeking to minimise resource use
and maximise self-sufficiency.

Finally, the Greens criticise the EC and European integration for
violating the principle of *non-violence*. According to the Greens, integration within the EC is a front for the 'wider integration and militarisation
of Europe under the control of NATO' [*die Grünen, 1984b: 12–13*]. The
Greens argue further that the EC is not a 'real community' and that 'the
demands for cooperation and solidarity do not stop at bloc borders' [*die
Grünen, 1989c: 3*]. In 1984 they went so far as to claim that the 'EC, in
essence never a political or a peaceful union of the nations of Europe, is
nothing more than an economic syndicate' [*die Grünen, 1984a: 28*].

Instead, the Greens maintain that close co-operation between communities and movements is needed to deal with issues of peace and
ecology. In a Europe of the Regions, boundaries would remain fluid,
allowing co-operation to 'transcend all borders and blocs' [*die Grünen,
1989b: 7*].

In sum, the Greens view the Europe of the Regions as their official
alternative to an 'EC of bureaucracies, bombs and butter-mountains' [*die
Grünen, 1984b: 38*]. Invoking the principles of decentralisation, grassroots democracy, ecological sustainability and non-violence, the EoR
promises to be a 'peaceful, nonaligned decentralised Europe made up of
manageable administrative areas' [*die Grünen, 1989b: 7*].

Certain aspects of the Europe-of-the-Regions conception put forth by
the Greens are politically and conceptually important. Conceptually, the
rapid, dramatic change occurring in Europe, much of which is linked to
regionalist or centrifugal forces, suggests the need for discussions of
alternative, contending models of the shape of Europe. Despite its
nascent formulation, the EoR conception offers one blueprint of such a
conceptual alternative.

Politically, some of the concerns addressed by the EoR conception are
widespread among Green supporters and non-supporters alike. In particular, the Green alternative conception of Europe appeals to regionalist
sentiments and responds to fears of centralisation and unchecked state
power.

Several unlikely allies of the Greens – including farmers in Bavaria and wine growers in the Rhineland – are attracted to aspects of the Greens' alternative conception. For instance, the EoR's emphasis on decentralisation and small-scale, sustainable farming methods, as well as its implicit critique of the CAP, attracts smaller farmers. The CAP favours larger farmers, whilst 'the farmer with little to sell, either because his farm is small or because he is situated in difficult farming country, benefits proportionately less' [*Marsh, 1989: 156*].

Established parties have been forced to take into account some of these concerns raised by the Greens. This was particularly true in the 1989 election to the European Parliament. Writing on the German campaign in that election, Kolinsky [*1990: 75–6*] argues that all major parties stressed environmental issues as one of their top priorities.

The EC itself has latched on to the concept of a EoR. At the December 1991 intergovernmental conference in Maastricht, government ministers gave the EoR a degree of recognition by accepting that an advisory 'committee of the regions' should be added to the Community structure [*Ascherson, 1992*]. In addition, the conference increased structural funds for disadvantaged areas and proposed a cohesion fund intended to finance environmental improvements in poorer regions suffering from environmental degradation. These funds create new possibilities for EC policymakers to deal directly with political actors in individual regions [*Marks, 1992*].

Yet the Greens' alternative conception may be criticised as contradictory, vague, and sloganistic. Above all, it enjoyed only limited acceptance or attention among the ranks of the Greens. During the 1984 European election the idea of a EoR was debated within the Green party, where it met with mixed reactions [*Dierker, 1987: 18*]. On one hand, the confederative aspect of the conception was well received by Green supporters (the *Basis*) because it corresponded with fundamental Green demands for decentralisation, regionalism, and grassroots democracy. On the other hand, this portion of the Greens' European programme met with widespread disinterest, was inadequately discussed, and lacked any concrete formulation. In an internal party memorandum outlining her thoughts on Europe, Petra Kelly wondered aloud about this lack of agreement: 'We strive for an alternative Europe – but which one? We must be clear on this' [*Kelly, 1984: 3*].

The Greens limited themselves to a critique of the EC and an extremely general exposition of the future 'Europe of the Regions'. Although Green representatives such as Antje Vollmer [*1984*] had much to say about the positive cultural and geographic diversity offered by a EoR, they offered no clear structural or procedural strategies for delivering it. 'Europe of the Regions' thus remained a vague abstraction.

Later attempts to make the EoR conception more concrete confronted the same obstacles of disinterest and disarray, and were no more successful. As Green member Brigitte Heinrich noted in 1986:

> What in the world might a green-alternative 'Europe of the Regions' look like concretely? Obviously, a decentralisation of the decisionmaking process, regional energy programs, etc. . . . But it's been two years and we are still facing these same vague conceptions (quoted in Wolf [*1986: 68*]).

These 'same vague conceptions' were still present in the 1989 European election campaign. A 'Europe of the Regions' was again presented as an alternative to the current EC structure. In their 1989 European election programme the Greens promised to campaign for: 'a Europe of dissolution of military alliances, of self restraint, of cooperation between regions and international solidarity' [*die Grünen, 1989b: 7*].

Yet such discussion remained as ambiguous as before. Nowhere, for instance, was a 'region' defined. Even in the area of environmental policy the party remained patently vague. The Greens advocated banning harmful chemicals and imposing environmental controls on industrial production. However, they specified no particular agencies or legislative procedures with which to realise their demands [*Kolinsky, 1990: 72*].

The Greens' lack of coherent theorising on Europe can be explained partly by their 'movement-party ambivalence' towards Europe and the European Community. Amidst attempts to 'think globally, act locally', the Greens neglected this middle sphere: the regional level of Europe. First, for many Greens emerging from the peace or local citizens' movements, Europe was an uncomfortable halfway house, neither international nor local and for that reason uninteresting.

Secondly, for many Greens the notion 'Europe' immediately conjured up the EC. It appears that their refutation of the EC was, for some Green members, carried over to a more general refutation of (or at least ambivalence towards) European policy in general. That some Green members made little distinction between Europe and the European Community is indicative of the scant attention given the European level in conventions, rallies, or party meetings. For example, in an internal party document of November 1988, a segment of the Green parliamentary group complained of the lack of coordination between the national and supranational level. In particular, the authors noted within the Green party a debilitating 'lack of a strong foundation on which to develop a coherent, long range European policy and programme' [*Jäcker and Hadamczik, 1988: 1–2*].

Green Strategy and Action in Europe

Despite the party's lack of conceptual interest in Europe, an active core of German Greens chose to work on the European level from an early stage. The first direct election to the European Parliament in 1979 provided an opportunity for Green activists to engage in formal, trans-national co-operation and activity. To participate in EP elections, movement activists had to constitute themselves as a national political party. In Germany, a heterogeneous national alliance of citizen action groups (*Bürgerinitiativen*), green lists, minor parties, and alternative groups formed the SPV: '*Sonstige Politische Vereinigungen. Die Grünen*' ('Other Political Alliances, The Greens').

The 1979 campaign of the SPV reflected the heterogeneous background and contentious character of the German Greens. Comprised of activists representing a wide variety of ecological and protest movements, the SPV campaign brought into the open conflicting parliamentary and extra-parliamentary strains within the Greens. The argument centred on the degree to which politics on the parliamentary plane strengthened or weakened the work and goals of the extra-parliamentary movements. Should the Greens remain true to their 'movement roots'? Or would an 'institutional route' better achieve green goals in Europe? This fundamental debate continued throughout the decade and was featured in the 1979, 1984 and 1989 EP campaigns.

On one side of the debate stood the 'parliamentarians', those activists advocating formal participation in the EC. This group provided the arguments and philosophy later used by the '*Realo*' wing of the Greens. Proponents of this route argued that parliamentary activity would allow the advantages of more media attention and more official access. Because German parties receive a cash reimbursement in relation to their share of the vote, substantial monetary gain would result from even a moderately successful voter return. One candidate went so far as to suggest candidly that the Greens' 'true' motivation for participating in the EP election was to 'happily cash in and invest in ecological funds and causes' (quoted in Nostitz [*1984: 18*]).

It also was hoped that many disgruntled voters now would 'have a reason to vote'. In the February 1984 issue of the Green party's newsletter, Green EP candidate Dietmar Spiegel [*1984: 26*] argued that movement activities alone were inadequate methods to mobilise the Euro-vote: 'Certainly, our knack at "spontaneous spectacle" (*Sponti-Spektakel*) no longer suffices to mobilise voters'.

Finally, parliamentarians expressed the more general hope that parliamentary campaigning and participation would force important issues onto parliamentary agendas and into the public consciousness. They viewed parliaments as a tool for consciousness raising, and the Greens as the 'yeast in the dough' [*Jäenicke, 1982*]. These advantages were especially important on the European level. The 'transcendence of borders' featured in a Europe of the Regions would be made easier by adopting supranational strategies with other European green parties. Crossnational activities within the EC would highlight the imperative to solve environmental problems transnationally.

Petra Kelly was a strong advocate of this strategy. She felt the EP campaign would provide an opportunity to publicise movement concerns:

> For me, taking part in an election – whether European, federal, or state level – is one of many methods, one of many peaceful possibilities, which remains open to us. I think we should assume that parliamentary work can enhance extra-parliamentary work, like it's done for the Italian Radicals[2] [*1980: 73*].

On the other hand, strong-willed movement activists and leaders demurred. The leaders of anti-nuclear and citizens' initiative movements in Germany were particularly sceptical of any parliamentary action. On the European level, four dangers of parliamentary activity and 'parliamentarisation' were depicted.

First, the movement 'energy' and vigour would be neutralised once the movement had gone through the necessary compromise and cooperation required of any parliamentary actor. This was seen as an even greater danger on the European level. Movement activists pointed out that the EC's decision-making process often allowed precious little direct parliamentary or public access. The movement's defining principle of democratic decision-making would not survive the process undiluted.

Secondly, it was feared that 'being there' would take on more importance than movement goals. And 'being there' on the European level meant being swallowed by the 'bureaucratic monstrosity' that was Brussels [*die Grünen, 1984a: 5*].

Thirdly, the mere appearance of movement representatives in the EP would create an illusion that conventional, institutional strategies really are influential and street action no longer necessary. The parliamentarians were accused of 'buying into' the illusion, and of wanting to make 'speeches for show (*Fensterreden*) just like the NATO parties' [*Widmer, 1984: 30*].

Finally, the charge of 'you cannot change the system if you are a part of it' was voiced. Only movements allowed for 'politics from below.' In short, movement members were intent on protecting their political integrity through strict and fundamental abstinence from conventional politics [*Schoonmaker, 1988*].

Despite their inherent mistrust, most movement activists agreed to participate in the 1979 and subsequent elections to the European Parliament. But they did so only out of limited logistical reasons – that is, to contest the upcoming election. It was assumed that after the election the movements would go their separate ways, far away from government structures and back to the grassroots.

In the course of this debate over strategy, both sides neglected the concept of Europe. On one hand, the movement activists lacked an institutional vision, a practical concept of what Europe should be and what methods could best achieve those aims. Additionally, the movement strategy arguments suffered from lack of positive alternatives. How should movements work transnationally, if not through a supranational body like the EC? Put another way: 'Radical charm will only turn into radical politics when the Greens realise and reflect upon the conditions and feasibility of their demands' [*Nostitz and Merkel, 1986*].

The 'parliamentarians', on the other hand, could be accused of putting method before aims, strategy before content. On the European level, Green members advocating participation in the EP election often considered these means to be ends in themselves. As a result, the substantive issues of the desirability or form of integration, or the conception of an alternative European 'community' were neglected.

The problems outlined here underscore the central importance of the increasing tension between a party and various extra-parliamentary social movements. From their emergence on the European level, the Greens were caught in the crossfire of conflicts between the demands of social movements and parliamentary structures. By 1984 the Greens had not yet decided whether to succumb to parliamentary advantages or maintain their 'political chastity' as movement representatives. They thus occupied the middle ground of a movement-party, but at a cost to strategic coherency and unified collective action.

An Inside View

The German Greens received only 3.2 per cent and no seats in the 1979 Euro-election. But in 1984 they captured 8.2 per cent of the German vote and seven seats in the European Parliament. The Green Members of the European Parliament (MEPs) chosen to fill these seats were given a mandate with distinct advantages and disadvantages. On one hand, they were bound by no rigid party programme or policy requirements. Green MEPs enjoyed an extraordinary amount of freedom and flexibility in their activities in Europe. On the other hand, the Green MEPs were sent off to Strasbourg and Brussels with conflicting messages from their movement-party, little direction from the party executive, and scant attention from the grassroots.

EC rules for the 1984–89 parliamentary term stipulated that official party groups within the EP had to include at least ten MEPs from a minimum of three different countries. Through the building of coalitions, the representatives of smaller parties were able to enjoy the significant financial, structural and procedural advantages offered to established groups in the EP [*Müller-Rommel, 1985: 394*]. For example, factions or party groups were given the resources to employ office staff, convene conferences, and provide translation services. Moreover, leaders of the party groups took part in drafting the EP's plenary agenda and allocating important committee chairs [*Lodge, 1989: 63*].

After several rounds of fierce negotiation with other green and non-green movement-parties, the 'Rainbow Group' was formed in 1984 as a parliamentary group in the EP. It was an extremely diverse collection of regionalist, green and protest representatives [*Rüdig, 1985*]. The main group within the Rainbow, and the only group to represent green and alternative issues in the EP, was the Green Alternative European Link (GRAEL). The two other sub-groups comprising the Rainbow were the European Free Alliance (a collection of regionalist groups) and the Danish movement against the EC.

In 1984 GRAEL included a total of 12 parliamentarians: seven from West Germany, two from Belgium, two from the Netherlands, and one from Italy. Shortly after the election GRAEL representatives met in Paris to draw up a common platform. The result was an extremely vague set of principles put forth in the 1984 Paris Declaration. GRAEL's vision of a 'new, neutral, decentralised Europe' was based on the following points: opposition to deployment of nuclear missiles in East and West Europe; a no-compromise policy on the environment; equal rights for women and minorities; a new economic policy on employment and social benefits; reorganisation of economic relations between Europe and the Third World; free exercise of fundamental civil rights; and ecological forms of agriculture [*GRAEL, 1984*]. Because the group was so diverse, the declaration was purposefully vague. The intention (and hope) was that GRAEL members would develop the specifics of these broad principles during their first term.

As a representative body of several different movement-parties, GRAEL's organisational structure was on purpose kept loose and non-conformist. Strategies were designed to encourage internal democracy and grassroots control within GRAEL. GRAEL meetings were generally 'accessible to the grassroots' (open to the public). New working groups were established to research political issues relevant to the grassroot movements. All staff members received equal wages and were responsible for preparing the political work within the working groups. Moreover, no staff was employed to do strictly auxiliary work such as typing, photocopying and similar services, since GRAEL's policy was 'not to separate manual and intellectual work' [*GRAEL, 1988b: 5*].

In addition, several specific measures were taken to encourage wide and equal participation within GRAEL. Most important was the emphasis placed on equality between the MEPs and their alternates or deputies (*Nachrücker*). All GRAEL MEPs and their alternates participated in the political work of the group with 'equal rights and duties' [*GRAEL, 1988b: 5*]. GRAEL members and their deputies both drew the same salary and both were entitled to vote within the group. Equality between MEPs and their deputies was also enforced through the rotation policy. Half-way into their first legislative period, the Green MEPs were expected to step down from their posts and be replaced by their alternates. The former members (*Weggerückten*) continued to work within the group as 'elder statespersons'.

Yet relations within GRAEL were difficult from the start. Even the supposedly minor issue of what to name the faction was resolved only after long and agonising debate. According to German GRAEL members, the German acronym for the original name, *Grün-alternative Europäische Bündnis* (GRAEB), was too similar to the German word *Grab* (grave) and thus not appropriate for the 'new beginning' of the green party in Brussels [*GRAEL, 1988a: 7*]. MEPs from other countries, however, disclosed another reason for a name change: they preferred a 'more neutral, non-Germanic' acronym (Kersten, interview, Brussels, 9 May 1989).

A more serious source of disputes stemmed from the movement-party measures erected to ensure internal democracy. The rotation policy caused particularly bitter disagreements within GRAEL. In an official account of his GRAEL activities (*Rechenschaftsbericht*), MEP Schwalba-Hoth [*1988: 2*] reported that the principle of rotation (and specifically those who refused to abide by it) hurt both the operation and atmosphere of GRAEL. When the first rotation deadline arrived, only he and one other of the seven German MEPs agreed to step down. Other Green MEPs argued that strict adherence to principles of grassroots democracy was not always possible if Greens were to assume positions of political responsibility. They emphasised further the need for experienced, qualified people to deal with the complex institutional and bureaucratic apparatus of the EC [*Bloch von Blottnitz, 1986b: 39*]. In other words,

MEPs continued the debate between 'parliamentarians' and 'movement-oriented' Greens which had emerged in the early stages of Green activity in Europe.

Throughout GRAEL's 1984–89 term, the West German Greens enjoyed clear numerical dominance within GRAEL. Following the 1984 EP elections, over one-third of GRAEL MEPs were German. A majority of staff members were also German since distribution of staff by nationality was roughly equivalent to that of the countries represented in GRAEL. Green MEPs from the Netherlands and Belgium expressed concern that the Germans, given their relative financial and organisational potency, tended to lean towards the 'arrogance of the mighty'. Indignant about the conduct of German GRAEL members, spokeswoman for the British Greens, Sara Parkin, complained that 'there is no real excuse for the arrogant and often contemptuous behaviour of some members of the German party' [*Parkin, 1989: 259*]. German MEPs themselves admitted that this was a problem: 'Yes, well, the Germans are known as rather addicted to "profiling" themselves. That took some time to work out' [*Ennich, 1986: 29*].

But this sheer numerical superiority was not matched by a dominant political influence. The German group was extremely heterogeneous in matters of content as well as strategy. Only rarely did the Germans present a 'German view' on matters of European policy.

This lack of consensus was attributable to the Greens' movement-party character. By 1984, Greens on the national and sub-national level were bitterly divided between the parliament-oriented 'Realists' and movement-oriented 'Fundamentalists'. The Germans inside GRAEL often displayed a disunity similar to that found on the national level. Among the MEPs, this factional debate often took petty forms. For instance, arguments over stipends, assistantships, travel priorities and other matters were especially noticeable among the German MEPs in the mid-1980s. According to MEP Bloch von Blottnitz (interview, Grabow, 13 May 1991), the quarrelsome atmosphere significantly damaged the work of the entire GRAEL: 'the situation in my own party wasted more energy than the battle against the Brussels monstrosity'.

Joining the Green group in the EP in 1988, Dutch member Wim Kersten was struck by the fierce bickering between wings of the German Greens. Kersten stated that by 1989, non-German members of GRAEL began insisting that the Germans 'settle their petty disputes at home' (Kersten, interview, Brussels, 9 May 1989).

Another hindrance to consensus-building was the unwillingness of the Greens at home to prioritise the political goals to be pursued at the

European level. The MEPs were given no definition of what key points to work for and implement through the EC. Specifically, MEPs received no guidance on how to turn the Europe-of-the-Regions conception into reality.

Untutored by their party on matters of Green Europapolitik, the German MEPs could not agree on aims and strategies to be pursued in Europe. Whilst Green MEPs agreed that the current EC was not an ideal instrument for implementing Green *Europapolitik*, attitudes towards the EC ranged from qualified acceptance to outright rejection. Or as another put it: attitudes concerning the EP varied from a shrug of shoulders to foaming at the mouth. Focusing on the Green MEPs in the 1984–89 parliamentary term, three broad categories are distinguishable.

For the first group, the *'obstructionists'*, the EC was an intolerable institution incapable of reform. The EC represented neither Europe (membership of the EC was limited to '12 market economies'), nor the positive connotations of 'community'. According to this view, even the representative body of the EC, the European Parliament, was considered unrepresentative and hopelessly undemocratic. Adherents to this view categorically rejected any expansion (horizontal or vertical) of the EC. This position was clearly represented by Dorothee Piermont who stated that:'[The] EC, in its reality and finality, is no community of the citizens ... Greater competence for the European Parliament can't change anything about this basic evil; it would only serve to hang a democratic cloak around it' [*Piermont, 1986: 17*]. According to another obstructionist, Wilfried Telkämper, the Green MEP's role in the EP was to 'disclose the European Parliament for what it is'. He argued that the real aims of the EP, the aims that need to be exposed, included 'the concentration of West European armament projects ... and the further relief for trade of goods for the benefit of transnational firms' [*Telkämper, 1986: 13*].

Obstructionists claimed to be most representative of the social movements and considered their approach as most sincere and loyal to the movement 'cause'. They hoped to exploit the institutions of the EC whilst serving as a fundamental opposition to the existing structures. To this end, the work of the obstructionists inside the EP focused on disrupting plenary sessions and criticising EC institutions and policies.

A second, somewhat larger number of the European group may be termed *'reformists'*. They recognised significant problems within the EC and campaigned vigorously against what they saw as the 'democratic deficit' of the institution. In particular, this group lamented the subordinate position of the European Parliament in relation to the EC's Council of Ministers. However, they did not view the institution as void of any value or incapable of reform. They pushed for reforms which they viewed as necessary and urgent. The best known advocate of this position was Frank Schwalba-Hoth [*1987*] who demanded a moratorium on EC expansion (that is, no new power for the EC) until a democratising and strengthening of the EP occurred.

To a reformist, justification of work within the EC was multi-faceted. According to MEP Benedikt Härlin, Green goals were to simplify the bureaucratic operations of the EC, to service the movements by offering EC facilities and translation services, and to disclose and penetrate the rhetoric of established parties. Their role, in Härlin's words, was 'to act as coarse gravel in the slippery smear of the parliamentary soap opera' (quoted in Wolf [*1986: 297*]).

Whilst exposing what he saw as the inadequacies of EC institutions, reformer Härlin complained of the lack of interest displayed by the public in general and the grassroots in particular. He was especially critical of the movement activists who categorically rejected EC institutions and the work of Green MEPs within them. 'What looks so simple from the safe distance of home becomes complex and perplexing in the routine of everyday life in Brussels' (quoted in Wolf [*1986: 297*]).

Other Green parliamentarians belonged to a third category. They are known as '*colluders*' or '*constructive co-workers*'. They accepted and attempted to work within the existing EC structures and saw their central task in the EP as publicity and 'damage limitation'. One member of this category, agricultural expert Friedrich Wilhelm Graefe zu Baringdorf, argued that the primary function of the Greens in the European Parliament should be to work within the institution and publicise the policies of the EC [*Wolf, 1986: 292*].

This group worried little about the lack of any overarching Green *Europapolitik*. When pushed on the need for such a blueprint by Green colleague Wolfgang Nostitz, the 'colluder' Bloch von Blottnitz allegedly responded 'What nonsense, I have absolutely no time for that!' (quoted in Nostitz [*1986: 6*]). Instead, Green MEPs in this category displayed a keen interest in learning about the EC's institutions and its bureaucratic apparatus. Whilst admitting that much of her work and research was wasted in the 'giant paper shredder of the EC', Bloch von Blottnitz [*1986a: 37*] claimed that the pay-off for her EP work was the tightening of EC environmental regulations.

As is typical for a colluder/co-worker, Bloch von Blottnitz claimed to serve as the active parliamentary arm of the grassroots movements. The MEPs' task was to 'be there, to pay attention, to stick our green nose into everything; to put forth demands in parliament that would otherwise stay confined to the street' [*Bloch von Blottnitz, 1986a: 37*]. She bemoaned the lack of attention and respect given the EC and MEPs by the grassroots. According to Bloch von Blottnitz and others in her category, the Greens underestimated the importance of the EC or the implications of EC policy. Bloch von Blottnitz [*1986a: 36–7*] warned that 'what's decided in Brussels and Strasbourg will be carried out in Bonn'.

Thus, significant differences in attitudes and beliefs concerning the European Community were visible among Green MEPs as they were within the party itself. All positions reflected a certain unease with the institutions of the EC; all claimed to best represent 'green interests'. But the variance in the three positions was considerable (see Table 1). Of the 14 Greens sent to the EP in 1984 (seven MEPs and seven *Nachrücker*), roughly 50 per cent belonged to the middle reformist position; about 30

TABLE 1

Category	Characteristics	MEPs
Obstructionists:	reject all EC institutions; participate in EP only to exploit EC resources and disrupt status quo	Piermont Telkämper
Reformists:	see an urgent need for 'democratic reform', in the EC but do not view the institutions as void of any value; favour the strengthening of the EP.	Schwalba-Hoth; Härlin
Co-workers/ 'Colluders':	pragmatists who accept and work within the existing 'imperfect' EC structures; see their main task as damage limitation and concrete policy results	Bloch von Blottnitz Graefe zu Baringdorf

per cent were obstructionists; and the co-worker/colluders comprised around 20 per cent of German GRAEL members.[3]

The rifts among the MEPs can be traced to the movement-party split itself. To a certain extent they also mirrored the divide on the national level between the '*Realos*' and '*Fundis*'. Broadly speaking, the 'obstructionists' paralleled the *Fundi* wing of the Greens, especially in their penchant for disruptive tactics. Conversely, the 'co-workers/colluders' shared the *Realos*' enthusiasm for pragmatic parliamentary work. Yet a simple correspondence of traits between the national and supranational level would be misleading. Primarily because there was so little contact and cooperation between the national and European Greens, MEPs were driven much more by individual preferences and values than by national party factions. The strongest explanation of these diverging views is the individualistic pattern of MEP activities in GRAEL.

These differences in positions had consequences for the Greens'

Europapolitik. Indeed, they precluded any development of a feasible alternative European policy [*Scheuer, 1989*]. Diversity of views and positions often produces creative alternatives to policy problems. In the Greens' case, however, a coherent set of Euro-political goals and strategies was blocked by the trenchant antagonism among the Greens and, specifically, between those who believed reform of the EC was possible and those who believed the EC system was neither tolerable nor reformable in its current state.

Contradictions, Conflicts, and the Collapse of GRAEL

The conflicts which beset the Greens during the 1984–89 parliamentary period were not resolved in subsequent terms. In the 1989 election to the European Parliament, widespread public concern about the state of the environment resulted in dramatic electoral success for green parties [*Lodge, 1990*]. New green contingents from France (eight seats), Italy (seven seats), Portugal (one seat) and Spain (one seat) entered the EP where they joined the German, Belgian and Dutch Greens already comprising GRAEL. The German Greens themselves increased their share of the German vote in the 1989 Euro-election, winning 8.4 per cent of the German vote and eight seats. But the German Greens' continued electoral success did not resolve internal tensions. Instead, existing conflicts were exacerbated by new ones.

With the entry of the French, Spanish, and Italian Greens into the EP for the first time, a conflict arose between more conservative or 'straight' green parties, as represented by the French Greens, and 'leftist-alternative' green parties such as the German Greens. Following the 1989 election, the German Greens felt outnumbered and discriminated against by the 'straight' French and Italian Green representatives. Several Germans complained that the French and Italian Greens had sent their 'conservative elites' to Europe [*Bullard, 1990: 5*]. These Mediterranean 'elites' moreover, held a particularly low opinion of the current status of GRAEL which they viewed as too leftist and quarrelsome (Boissière, interview, Brussels, 29 May 1991; Lapa, interview, Brussels, 28 May 1991).

These new conflicts may have been annoying to the German Greens, but they were hardly insurmountable. Some German Green MEPs welcomed the added representation, noting that GRAEL was diverse and flexible enough to accommodate a wide variety of green positions. The more destructive conflicts and contradictions came from inside the German group. Put another way, internal conflicts proved more debilitating than external ones.

First, the 1989 election did not provide the Green MEPs with any clearer notion of the policies they were to pursue in Europe. This lack of clarity from the party made it especially difficult for Green MEPs to uphold movement-party principles. For instance, the Green principle of 'imperative mandate' was impossible to sustain in the EP. Designed to ensure grassroots control, this principle required the resignation of any deputy who deviated from policy resolutions of the party assembly. But because there was no coherent *Europapolitik*, there were no coordinated policy resolutions from which to deviate. Consequently, the Greens' fundamental emphasis on grassroots input and participation was missing at the European level.

This problem was made even more intractable by the MEP's ambivalent relationship with the party executive and party base. MEPs felt that despite their 'international worth and reputation', they were often 'treated as second-class representatives at home' [*die Grünen, 1989a: 1*].

Secondly, the ambivalence of the Greens towards the EC became more apparent after the 1989 election. The new German MEPs continued to straddle uncomfortably movement and party imperatives. On one hand they could resume 'business as usual' within the European Parliament. The Greens' relationship with social movements had provided them with unique opportunities within the EP. Several GRAEL members used the Parliament as a platform through which to bring new movement issues and ideas on to the EC's agenda. One observer writes that 'flowers on the plenary desks, ... leaflets in the plenary sessions' as well as 'happenings' to denounce scandals in European agricultural and environmental policy were all characteristic of the Green group in the EP [*Buck, 1989: 170*]. These tactics initially attracted media attention and helped raise movement issues ignored by the larger party groups within the EP.

A related parliamentary advantage enjoyed by GRAEL MEPs was the liberty to pursue individual policies and interests within the EP. Whereas members of most national parliaments were expected to vote and act with their party, MEPs were under no comparable pressure. In seeking to encourage party unity within the EP, no sanctions could be invoked against those who did not 'fall into line' [*Nugent, 1989: 129*]. Consequently, several GRAEL members, especially those of the 'colluder/co-worker' category, pursued special projects and campaigns in the area of EC environmental, energy, or agricultural policy.

For instance, German Green MEP Bloch von Blottnitz had several successes in targeting key environmental issues. Her report on the carcinogenic substances released in the vicinity of Windscale Sellafield was adopted by the EP. This was the first EP report to attack the nuclear industry; its positive reception in the EP caused an outburst of publicity within Britain and led the Council of Ministers to call a special session on the issue (*The Times*, 21 Feb. 1986).

Yet being 'effective' carried its own consequences for representatives of a movement-party. GRAEL member Wolfgang Nostitz expressed the concern of several of his colleagues when he recognised that Green MEPs often

> behaved more like hamsters on a wheel spun by our opponents ... The proposals, meetings, questions, daily flood of paper, the appointments that appear so important, ... all this (gave us) the feeling that we had become politically indispensable (quoted in Esders [*1988: 13*]).

Thus, many Green MEPs feared they were in constant danger of becoming seduced by the parliamentary process and losing sight of their movement-party mandate and green goals.

Moreover, the Green MEPs were still under extreme pressure to legitimise their work to the grassroots. When asked what the ecology movement wanted from GRAEL, MEP Schwalba-Hoth responded that the movements demanded disruptive and radical behaviour. 'They expected us to behave as "ecological Rambos"' in representing movement and grassroots interests [*Schwalba-Hoth, 1989: 204*].

In short, Green MEPs were still expected to represent the wishes of both the Green party and the wider green movement. The Green MEPs' mandate thus involved reconciling an apparent incongruity of structures – parliamentary, centralised – and principles – grassroots, decentralised. The movement proponents demands for more grassroots participation within GRAEL often conflicted with the party's desire to act effectively in parliament. One frustrated MEP described the legitimation dilemma this way: 'to be effective in the institutions, to exploit them, essentially means to serve the institutions, to feed them' [*Ennich, 1986: 30*].

Neither the Germans nor the body GRAEL could withstand the push-and-pull of these multiple dilemmas. The GRAEL group did not become parliamentarised, nor did it remain completely loyal to its movement-roots. It hovered between the two poles, adrift in the grey zone of movement-party existence. Under the pressure of both internal and external conflicts, GRAEL dissolved in summer 1989.

Conclusion: Lessons from GRAEL

The defunct GRAEL was replaced by the Green Group in the European Parliament (GGEP) on 25 July 1989. The GGEP consists of 29 MEPs and is the fifth largest of the ten organised EP political groups.[4] Unlike

GRAEL, the GGEP formed its own parliamentary group and is not a part of the Rainbow group. No longer including the anti-EC or regionalist parties which helped make up the Rainbow, the GGEP is a more cohesive green group rather than a expedient collection of leftist alternative groups. It is thus a 'political rather than a technical group' [*Lannoye, 1991: 1*].

German Greens still make up the second largest national contingent in the GGEP. But numerically and otherwise, the Germans no longer enjoy a leadership position. Structurally, the GGEP's primary decision-making body is an executive committee (*bureau*) with eight members and two presidents. Compared to the German-dominated GRAEL, the GGEP is clearly French-led. GGEP's first eight-member executive committee had one French and one Italian president; the only German member served as a 'co-vice president'. In short, the new Green Group in the European Parliament, and the Germans' role within it, have changed significantly. Yet despite GGEP's electoral support and larger size, German and other Green MEPs encounter the same opportunities and dilemmas facing GRAEL.

The German GGEP members thus would do well to heed the lessons from GRAEL's experience. The success of GGEP depends in part on its ability to reconcile movement and party imperatives in their European policy. To do so, the GGEP must meet a number of prerequisites not fulfilled by GRAEL. First, for a movement-party, such a strategy re-quires interest and engagement from the grassroots. Like GRAEL, the GGEP seeks to avoid the rigid structure of established party groups. Instead, it emphasises its support of alternative politics and grassroots principles. First GGEP co-president Paul Lannoye explains [*1991: 1*] that the chosen strategy of the GGEP, 'is a constant pedagogy of political ecology ... Fulfilling this demanding task in coordination with the whole ecological movement is a constant challenge – a challenge we must take up'.

Yet the GGEP may underestimate the difficulty of this 'movement-party challenge'. The GRAEL example illustrates that grassroots demo-cracy generally has not provided MEPs with the necessary coherence or engagement to carry out their movement-party mandate. Continual contact and input from the grassroots is critical if the Greens are to uphold their distinguishing principle of grassroots democracy. But clearly, it is not easy to achieve and maintain such links.

Alternatively, the GGEP could consciously embrace the 'parliamen-tarisation' forces in the EP. There are signs that this may be the direction followed by the GGEP, and accepted by its German members. In their dealings with the EP the GGEP has shifted away from the confrontational tactics employed by GRAEL. Instead, the GGEP has chosen to work more closely with other parliamentary groups, even if this means compromise and accommodation. Indeed, one-time 'obstructionist' Wilfried Telkämper is now serving as one of the vice presidents of the EP. Moreover, the GGEP has devised 'conventional' and co-operative strategies of a sort shunned by GRAEL. For instance, the GGEP is pushing hard for the use of economic incentives as a tool for environmental policy [*de Roo, 1991*; *EP, 1990*; *GGEP, 1991c: 7*].

A final lesson from the GRAEL experience applies regardless of whether the GGEP emphasises movement or parliamentary strategies. Above all, a successful European policy requires some shared interest in developing a clear, detailed conception of green goals in Europe. The GGEP claims that 'the Greens are the only bearers of a coherent and innovative project for society' [*Lannoye, 1991a: 2*]. But internal conflict, national differences, and lack of coordination continue to preclude the formation of a coherent *Europapolitik*. Bowler and Farrell [*1992: 134*] observe that:

> while the individual [GGEP] MEPs may have a high profile within the Parliament and its committees, there is an absence of an adequate *group* dimension. The individual MEPs tend to bring their individual national identities with them to the EP; they seem unwilling or unable to adequately pool their strategies and resources as a group (emphasis in original).

This is a serious impediment to sustained green success. The GRAEL experience demonstrated that immediate needs might be served by an individualised, *ad hoc* approach to policy. But larger issues and fundamental questions such as enlargement of the EC, the green response to completion of the internal market, and ecological disasters in the East require a collective, long-range plan and a coherent alternative conception of a future Europe.

Lack of a coherent European policy is a problem shared by other parties operating on the European level. However, for the Greens it is especially damaging. The German Green party platform has always been characterised by a strong emphasis on crossnational issues, especially environmental concerns. The Greens also claim to provide non-conventional answers to current concerns, answers that are 'neither right nor left but forward looking'. Moreover, these answers are said to emerge out of the diverse views of the grassroots.

If German Greens are to exercise any continued influence in Europe, be it in the way of reforming current structures or establishing new ones, they first must develop a *Europapolitik* coherent in formulation and acknowledged by the grassroots. Without a comprehensive and comprehensible conception of Europe, the impact of the growing green consciousness in Europe will remain muted.

NOTES

1. This explains, for instance, why the Greens had always been opposed to German unification. They instead emphasised the need to correct and restructure the international political configurations so that unification would become unnecessary and the borders between the two Germanies would lose their divisive effect [*Gransow, 1989: 143–4*].
2. Also a movement-party, the Italian Radicals received strong support from movement activists. They gained parliamentary representation in Italy in 1976 and enjoyed a dramatic breakthrough in 1979 with 1.25 million votes and eighteen seats.
3. One MEP, Michael Klöckner, left the group in late 1984, before his 'tendency' could be established.
4. To counter what the Greens view as Britain's unjust first-past-the-post electoral system, the GGEP also includes one British representative, Jean Lambert. In addition, Hans Meisel, a member of the former East German 'Neues Forum', joined as an observer in February 1991.

REFERENCES

Ascherson, Neal (1992), 'The New Europe', *The Independent on Sunday Magazine*, 9 Feb. 1992, pp.31–4.
von Beyme, Klaus (1982), 'Krise des Parteienstaats – ein internationales Phänomen?', in J. Raschke (ed.), *Bürger und Partein*, Opladen: Westdeutscher Verlag, pp.87–100.
von Beyme, Klaus (1984), 'Die ökologische Bewegung zwischen Bürgerinitiativen und Partieorganisation', in B. Guggenberger und U. Kempf (eds.), *Bürgerinitiativen und Repräsentatives System*, 2nd ed., Opladen: Westdeutscher Verlag, pp.371–92.
Bloch von Blottnitz, Undine (1984), 'Was soll der Quatsch – Grünen nach Europa?' *Grüne Informationen*, Vol.7, p.5. Niedersachsen.
Bloch von Blottnitz, Undine (1986a), 'Auch in Brüssel die grünen Nasen überall reinstecken', *Grüner Basis-dienst*, Vol.10, pp.36–7.
Bloch von Blottnitz, Undine (1986b), 'Alternativer Forschungspolitik: Die EG als "Eisbrecher?"', *Grüner Basis-dienst*, Vol.10, pp.38–9.
Bowler, Shaun and David Farrell (1992), 'Profile: The Greens at the European Level', *Environmental Politics*, Vol.1, No.1, pp.132–7.
Buck, Karl (1989). 'Europe: The "Greens" and the "Rainbow Group" in the European Parliament', in F. Müller-Rommel (ed.), *New Politics in Western Europe. The Rise and Success of Green Parties and Alternative Lists*, Boulder, CO: Westview Press, pp.167–72.
Bullard, Michael (1990), 'Oberwasser für Euro-Grüne', *die Tageszeitung*, 12 December 1990, p.5.
Dierker, J. (1987), 'Die Grünen und die europäische Integration', unpublished manuscript, Westfälische Wilhelms-Universität.
Dobson, Andrew (1990), *Green Political Thought*, London: Unwin Hyman.
Ennich, Edeltraud (1986), 'Regenbogen oder Wurstmaschine?' *Grünen Basis-dienst*, Vol.10, pp.28–31.
EP (1990), 'Economic and Fiscal Incentives as a Means of Achieving Environmental Policy Objectives', European Parliament Directorate-General for Research. Research and

Documentation Paper – Environment, Public Health and Consumer Protection Series, No.16. Luxembourg.

Esders, Jürgen Peter (1988), 'Gefangen im Parlamentsbetrieb?' in GRAEL, *Politik im Regenbogen. Grün-alternatives im Europäisches Parlament*, pp.12–15.

Franken, Michael and Walter Ohler (eds.) (1989), *Natürlich Europa. 1992 – Chancen für die Natur?*, Köln: Volksblatt Verlag.

Frankland, E. Gene (1989), 'Parliamentary Politics and the Development of the Green Party in West Germany', *Review of Politics*, Vol.51, No.3, pp.386–411.

GGEP (1991a), *Green Leaves: Bulletin of the Greens in the European Parliament*, No.0, Brussels.

GGEP (1991b), *Green Leaves. Bulletin of the Greens in the European Parliament*, No.1, Brussels.

GGEP (1991c), *Green Leaves. Bulletin of the Greens in the European Parliament*, No.2, Brussels.

GRAEL (1984), *Paris Declaration*, Paris.

GRAEL (1988a), *Politik im Regenbogen. Grün-alternatives im Europäisches Parlament*, Brussels.

GRAEL (1988b), *Rainbow Politics: Green alternative politics in the European Parliament*, Brussels.

Gransow, Volker (1989), 'Greening of German–German Relations?' in E. Kolinsky (ed.), *The Greens in West Germany. Organisation and Policymaking*, Oxford: Berg, pp.141–58.

die Grünen (1980), *Programme of the German Green Party*, London: Heretic Books.

die Grünen (1984a), *Common Statement of the Greens for the 1984 Election to the European Parliament*, Bonn.

die Grünen (1984b), *Global Denken – vor Ort Handeln: Erklärung der Grünen zur Europawahl 1984*, Bonn.

die Grünen (1989a), *Extra Blatt zur Europawahl*, Bonn.

die Grünen (1989b), *Kurzprogramm der Grünen zur Europawahl '89*, Bonn.

die Grünen (1989c), *Plattform der Grünen zur Europawahl '89*, Bonn.

Härlin, Benedikt (1984), 'Eine Stimme für die Freiheit', *Grüner Basis-dienst*, Vol.4, pp.10–11.

Heuglin, Thomas (1986), 'Regionalism in Western Europe: Conceptual Problems of a New Political Perspective', *Comparative Politics*, Vol.18, No.4, pp.439–58.

Jäcker, B. and M. Hadamczik (1988), 'Vorstellungen zur Arbeit und Struktur einer (B)AG Europa/EG', Green unpublished memorandum. Bonn.

Jäenicke, M. (1982), 'Parlamentärische Entwarnungseffekte? Zum Ortsbestimmung der Alternativbewegung', in J. Mettke (ed.), *Die Grünen – Regierungspartner von Morgen?*, Reinbek: Rowohlt, pp.69–81.

Kelly, Petra (1980), 'Die Vierte Partei – Eine wahlbare ökologische, gewaltfreie, soziale und basisdemokratische Anti-Partei', in H. Lüdke (ed.), *Die Grünen, Personen – Projekte – Programme*, Stuttgart: Kröger, pp.62–80.

Kelly, Petra (1984), 'Gedanken zur gegenwärtigen Europadiskussion 1984', unpublished memorandum, Bonn.

Kolinsky, Eva (1984), 'Ecology and Peace in West Germany: An Uneasy Alliance', *Journal of Area Studies*, Vol.9, pp.23–8.

Kolinsky, Eva (ed.) (1987), *Opposition in Western Europe*, New York: St. Martins Press.

Kolinsky, Eva (1990), 'The Federal Republic of Germany', in J. Lodge (ed.), *The 1989 Election of the European Parliament*, New York: St. Martins, pp.67–89.

Lannoye, Paul (1991), 'A Green Group in the European Parliament: What For?' *Green Leaves: Bulletin of the Greens in the European Parliament*, No.1, pp.1–2.

Lenk, Kurt (1983), 'Institutionalisierung – Endstation sozialer Bewegungen?', *Frankfurter Hefte*, Vol.5, pp.56–66.

Lodge, Juliet (1989), 'The European Parliament: From "Assembly" to Co-Legislature: Changing the Institutional Dynamics', in J. Lodge (ed.), *The European Community and the Challenge of the Future*, London: Pinter, pp.58–82.

Lodge, Juliet (ed.) (1990), *The 1989 Election of the European Parliament*, New York: St. Martins.

Marks, Gary (1992) 'Structural Policy in the European Community', in A. Sbragia (ed.), *Euro-Politics. Institutions and Policymaking in the 'New' European Community*, Washington, DC: Brookings Institution, pp.191–224.

Marsh, John S. (1989), 'The Common Agricultural Policy', in J. Lodge (ed.), *The European Community and the Challenge of the Future*, London: Pinter, pp.148–66.

Müller-Rommel, Ferdinand (1985), 'Das grün-alternative Parteibündnis im Europäischen Parlament. Perspektiven eines neuen Phänomens', *Zeitschrift für Palamentsfragen*, Vol.16, pp.391–404.

Narr, Wolf-Dieter (1982), 'Andere Partei oder eine neue Form der Politik?', in J.R. Mettke (ed.), *Die Grünen – Regierungspartner von Morgen?*, Reinbek: Rowohlt, pp.270–306.

Nitsch, Egbert (1986), 'Wer wildert in welchem Erbhof?', *Grüner Basis-dienst*, Vol.10, pp.55–6.

Nostitz, Wolfgang von (1984), 'Die Europäischen Gemeinschaften aus der Sicht der Grünen', *Grüner Basis-dienst*, Vol.4, pp.18–19.

Nostitz, Wolfgang von (1986), 'Die Grünen im Europäische Parlament – eine weitere vertane Chance?', *Grüner Basis-dienst*, Vol.10, pp.4–7.

Nostitz, Wolfgang von and Merkel, Christine (1986), 'Vorwort. Europagruppe der Grünen/Regenbogenfraktion', *Grüne Inhalt*, (foreword without page numbers).

Nugent, Neill (1989), *The Government and Politics of the European Community*, London: Macmillan.

Parkin, Sara (1989), *Green Parties: An International Guide*, London: Heretic Books.

Piermont, Dorothee (1986), 'Die EG ist eben ganz anders', *EG Magazin*, Vol.2, pp.17–18.

Raschke, Joachim (1988), 'Bewegung und Partei', *Forschungsjournal Neue Soziale Bewegungen*, Vol.4, pp.6–16.

Roo, Alexander de (1991), 'Towards a Green EC-Strategy Against the Greenhouse Effect: A Tax on Non-renewable Energy Sources', Green Discussion Paper, GGEP, Brussels.

Rüdig, Wolfgang (1985), 'The Greens in Europe: Ecological Parties and the European Elections of 1984', *Parliamentary Affairs*, Vol.38, No.1, pp.56–72.

Scheuer, Thomas (1989), 'Tanz auf dem Regenbogen. Der GRAEL im Europaparlament', in M. Franken and W. Ohler (eds.), *Natürlich Europa: 1992 – Chancen für die Natur?*, Köln: Volksblatt Verlag, pp.185–98.

Schoonmaker, Donald (1988), 'The Challenge of the Greens to the West German Party System', in K. Lawson and P. Merkl (eds.), *When Parties Fail. Emerging Alternative Organizations*, Princeton N.J.: Princeton University Press, pp.41–75.

Schwalba-Hoth, Frank (1987), 'Thesenpapier zur Europäischen Gemeinschaft', GRAEL internal memorandum. Brussels.

Schwalba-Hoth, Frank (1988), *Rechenschaftsbericht*, April 1988.

Schwalba-Hoth, Frank (1989), '1992 droht ein ökologisches und soziales Dumping', in M. Franken and W. Ohler (eds.), *Natürlich Europa: 1992 – Chancen für die Natur?*, Köln: Volksblatt Verlag, pp.199–208.

Smith, Gordon (1984), *Politics in Western Europe*, 4th ed., New York: Holmes & Meier.

Spiegel, Dietmar (1984), 'Grünen Politik im Europa-Parlament', *Grüner Basis-dienst*, Vol.2, pp.26–7.

Spretnak, Charlene and Fritjof Capra (1986), *Green Politics. The Global Promise*, Santa Fe, New Mexico: Bear & Co.

Stuth, R. (1984) 'Die Außen-und Deutschlandpolitik der Grünen' in K. Gotto and H. Veen (eds.), *Die Grünen – Partei wider Willen*, Mainz: von Hase & Koehler Verlag, pp.54–72.

Telkämper, Wilfried (1986), 'Das vereinnahmende Ungeheuer', *Grüner Basis-dienst*, Vol.10, pp.13–16.

Vollmer, Antje (1984). 'Für ein Europa der Mutterländer', *Grüner Basis-dienst*, Vol.4, pp.3–5.

Widmer, Günther (1984), 'Europa – wo sind deine Reize? Die Europäischen Institutionen und Organe', *Grüner Basis-dienst*, Vol.2, pp.29–30.

Wolf, Frieder (1986), 'Dossier über "Die Grünen im Europaparlament"', in E. Jurtschitsch, A. Rudnick and F. Wolf (eds.), *Grünes und alternatives Jahrbuch 1986/1987*, Berlin: Elefanten Press, pp.290–316.

Zeuner, Bodo (1985), 'Parlamentarisierung der Grünen', *Prokla*, No.61, pp.13–18.

'Predestined to Save the Earth': The Environment Committee of the European Parliament

DAVID JUDGE

Despite an increase in the influence of the European Parliament in the decision making process of the European Communities in recent years some commentators still maintain that the EP's impact on EC legislation remains marginal. Taking the Environment Committee of the European Parliament as its focus this article assesses the contribution made by the EP to EC environmental policy. While it is often asserted that the EP's legislative role in relation to environmental policy began with the Single European Act, in fact the EP performed a legislative role, including the right of initiative, before 1987; a role subsequently enhanced by the SEA. Tracing the decision making process through the various stages of initiation, consultation, cooperation and implementation, and using case studies to illustrate the Committee's contribution to this process, the variable impact of the EP upon EC environmental policy is revealed. The role of the Environment Committee as a promoter of 'environmentalism' within EC policy and institutions, and the shared consensus within the committee which assists the Committee in its efforts to influence policy is also noted.

That the influence of the European Parliament (EP) in the decision making process of the European Communities (EC) has increased in recent years is generally acknowledged, but the exact extent of that increase remains the subject of significant controversy. This division of opinion is clearly manifested in two of the most recent texts on the EC (American in both instances – reflecting the seriousness with which US academics now treat the EC). On the one side, Harvard Professor Shirley Williams [1991: 160] states: 'When it comes to initiating proposals or

The author's especial thanks to Ken Collins MEP and David Earnshaw, without whose generous assistance this study would not have been written. Thanks also to Dr Hans Herman Kraus of the EP's DG IV for providing research documents; and also to Jane Aitken, and Dr Tricia Hogwood. To those members of the Commission, MEPs, parliamentary consultants, and EP committee secretariats who gave so generously of their time in interview the author hereby expresses his gratitude. The Nuffield Foundation provided a grant to enable these interviews to take place.

influencing them, the EP's input remains marginal.' While acknowledging the enhanced powers conferred upon the EP by the Single European Act, Williams still, none the less, sees them as 'grudgingly' given and thus leaving 'the whole cloth that the EP is trying to make (to be) woven out of sparse fragments' [*Williams, 1991: 166*]. On the other side, Guy Peters [*1992: 90*], Professor at Pittsburg, maintains that: 'the Parliament has evolved to the point that it can compensate for some of the democratic deficit of the Community.... The Parliament is also attempting to emulate the role of a legislature in a conventional parliamentary democracy. There is still a good bit to be done ... but progress has been steady and substantial and sustained.' The intention of this paper therefore is to contribute towards the assessment of the degree of progress by examining the contribution of one part of the EP – the Environment Committee[1] – to one part of EC policy – environment policy. The first reason for examining the Environment Committee is that much of the major work of the EP is carried out through its committee structure [*Jacobs and Corbett, 1990: 91; Nugent, 1991: 159*].

The logical starting place, therefore, to understand the intricacies of the EP's contribution to environmental policy is in the committee. But a second reason arises from the very intricacies of the process itself; for general observations or conclusions about the EP's 'influence' or 'contribution' to policy making are often misleading, over-legalistic, invariably anachronistic, and under-researched. What is required instead are more detailed studies of specific issue areas, studies which examine the details of the interinstitutional connections within the EC – especially the informal flows of influence as well as the formal, treaty-prescribed contours of power. Thus, given the intrinsic importance of environmental policy to the EC (recognised formally, and belatedly in the Single European Act and the Maastricht treaty), and given the political importance of the Environment Committee within the EP this is an area worthy of detailed study.

Environmental Action Programmes

The evolution of the EC's environmental policy has been described above in this volume by Philipp Hildebrand, and there is no need, therefore, to repeat the details here. Instead, it is proposed merely to chronicle the changing emphases apparent within that evolution and to note how pressure from within the EP, especially from the membership of its Environment Committee contributed to a dynamic of policy development.

The first phase identified by Hildebrand is the period 1956–72 and is one essentially of incidental environmental measures. The absence of an explicit legal basis for the development of environmental policy within the EEC treaty, combined with the overwhelming market orientation of the community, meant that 'environmental' measures were pragmatic and incoherent. The second phase, termed the 'responsive period' by Hildebrand, was launched at the Paris summit in 1972. At that summit, leaders of the member states, either out of a cynical recognition of the distortions to competition that divergent national rules on pollution could cause, or out of an awareness that environmental problems needed an international dimension for their resolution, or in fact both, requested the Commission to draft a programme for environmental action. It should also be noted in passing that 1972 witnessed the decision to establish the EP's Environment Committee. In November 1973 the First EC Action Programme on the Environment was approved by the Council of Ministers and marked the adoption of a formal EC environmental policy.

The First Action Programme was primarily concerned with the reduction and prevention of pollution and was characterised generally by a 'remedial' orientation to EC environmental issues [*EC Documentation, 1990: 7*]. Importantly, it adopted the principle that the cost of prevention and elimination of environmental 'nuisances' should be borne by the polluter. The Second Action Programme adopted in 1977 was a continuation and reinforcement of the remedial policy perspective of its predecessor. Only with the adoption of the Third Action Programme in 1983 did the focus move from remedial to preventive action [*Johnson and Corcelle, 1989: 17–18*]. The Third Action Programme emphasised the need for, first, environment policy to be integrated into other sectoral policies such as agriculture, energy, industry and transport; second, environmental assessment procedures; and, third, the reduction of pollution and nuisance at source.

The Fourth Action Programme, negotiated throughout 1985–86 and formally adopted in October 1987, sought to develop the principles of the Third Programme whilst introducing a number of new principles and concerns including the introduction of sufficiently strict environmental standards; the need for greater control over the implementation of EC directives; and the progressive introduction of a genuine environmental information policy. In parallel, the Single European Act (SEA) was being drafted [*Lodge, 1984; Bouguignon-Wittke et al., 1985*]. The subsequent insertion of the title 'environment' into the EEC treaty ensured that, for the first time, environmental policy was given a constitutional base and legal definition within the EC [*Vandermeersch, 1987; PE 140.600, 1990*].

What is important for present purposes, however, is the role of the EP in helping to secure the incorporation of environmental protection provisions within the SEA. At a general level, as Juliet Lodge [*1990: 68*] observes, 'without ... the constant pressure from the EP it is doubtful that the SEA would have seen daylight'. At a specific level, the incorporation of environmental policy into the treaties was a major concern of the EP [*Arp, 1992: 46*]. As an increasingly high-profile policy area, environment fitted into the strategy, identified by the 'Crocodile Club' [*Capotorti et al., 1986: 11–17; Lodge, 1986: 203–7*] immediately after direct elections, of heightening public awareness within member states of the need for, and commitment to, enhanced democratic control of transborder policies at the EC level. Hence the Draft Treaty Establishing the European Union, approved by the EP in February 1984, included the statement in Article 59:

> In the field of the environment, the union shall aim at preventing or, taking into account the 'polluter pays' principle, at redressing any damage which is beyond the capabilities of the individual member state or which requires a collective solution. It shall encourage a policy of rational utilisation of natural resources, of exploiting renewable raw materials and of recycling waste which takes account of environmental protection requirements [*EP, 1985: 39*].

The subsequent Ad Hoc Committee for Institutional Affairs of the European Council, commonly known as the Dooge Committee, accepted that a 'high priority must be given to the protection of the environment' [*HL 226, 1985: lxxii*]. When the Single European Act was eventually agreed by member states it included for the first time, as noted above, an explicit commitment in Title VII to 'action by the Community relating to the environment' [*SEA, 1986*]. Though the EP itself was dissatisfied with the actual outcome of the SEA, criticising in particular its 'vagueness and inadequacy ... in defining Community environmental policy' (OJ C 68/45, 24 March 1986), none the less the EP had been of some importance in exerting pressure which culminated in the inclusion of Title VII and Article 130 [*Haigh and Baldock, 1989: 20*] (see below on Article 130).

Legislative Role: Formal Powers and Informal Processes

It is often asserted that the EP's legislative role in relation to environmental policy began with the SEA, and moreover that this role is essentially negative as conceptualised in the 'co-operation' procedure. Such assertions are inaccurate on both counts: first, the EP performed a 'legislative' role in environmental policy *before* 1987, a role that was *enhanced* and not initiated by the SEA; and, second, the EP performed a positive legislative role of initiation which again predated the SEA.

Initiation of Legislation

Under Article 155 of the Treaty of Rome the Commission alone is empowered to formulate recommendations for legislative action. In the 1957 treaty it was not envisaged that the 'Assembly' would have anything other than consultative status [*Lodge, 1989: 59*]. None the less, and especially since the introduction of direct elections to the EP in 1979, Members of the European Parliament (MEPs) came to adopt procedures[2] which enabled them to forward draft proposals for legislation to the Commission. Any MEP may table a short, 200 word, motion for resolution on any matter falling within the sphere of EC competences. These resolutions are then referred to the appropriate EP committee for consideration whether or not to produce a report or an opinion. Only a minority of individual resolutions become the subject of a committee report and an even smaller number become the basis of 'Rule 63' reports proposing legislation. In addition, committees themselves may independently seek to draw up a report on an particular issue. In these circumstances the committee concerned must seek authorisation from the bureau of the parliament to draw up an 'own-initiative' report[3]. The first point of significance, therefore, is that, although there is no mention in the treaties of an EP involvement at the initiation stage of EC legislation, the EP has established procedures to insert its ideas into the formulation stage of legislation. The second point is that, even before the SEA, 'own-initiative' reports constituted 'a major source of Community initiatives' [*HL 226, 1985: 167*]. And the third point of significance is that the Environment Committee is exceptional amongst the major 'legislative'[4] EP committees in continuing to produce a considerable flow of 'own-initiative' reports [*Jacobs and Corbett, 1990: 106*]. Indeed, the Environment Committee has had several notable successes in prompting the Commission into legislative action. Again, it is important to make the point that several of these successes *pre-date* the SEA. Thus, before 1987, initiatives taken within the EP contributed to the genesis of directives on major industrial hazards (*82/501/EEC*), the lead content in petrol (*82/884/EEC*), the importation of seal pup skins (*83/129/EEC*), and transfrontier shipment of waste (*84/631/EEC*). Since 1987 the Environment Committee has also been able to claim 'parentage' of the proposals, amongst others, on a Financial Instrument for the Environment (LIFE) (Com (91) 0028 final; for details of inception [*PE 146.246/fin., 31 July*]

1991: 28–9]), and on minimum standards for keeping animals in zoos (Com (91) 0177 final).

Agenda Setting

In addition to overtly 'legislative' initiatives the EP has used 'own-initiative' and 'Rule 63' reports to 'bring up a new issue on the policy agenda, to give a view on a Commission Communication on which Parliament has not been formally consulted' [*Jacobs and Corbett, 1990: 106*]. Indeed, the Environment Committee has consistently sought to involve itself at the *pre-legislative* stage through a conscious strategy of agenda setting. There are several dimensions to this strategy. One is to use 'Rule 63' reports to encourage action on the part of the Commission. On many occasions the Commission might already be considering such action, and so the intention of the committee is either to accelerate this process, and so advance the issue up the Commission's overcrowded agenda, or to focus the Commission's attention upon an issue and so determine the priorities and relative policy-weighting of the Commission.

Indeed, since 1989 it is apparent from the 'Rule 63' reports emanating from the Environment Committee that it, or its presidency at least, has a clear vision of what the priorities of the Commission should be in the early 1990s. Aware, for example, that the Commission was formulating proposals on waste management, the Environment Committee initiated its own investigation into the subject [*PE 144.135/fin., Dec. 1990*] with the intention of 'guiding' the Commission's own internal deliberations. The influence of the Committee's report is partially observable in the Commission's eventual proposals on the incineration of hazardous waste (Com (92) 9 final, 19 March 1992) and on landfill of waste (Com (91) 102 final, 23 January 1992). Similarly, since 1989, the Committee has launched a series of its own reports on the issues of Economic and Fiscal Instruments [*PE 145.367/fin., 13 May 1991*], eco-labelling [*PE 152.137/ fin., 5 Nov. 1991*], and the implementation of EC environmental law [*PE 152.144, 28 Aug. 1991*]. Clearly, in this exercise the Environment Committee has been engaged in a *pro-active* strategy of articulating its own policy concerns to the Commission, rather than simply waiting to react to formal Commission proposals as part of the consultation process (see below). Equally clearly it is difficult, if not impossible, to assess the direct influence of this strategy upon the final Commission proposals, and, indeed, the Committee itself would probably claim no more than that it seeks to get the voice of the EP heard as part of the chorus of interests considered by the Commission at the formative stage of legislation.

There are, however, notable examples where EP initiatives are openly acknowledged by DG XI itself as prompting action or changing its own priorities. Perhaps the clearest, and most publicly acknowledged, example is the genesis of the Commission's *Green Paper on the Urban Environment* [*EUR 12902 EN, 1990*]. In the preface to the *Green Paper* Commissioner Ripa Di Meana openly records that the paper is 'a practical response to the resolution tabled in December 1988 by a Member of the European Parliament, Mr Ken Collins, urging that the problems facing the urban environment be studied in greater detail' [*EUR 12902 EN, 1990: 5*]. Moreover, the DG XI official responsible for drafting the paper was in no doubt as to the 'importance of the Collin's report', and was willing to attribute to the EP 'a considerable share of responsibility' (alongside Ripa di Meana's own commitment to putting urban issues on the environmental agenda) for the introduction of the *Green Paper* (interview, Brussels, 20 May 1992). As the Commission official went on to state: 'the Commission could have easily ignored the Collin's report, but chose not to do so. It is a good example of the coming together of interests within two institutions to advance policy.'

A less publicly documented recent example of EP influence over the Commission's pre-legislative agenda concerns the Environment Committee's reports on tropical rainforests [*PE 139.166/fin., 5 July 1990*]. A member of the Directorate of DG XI noted in interview (Brussels, 19 May 1992) that: 'The EP has been pressing very hard for a ban on all tropical hardwoods. As a result, it is true to say that thinking within the Council and Commission has developed on tropical forests. There is no Commission legislation yet, but the EP has been in early pushing this item up the agenda'.

The problem in assessing the precise impact of the EP's agenda setting and initiation roles is that they are largely unquantifiable.[5] As such they are often overlooked in standard texts on, and 'guides' to, the EC decision-making process (see, for example, Budd and Jones [*1990*]; de Rouffignac [*1991*] which make no mention of the EP's informal contributions to the initiation stage of legislation). None the less, as more perspicacious commentators have observed 'astute interpretation of the Treaty and its own rules allowed the EP to find, for itself, a right of legislative initiative' [*Lodge, 1989: 66*], and the 'Commission pays a great deal of attention to the views of the Parliament in its preparation of draft legislation' [*Pinder, 1991:37*].

Indeed, the transmission of information between Commission and EP at the pre-legislative stage is not simply a one-way process. Nugent [*1991: 286*] points out that Commission officials may informally 'sound out' EP committees on draft legislation. This process has to remain informal because as one senior member of the Directorate-General of DG XI commented:

You have to remember that there is an institutional relationship: the Commission proposes, the Council accepts and the EP adopts. In which case there cannot be formal consultation with the EP until the Commission announces its proposal. National parliaments are already critical of the Commission for not consulting them; if we don't talk to the EP then we shouldn't talk to national parliaments (interview, Brussels, 20 May 1992).

Another DG XI senior official was even willing to acknowledge informal 'soundings' at the pre-legislative stage and stated categorically that: 'The Commission does not want to get involved with the EP at the preparatory stage of legislation' (interview, 19 May 1992). None the less, the same official held the personal belief that there was a case for providing the chairman of the Environment Committee with a copy of draft proposals circulated by the Commission.

The Committee's chairman understood the Commission's reluctance to include the EP in the formal process of consultation. Indeed, he argued that the Committee itself did not wish to be a part of this process as it would 'reduce Parliament's pre-legislative contribution to that of merely another lobby'. Instead, what the committee sought to maintain was informal contact whereby 'the Commission was well aware of what was likely to be acceptable to Parliament. So that when the Commission sought the opinion of Parliament it was already running with the tide' (interview, Brussels, 21 May 1992).

Consultation, Conciliation and Co-operation

Consultation: The founding treaties of the EC allowed for the involvement of the EP in the legislative process only to the extent that the Council was required to consult Parliament on Commission proposals (relating to 33 treaty articles) before their adoption. As is well documented [*Jacobs and Corbett, 1990: 162–6; Lodge, 1989: 65–6; Nugent, 1991: 130–31*] the EP successfully maximised the significance of the consultation procedure, both formally and informally. Informally, in response to pressure from the EP, the Council in successive steps in the 1960s and 1970s committed itself to consulting Parliament on all important matters whether or not required to do so by the treaties. In addition, by the early 1970s the Council had agreed, when adopting community legislation that departed from an EP opinion, to inform Parliament of its reasons for doing so.

Formally, the right of the EP to be consulted in designated areas was upheld by the Court of Justice's ruling on the celebrated 'isoglucose' case in 1980 [*Kirchner and Williams, 1983*]. This ruling made it clear that the

Council of Ministers could not adopt a Commission proposal without awaiting the EP's opinion. In 1981, in the wake of the 'isoglucose' ruling, Parliament amended its procedures to enable its committees to postpone a vote on a Commission proposal until the Commission had taken a position on Parliament's amendments. Under the present rule 40 [*EP Rules of Procedure, 1992*] a committee is enabled to postpone a vote if the Commission does not adopt all of Parliament's amendments. The significance of this rule is that without a positive vote for a motion for resolution an opinion of Parliament cannot be expressed. In turn, in the absence of an opinion the Council cannot act upon a Commission proposal and so the legislative process stalls on that particular issue. As the chairman of the Environment Committee noted in his evidence to the House of Lords' Select Committee on the European Communities [*HL 226, 1985: 168*] this rule 'enables the EP to move beyond a formal right to be consulted and propels Parliament into something more akin to a bargaining relationship'. The Commission rapidly recognised the potential of this delaying power, so making it more receptive to EP views and more willing to engage in a dialogue with the relevant parliamentary committee to avert later delay [*Lodge, 1989: 64*] (also see below).

Conciliation: A further formal extension of the EP's contribution to the legislative process has been the development of the 'conciliation procedure' between the Council and Parliament. The stated aim of the procedure is to reach 'an agreement between the European Parliament and the Council' on 'acts of general application which have appreciable financial implications' (Joint Declaration of EP, Council and Commission, 1975). However, the deficiencies of the procedure were illustrated in 1985 when the Environment Committee sought to activate the conciliation procedure in response to the EP's opinion on the car exhaust emissions proposal. The chairman and rapporteur of the Committee met with the President of the Council and expressed the Committee's disquiet over the Council's decision on this proposal. As the Committee's chairman noted at the time: 'At that meeting the President did not concede the principle that the Committee should be informed of the grounds for Council's decision nor that Parliament had the right to a conciliation procedure on general legislative matters' [*HL 226, 1985: 171*]. If anything, since 1985, the position has worsened with the increased propensity of the Council to adopt resolutions on the basis of papers presented by the Council presidency or on the basis of Communications from the Commission, upon neither of which is the EP formally consulted. In February 1991 the Environment Committee unanimously requested the renegotiation of the 1975 joint declaration. This specific request met with no direct positive response, though it is notable that the Maastricht treaty embodies, in Article 189b, a new codecision procedure which incorporates conciliation between Council and Parliament.

Co-operation: Concern with the restricted formal legislative powers of the EP, and the Council's often cavalier attitude even to those powers, was one of the stimuli for the EP's draft treaty on European union and subsequently for the Single European Act itself [*Pinder, 1991: 37*]. The SEA introduced a new 'co-operation' procedure for ten articles of the EEC treaty dealing with harmonisation measures necessary for the completion of the single market, regional fund decisions, some social policy matters and specific research programmes. In the case of environmental legislation the SEA distinguishes between measures introduced under Article 130s of the new Title VII on the environment, and those introduced under Article 100a. The former are subject to the established consultation procedure, where the Commission proposal is considered by the EP in a single reading in which amendments are voted upon and an opinion formally delivered (with recourse if necessary to the *de facto* delaying powers noted above). Measures dealing with the harmonisation of environmental standards necessary for the completion of the internal market under Article 100a are subject however to the new cooperation procedure.

Given the different 'legal base' available to the Commission in the introduction of environmental proposals under the SEA, the EP has been anxious to ensure that Article 100a is used wherever possible. As Jacobs and Corbett [*1990: 170*] note 'the Commission has usually been willing to co-operate closely with the Parliament on this'. Indeed, since 1989, of the 29 environmental directives proposed by the Commission, 15 have been based on Article 100a. Hence the Commission has already demonstrated its willingness to invoke the co-operation procedure on major environmental proposals. The quantitative significance of the co-operation procedure in both the volume of environmental and related public health and consumer legislation and in the work of the Environment Committee itself can be gauged from Table 1.

TABLE 1

TOTAL CO-OPERATION PROCEDURES BEGUN BY THE EP, BY COMMITTEE
(JULY 1987–NOV. 1991)

Environment	80
Energy	72
Economic Affairs	66
Legal Affairs	52
Social Affairs	11
Other Committees	18
Total	299

Source: EP Dossiers d'études et documentation, Series 4-A, Jan. 1992.

The Environment Committee alone accounted for 27 per cent of co-operation procedures up to November 1991, and in combination with the Energy, Economic and Legal Affairs Committees accounted for 90 per cent of the total.

The fact that the majority of environmental proposals have been adopted under Article 100a has not prevented the Environment Committee from pressing the Commission for still further use of the co-operation procedure. One of the first and most dramatic disagreements between the Commission and the EP arose out of the Environment Committee's insistence that the regulation (3954/87) laying down maximum permitted radioactivity levels for foodstuffs after Chernobyl should come under Article 100a. The Commission chose instead to use Article 31 of the Euratom Treaty which required only consultation with the EP. In response the Committee sought to amend the legal base. When the Commission refused to accept this amendment, the Committee then delayed giving its opinion. And at the December 1987 Plenary session the EP finally rejected the Commission's proposal. The Council then acted on the basis of the Commission proposal and Parliament responded by taking the Council to the Court of Justice on the grounds of an incorrect legal base [*Corbett, 1989: 361–2; Jacobs and Corbett, 1990: 172*]. The outcome was that in October 1991 the Court ruled that the contested regulation was correctly based on Article 31 of the Euratom Treaty. In the interpretation of the EP's Directorate General for Committees [*PE 200.380, 22 March 1992*] this simply means that: 'This judgement should not however be regarded as limiting of the scope of Article 100a except in respect of health protection measures against radioactive contamination'.

Despite the occasional public disputes between the EP and the Commission over the appropriate legal base to be adopted (and the innumerable informal disputes – as one senior Commission official commented 'one thing you can be sure of is that the Environment Committee wants 100a as many times as is possible'), nevertheless, the EP has consistently supported the Commission in its own battles with the Council over the legal base of proposals. This was demonstrated in 1991 when the Commission, supported by the EP, took the Council to the European Court for its adoption of Directive 89/428/EEC on pollution reduction measures in the titanium dioxide industry. The Commission had proposed Article 100a as the legal base for the directive on the grounds that its proposal was essentially concerned with the harmonisation of pollution control standards. The Council changed the legal base to Article 130s maintaining that the main aim of the measure was 'environmental' in that it sought to eliminate pollution [*PE 200.380, 25 March 1992; Wilkinson, 1992: 10–11*].

In June 1991 the Court ruled in favour of the Commission pointing out that under the SEA the Commission was obliged under Article 100a to take as its basis a high level of environmental protection when proposing measures for approximating the laws of member states. Equally Article 130r stated that environmental protection should be a component of the Community's other policies. In which case the court ruled that the removal of market distortions and the goals of environmental protection could not be separated in this case (the Court talks of *la double finalité*). The decision has been greeted by one commentator at least as a 'benchmark ruling' [*Wilkinson, 1992: 11*], and the expectation is that 'the Commission (will) make a generous interpretation of the applicability of Article 100a'. None the less, disputes between the Commission and Council over the appropriate legal base still continue. Thus, in mid-1992, the two institutions disputed the legal base of the proposal for a regulation on the supervision and control of shipments of waste (Com (90) 0415 final). The EP was consulted under Article 100a, the Environment Committee produced a report in November 1991 [*PE 151.226/A/fin. 5 Nov. 1991*; rapporteur Florentz], and the proposed regulation received its first reading in the EP in March 1992. At the Environment Council of 23 March, however, ministers failed to reach agreement on the key issues on the export of waste to certain developing countries and on the movement of waste within the EC. In asking the Commission to bring forward an amended text, the Council also argued for the new text to be dealt with under Article 130s. If the proposal is reintroduced in late 1992 under Article 130s then there is every probability that the Environment Committee, on being reconsulted, would seriously question the text's legal base under the SEA. The intriguing prospect, therefore, is that in taking its time in considering the amended proposal the committee knows that if the Maastricht treaty is ratified in 1993 then even regulations introduced under Article 130s will be subject to a co-operation procedure (see below).

At the same time as the EP (and its Environment Committee) has been actively promoting a creative interpretation of the SEA to maximise the use of Article 100a, it has also sought to maximise, through informal means, the formal legislative influence conferred upon it by the co-operation procedure. In other words, the true significance of the SEA rests not merely in the specification of a formal legislative role for the EP but in the enhanced capacity of its committees and individual MEPs to negotiate and bargain informally with other EC institutions. An increase in formal legislative power has thus served to enhance the informal influence of the EP to a cumulatively greater degree than can be gauged simply by looking at the treaty-prescribed institutional relationship.

The co-operation procedure itself is specified in the revision to Article

149 of the EEC treaty enacted by the SEA. The elaborate details of the procedure need not detains us here [*SEA, 1986: Article 7; Jacobs and Corbett, 1990: 169–71; Nicoll and Salmon, 1990: 38–40; Nugent, 1991: 131–4*]. In essence the cooperation procedure accords to the EP two legislative readings linked to deadlines, so breaking the 'rolling non-decisions and deliberations extending over many years that typified traditional decision making' [*Lodge, 1989: 70*]. Whilst much academic attention was initially focused upon the novelty of the second reading, the real significance of the second reading is the enhancement of parliamentary power *before* legislation reaches that stage. As much is recognised in the EP's changed rules of procedure in the wake of the SEA. Hence under current rule 51 [*EP Rules of Procedure, 1992*] amendments to

TABLE 2

CO-OPERATION PROCEDURE: ACCEPTANCE OF EP AMENDMENTS BY THE COMMISSION AND COUNCIL (JULY 1987–SEPTEMBER 1991)

| | First reading | | Second reading | |
	n	%	n	%
Amendments adopted by EP	2734	–	716	–
Amendments retaken by Commission	1626	60	366	48
Amendments retained by Council	1216	45	194	27

Source: EP dossiers d'études et documentation, Series 4-A, Jan. 1992.

Council's 'common position' [6] are only accepted at second reading if they seek to restore some or all of the position adopted by the parliament at the first reading; if they are compromise amendments based on agreement between the Council and the EP; or if they seek to amend content changes in the common position not included in the original text at first reading. The main focus of parliamentary attention remains therefore the first reading; with second reading providing spectacular, if ultimately limited, examples of EP influence over the Council. Generally, there is far less chance of parliamentary amendments being accepted at second reading than at first reading (see Table 2).

Only rarely has the parliament sought to reject a common position, and only on three occasions has it succeeded. Significantly, two of these rejections involved the Environment Committee. Indeed, the first rejection came in November 1988 after the Commission refused to accept the Environment Committee's amendments to the common position on a proposed directive on the protection of workers from benzene in the workplace (OJ C 290/36 14 Nov. 1988). Most recently in May 1992 the EP, on the advice of the Environment Committee, rejected the common position on a proposal for a Directive on Artificial Sweeteners [*Earnshaw and Judge, 1993*]. In both instances the Environment Committee was at the forefront of procedural innovation and the testing of the formal powers of the EP.

More routinely, but ultimately perhaps more importantly, the Committee has used the formal powers conferred by the co-operation procedure to strengthen its informal negotiating position with both the Commission and Council in the stages of the legislative process *prior* to second reading. In terms of its relationship with DG XI, the Committee has benefited from the existence of something resembling a shared inter-institutional ethos. Indeed, four senior officials from within the Directorate General and Ripa di Meana's cabinet (interviews, Brussels, 19 May, 20 May, 16 June and 17 June 1992) readily identified the EP and its Environment Committee as allies of the Commission in the legislative process. One member of the Commissioner's cabinet noted how Ripa di Meana 'sees the parliament as a natural ally, they are both supra-national bodies against the Council'. In the next breath he went on to observe that 'Ripa also sees the Parliament as an ally against the Commission itself. Parliament is much greener than the Commission and offers a surprising degree of support for Ripa and DG XI'. Similarly, a member of the Directorate-General noted:

> You have to remember that environment policy within the community was very much seen as a 'bolt-on' policy. For a long time DG XI wasn't taken too seriously within the Commission. In this context DG XI would lobby the EP to act on its behalf . . . In fact the Council still sometimes thinks that there is an incestuous relationship between the EP and DG XI, with the Environment Committee used to turn the screw.

One commonly used tactic in jointly 'turning the screw' on the Council is for officials in DG XI to assist committee rapporteurs in the drafting of reports and resolutions on legislative proposals. Indeed, Commission officials in interview could only recall one recent incident of an Environment Committee rapporteur rejecting outright the offer of informal assistance. The flow of influence between Commission and EP at this stage of the legislative process is apparent from the statement of an official in the Directorate-General: 'We will ask Parliament to do things, to look at things. If we need things to be changed in the Council then we might ask the EP to take an amendment on board. We then go back to Council and say "look this is what parliament is pressing for" . . . This is a legitimate tactic on our part' (interview, 20 May 1992). Equally, officials within DG XI will seek the support of the Committee in internal

Commission negotiations: 'In helping draft a report, Commission officials who have been involved with the proposal from the outset, and who may have seen their own pet proposal skinned at third and fourth floor levels at the Commission, will attempt to get their initial active proposal back in play as an amendment in the Parliament' (interview, 17 June 1992).

The capacity of the EP to amend legislative proposals is of course recognised by other organisations beyond the Commission and parliament itself (see Mazey and Richardson, this volume). Organised interests – industrial, environmental, and consumer groups alike – acknowledge the significance of the Environment Committee in the promotion of their specific interests. This acknowledgement takes several forms. The first is the sheer number of lobbyists who regularly attend and monitor the Committee's meetings. The second is the opinion of members of the Committee themselves. In interviews and discussions with nine leading members of the Environment Committee (interviews, Brussels, May and June 1992) all could point to instances where lobbyists had drafted amendments for them to include in their reports as rapporteurs and all recorded that contact with lobbyists was a daily occurrence. Indeed, most MEPs actively sought the opinions of lobbyists in drafting reports. As one EP member stated: 'MEPs need a network, we all need information, and, as a rapporteur, groups will come to you. Of course they don't provide disinterested information. All information is biased. But what some of them do provide is good analysis of what the proposal is about, and all provide ideas for change' (interview, Brussels, 22 May 1992). Carlos Pimenta as Liberal Group Coordinator on the Committee, and ex-environment minister in Portugal, brought a comparative dimension to the assessment of lobbying:

> In Portugal, as national environment Minister, I wasn't lobbied very often, and when I was it was only by small national groups. Now in the European Parliament I am lobbied all the time, every day, by multinational groups, by energy groups, by environmentalists, by industry: you name it. What this reflects is the lobbyists' own view of the influence of the Environment Committee. It does have a legislative impact (interview, 22 May 1992).

This view was indeed confirmed by one consultant from a UK-based lobbying company:

> The Environment Committee is a high profile activist committee. The commission is always our first port of call when we want something done; but the EP provides an extra wing to our activities

... The Committee is particulary useful for inserting into a proposal what we failed to get inserted at the drafting stage. On some resolutions you can see chunks of it written by groups and lobbyists (interview, 16 June 1992).

Clearly, therefore, in the perceptions of those members of the Commission, of MEPs and of lobbyists interviewed for this study, the EP is of some significance in its potential for affecting the content of EC legislation. But how, and how often, is this potential realised? Table 2 has already revealed the overall success rate of EP amendments under the co-operation procedure. The simple proportion of amendments accepted by the Commission and Council does not, however, indicate the magnitude of change effected by the EP upon the initial legislative proposal. A large number of amendments might be accepted to little substantive effect, or vice versa. In this respect the influence of the EP can only adequately be assessed through detailed case studies. Whilst bearing in mind the methodological difficulties involved in such an exercise[7] what is offered below is a summary of documented cases from within the EP itself. No claims are made that these cases are necessarily 'typical' (as there is no such thing as a typical legislative environmental proposal in the EC). Instead, these cases point to the diversity of policy issues covered by the Environment Committee and the differential impact achieved on these issues. At most, all that is claimed here is that the Committee and its resolutions has *some* impact, and that in many instances, *pace* Shirley Williams, its influence upon EC legislation is far from marginal.

The first case concerns exhaust emissions for small cars. The changes wrought by the EP to the draft directive on small car emissions in 1987 provide the exemplar, to date, of how parliament can use its powers of amendment [*Jacobs and Corbett, 1990: 170; Arp, 1992: 31; Peters, 1992: 92*]. The genesis of the legislative proposal and its specification of emission standards are both convoluted and complex, and need not detain us here [*Johnson and Corcelle, 1989: 127–34*]. The important point is that the emission standards initially specified in the 1984 draft directive of the Commission, of 30 grammes/test of carbon monoxide and 8 grammes/test of unburnt hydrocarbons and nitrous oxide combined, were far from exacting in comparison with standards enforced in the US since 1983. The proposed standards were blocked in the Council by Denmark in 1985 for being too lenient. It was not until the introduction of the SEA and qualified majority voting under Article 100a that the Council was able to adopt a 'common position' (against the votes of the Netherlands, Denmark and Greece) on 24 November 1988. The EP provided its opinion on 14 September 1988, and proposed far more stringent emission standards in accordance with the 1983 US norms and the introduction of catalytic converters to all classes of cars (OJ C 262/89, 10 Nov. 1988). In reaching its common position in November the Council ignored the opinion of the EP. With the EP threatening to reject the common position at the plenary session in April 1989, and with the Dutch government's introduction in January 1989 of tax breaks on cars which met the US standards, followed immediately by the Commission beginning formal infringement proceedings against the Netherlands under Article 169 EEC, Ripa di Meana seized the opportunity to convince the Commission of the desirability of revising the common position on the draft directive to take account of the Environment Committee's preference for the 1983 US standards. In addition, DG XI was also aware that many car manufacturers in Europe were capable of meeting the new standards, and with the weakening of the main source of resistance within the industry, Peugeot in France, DG XI was able to gain acceptance within the Commission, 'over many meetings and protracted discussions' (interview, Commission official, 17 June 1992) of the stricter emission standards. In return, the Environment Committee compromised by dropping two amendments unacceptable to the Commission. And so the amended common position was returned to the Council, where it was adopted by a qualified majority in June 1989 (Directive 89/458/EEC). This outcome was evidence, in Ripa di Meana's view, of the capacity of Commission and EP to 'coordinate their action in order to establish the necessary conditions to reach the objectives they have in common' (*Europe Bulletin*, 14 April 1989, p. 8). It was a '*résultat remarquable*' in the opinion of the Directorate-General for Research of the EP [*WIP 91/071/176, 1991:14*], and was 'to be seen as a victory both for the growing environmental movement and for the European Parliament' according to Johnson and Corcelle [*1989: 132*].

The second case was that of the European Environment Agency. On 7 May 1990 the Council adopted a regulation (1210/90, 7 May 1990) on the establishment of the European Environment Agency and a European Environment and Observation Network. Agreement was only reached, however, after months of protracted argument between the EP, the Commission and the Council. The intention was to create an agency as a source of reliable, objective and comparative – cross-EC – information on the basis of which the EC institutions, member states and other third countries could make 'scientifically' informed decisions. To this effect, in June 1989, the Commission proposed the creation of an Environmental Agency (Com (89) 303 final). By November the Council had agreed a compromise proposal on the Agency, based upon the original Commission text. As the Environment Committee chairman observed:

Not surprisingly, the European Parliament which had only been elected four months before and whose Committees were not formed until two months before that Council decision, did not find this acceptable. We had not even discussed it properly and a rapporteur had only been in place for about eight weeks. We were frankly appalled at the insensitivity of the Council in agreeing a proposal as important as this without any real critical evaluation of it [*Collins, 1991: 2*].

Between November 1989 and February 1990 the Environment Committee's rapporteur, Beate Weber, drafted an opinion which sought the extension of the role of the Agency far beyond that envisaged by the Commission or the Council. Indeed, subsequent efforts by the Committee to force its opinion on the Commission were not welcomed by the Environment Commissioner. As one of his closest advisers put it: 'The case of the European Environment Agency is, if you like, an example of the negative side of the relationship between the EP and the Commission. From Ripa's view this was a case where the ambivalent relationship with the Environment Committee had a minus sign in front of it. It was felt that the EP was playing a demagogic role' (interview, Brussels, 17 June 1992).

None the less, the Committee pressed its case remorselessly. Having prepared and agreed a parliamentary opinion, the decision was then taken to suspend the final vote for one month. In this period the rapporteur and Committee chairman engaged in discussions with national ministers in order to effect a compromise. Although there is no institutional provision for such direct contact between Council members and EP Committee chairmen, this did not dissuade the Environment Committee chairman:

In February 1990, I toured a number of Community capitals and was in practically daily and certainly weekly discussion with Carlo Ripa di Meana ... In March 1990, the Parliament gave its formal Opinion and Commission and Council eventually accepted, and then incorporated in the Regulation itself, word for word, three crucial so-called 'compromise amendments', which had been *negotiated* with the Irish Presidency and with other ministers during the previous month [*Collins, 1991: 3*; emphasis added].

These three compromise amendments (OJ C 96/112–3, 17 April 1990) incorporated vital parliamentary demands. First, that the agency should work at Community level to guarantee the implementation of EC law. Second, that the EEA should develop 'uniform assessment criteria' for the measurement, recording and evaluation of data, and produce reports on the quality, sensitivity of, and pressures on the Community environment. The ultimate objective, however, was to guarantee the effective implementation of Community law in the environmental sector and so open the door for the coordination of national environmental inspection. In this respect the EP did not entirely get its way. The Council refused to award inspection competences to the Agency outright, but did concede, nevertheless, that within two years of the adoption of the regulation it would consider proposals for the enlargement of the Agency's tasks. Particular attention was to be paid in this review to the 'granting of powers of inspection with regard to the implementation of Community environmental legislation' and the 'development of criteria for the environmental impact assessments necessary for the application of Directive 85/337/EEC' (OJ C 96/112–3, 17 April 1990).

Hence, the case of the EEA provides another example of the capacity of the EP to influence EC legislation.[8] What it also shows is the 'creative use of procedure'. As the EP's Directorate-General for Research [*WIP 92/01/142, 1992: 25*] concludes: 'On the whole this (example) demonstrates considerable parliamentary influence on the content of the regulation. This is remarkable, because, in accordance with the underlying Article 130, the Parliament need only be consulted and not given the authority of the cooperation process according to Article 149(2) EC'. Furthermore, this case also underscores the tenacity of the Environment Committee in pursuit of 'green' policy resolutions. Policy issues are conceived in a dynamic way in the Committee. Thus, not satisfied with the compromise reached on the allocation of functions to the Agency, the Committee has already indicated its intention to operationalise Article 20 in the regulation – to review the Agency's tasks after two years – and so to influence the precise form of 'the enlargement of the Office's tasks'. 'In other words, the Agency is not to be a static phenomenon at all. It is expected to be dynamic' [*Collins, 1991: 4*].

The third case concerned genetically modified micro-organisms. In 1988 the Commission, strongly influenced by OECD guidelines of 1986, proposed a directive aimed at harmonising the regulation of recombinant biotechnology in the EC (COM (88) 160 final; for details see Lake [*1991*]). One obvious impact the Environment Committee had upon this directive was that it decided that the original draft directive would better be considered as two separate proposals: one dealing with the 'contained use of genetically modified micro-organisms' (GMMOs) and the other concerning the 'deliberate release of genetically modified organisms' (GMOs). Thereafter this division was maintained by the Council. In essence the 'contained use' directive sought to establish a regulatory regime where GMMOs would be classified according to risk, and establishments operating with GMMOs classified according to size and purpose (whether operations are research-based or commercially-based prototype/production). National competent authorities would have to be informed of the contained use and where necessary explicitly authorise such use. The 'deliberate release' directive on the other hand is concerned with the intentional release of GMOs into the environment.

In its detailed assessment of the impact of the EP upon the final directive on 'deliberate release' the Directorate General for Research [*WIP 92/01/142, 1992: 22*] found that 10 of the 17 amendments put forward by Parliament at first reading were worked into the revised Commission proposal and that in turn the Council, in adopting its common position, 'substantially adopted the draft of the Commission'.

At the outset it should be noted, however, that the Environment Committee had little success in contesting the definition of key terms in the directive such as 'registration', 'registrant' and 'authorisation'. Similarly it had no success in trying to incorporate into the directive questions of legal liability and compensation which were absent from the original proposal. Nevertheless, Parliament managed to convince the Commission of the need for residents in the vicinity of a planned release to have advance notification, but the Council did not incorporate this into the final directive. Likewise, the Commission was also willing, but the Council was not, to meet the EP's demand for the alteration of a technical specification (of hydrologic characteristics) contained in the technical appendix.

Parliament did succeed, however, in influencing both Commission and Council on the necessity for adequate practical testing of the effects on other eco-systems prior to the lifting of controls on GMOs (amendment 7). Equally the EP had some success in ensuring that a deliberate release might only take place with the agreement of the responsible authority; and that a prerequisite for authorisation was adequate proof that the environment and human health was not endangered (amendment 9). The final directive also reflected the EP's demand for a more exact definition of a GMO. Amendment 30, that release should not take place without the written authorisation of the responsible authority was reproduced in slightly different wording in Article 6(4) of the directive; amendment 29, on the obligations of notification of changes in the release was included in Article 5(6); and amendment 78, on the prohibition of the transmission of confidential information to third parties was reproduced as Article 19(1) of the directive.

What this example shows is the differential impact the EP has upon certain parts of directives: making outright changes to some Articles, modifying others, and having no impact whatsoever on others. Overall, however, the verdict of the Directorate-General for Research [*WIP 92/01/142, 1992: 22*] is that 'the influence of the Parliament was considerable'. Similarly, Lake [*1991: 12*] concludes that the 'EP did have the satisfaction of seeing amendments (on explicit authorisation and penalties for infringement) included in the final Council text'. But Lake then proceeds to make the wider point that:

> a significant impact of the EP's deliberations has not so much been on the legal detail of the directives, but rather on the prevailing consensus within the Commission. Thus (the Environment Committee's) concerns over the mobility of genetic elements are now reflected by increased funding for further studies in these areas from DG XI and DG XII, which will be significant in the development of working guidelines for national competent authorities ... Indeed, it is in the practical implementation of these directives that the real efficacy of this European legislation will be established, and the EP has been concerned for some time about what its own role should be (in this process) [*Lake, 1991: 13*].

Before examining the role of the EP in the implementation process, however, one further point about the EP's legislative role, an issue raised above in the discussion of agenda setting, is worthy of note; and this concerns the ability of the Environment Committee to signal its aspirations for future policy whilst reporting on current legislation. One example will suffice here. In February 1990 the EP was requested to deliver an opinion on a proposal from the Commission for a Directive amending Directive 76/464/EEC on 'pollution caused by certain dangerous substances discharged into the aquatic environment of the Community'. Without going into the details of the resolution itself [*PE 143.032/fin, 18 July 1990*] the important point is that the Commission's 1990 draft proposal was a direct response to the Environment Committee's earlier demands voiced in its resolution on Com (87) 457 on limit values for discharges [*PE 119.413, 18 Feb. 1988*]. As much was gleefully pointed out by the Committee's rapporteur: 'The rapporteur congratulates the Commission wholeheartedly for submitting this proposal along the lines first suggested by Parliament.... The rapporteur proposes that Parliament approve the Commission's proposal without amendment. The proposal submitted by the Commission reflects entirely the commitment made by the Commission to Parliament' [*PE 143.032/final, 18 July 1990: 6–9*].

Despite the obvious successes noted above of the EP and its Environment Committee influencing legislation, an accurate audit of the Committee's activities would also reveal instances where the effects of its attempts 'to guide' the Commission's internal deliberations were not particularly apparent (for example, recently on eco-labelling); where its legislative amendments were largely ignored by the Commission (for example, trans-shipment of hazardous waste); or where its recorded influence on the final Council directive was marginal (for example, 88/609/EEC on large combustion plants). This is hardly surprising, for, in the context of institutional fluidity and legislative substantive complexity in which the Environment Committee operates, it is only to be expected that in the words of its chairman: 'You win a few and you lose a few. The important point is that the Committee continues trying to win' (interview, 22 April 1991).

Implementation

One stage of the legislative process at which the Committee considers that it (along with the EP and the Commission) has traditionally 'lost' is that of implementation. The importance of the implementation stage in the EC policy process is dealt with more fully by Collins and Earnshaw in this volume, but it is worth highlighting the specific contribution of the Environment Committee at this point. Quite simply the Environment Committee has been perhaps the collective memory and conscience of the Community on the subject of the implementation of EC environmental legislation (the Legal Affairs Committee can also claim such a role). Thus as one member of DG XI's Directorate General observed: 'The Environment Committee sits on our backs and watches things. It is concerned with the systematic enforcement and application of legislation, and consistently reminds us of our own role in this respect' (interview, 20 May 1992).

This concern is of relatively recent origin[9] and dates back essentially to the Committee's 1988 reports on the implementation of EC legislation relating to water and to air (OJ C 94/151–8, 11 April 1988). These reports coincided with the introduction of the Fourth Action Programme and the Commission's stated objective of securing the implementation of environmental directives. The report on water was particularly transparent in its intent: 'Parliament . . . has a responsibility to assist the Commission in this (implementation) exercise, as well as ensuring that each aspect of the Commission's work is subject to democratic supervision' [*PE 116. 085/fin, 14 Feb. 1988: 14*]. The report examined the EC implementation process as it related to three specific directives on the quality of bathing water, the quality of drinking water and the discharge of dangerous substances into the aquatic environment. In detailing the deficiencies of the implementation process the rapporteur concluded that 'the implementation of environmental legislation should henceforth be assessed systematically by Parliament's Committee on Environment, Public Health and Consumer Protection [*PE 116.085/fin., 14 Feb. 1988: 54*]. Since the first reports the Committee has produced further reports including an overview of the implementation of environmental legislation (OJ C 68/183–4, 19 March 1990), and most recently a major report on the application of environmental legislation by Jacques Vernier [*PE 152. 144, 28 Aug. 1991*].

The consistent theme of these reports from the Environment Committee, and one elaborated by its chairman in his evidence to the House of Lords Select Committee on European Communities [*HL 53–11 1992: 27–38*], is that more attention needs to be paid to the implementation of EC legislation. In practical terms this means: less secrecy where the Commission has recourse to Article 169 EEC; the systematisation of reporting requirements under environmental directives; the introduction of an environment inspectorate; enhancement of DG XI's monitoring role; and the 'democratisation' of the EC's legislative process.

Undoubtedly the Committee has been of some importance in raising the profile of the issue of implementation, as the creation of the European Environment Agency partially testifies, but as its chairman observed in November 1991: 'we are perhaps a little bit clearer about why implementation is a problem, but we have not solved the problem by any stretch of the imagination' [*HL 53–11 1992: 33*]. Whilst reaffirming the importance of monitoring both the legal and practical dimensions of compliance and of addressing the issue of enforcement, he proceeded to argue that: 'The Environment Committee is necessarily the best place to do that. The Environment Committee is the right place to do it ... I would like to think that [the] Committee at least once every five years will do a general report on implementation, but will also do individual reports on the implementation of specific Directives' [*HL 53–11 1992:36*].

Given its concern with the problems of implementation, it is not perhaps surprising that the Environment Committee reacted angrily in mid-1992 to suggestions from within the Commission, most particularly from Jacques Delors and Leon Brittan, that 1992 might be an appropriate time to reconsider the competences of the EC institutions in regard to environmental policy. The concerns of the Committee were forcibly expressed through the medium of a letter from its chairman to the President of the European Parliament. The contents of this letter were agreed unanimously at the Committee session of 25 June 1992:

In our view subsidiarity does not entail a zero-sum ('or winner take all') trade off over the allocation of power to different levels of government ... implementation is, of course, primarily the responsibility of Member States. However, Member States must examine honestly their own records of implementation ... the Community should, of course, retain powers to scrutinise implementation and in exceptional cases have the possibility, as at present, of recourse to the Court of Justice. This is essentially the philosophy agreed by the Council in the regulation establishing the European Environment Agency, itself an idea proposed by President Delors.

Clearly, the Committee will have to work hard in the aftermath of the May 1992 Danish referendum to ensure that the concept of subsidiarity is not redefined to legitimate the dilution of standards and control of environmental policy by returning 'competence in this area to national parliaments' [*Brittan, 1992: 18*].

Conclusion

One role traditionally performed by the Environment Committee has been the promotion of 'environmentalism' within EC policy and institutions. As one member of the Committee commented: 'the Environment Committee is different from most other committees, it sees itself as a crusader, at the cutting edge of one of the most important policy areas of our time ... Occasionally you get the impression that some of its members feel that they are predestined to save the earth' (interview, Brussels, 21 May 1992). This zeal, some might say zealotry, has not always endeared it to other committees within the EP (interviews, Brussels, 15 and 17 June 1992, with members of the Secretariat of two other Committees) nor to other Directorate-Generals within the Commission (interview, official of DG VI, 22 May 1992). Within the Committee, however, there appears to be a fundamental consensus, universally acknowledged by all of the Committee members interviewed for this study, which basically transcends political groupings and nationalities. Indeed, a typical response was: 'You have a look at the (political) groups: the Liberals are pro-environment; the socialists are pro-environment; the Christian Democrats are pro-environment; even the British Conservatives are!!' (interview, Brussels, 22 May 1992). A shared recognition of the importance of environmental issues has undoubtedly assisted the Committee in its efforts to influence EC policy. As a result, the practical legislative impact of the Committee stands in stark contrast to the academic assessment (American again in this instance) which still maintains that the 'European

Parliament itself is not very powerful, lacking true legislative capabilities
... MEPs have so little structural influence in their own policy domain'
[*Thomas, 1992: 4–5*]. Environmental policy is one policy domain where
this assessment sits uneasily with current reality.

NOTES

1. The official title is the Environment, Public Health and Consumer Protection Committee; hereafter, for the sake of brevity, referred to as the Environment Committee.
2. Currently Rules 63 and 121, *Rules of Procedure*, 7th edn., Feb. 1992.
3. Since 1989 the Environment Committee has not sought approval from the EP's bureau for legislative initiatives under Rule 121, preferring instead to use Rule 63, which does not require authorisation by the bureau.
4. 'Legislative' in the sense of having a heavy legislative burden. The Environment Committee is presently the most heavily burdened Committee.
5. The statistics that are available are largely inconclusive [*Arp, 1992: 14*].
6. Under the cooperation procedure, once the EP has given its opinion the proposal then goes to the Council with the Commission's views on the opinion. The Council then adopts by a qualified majority a 'common position' which it then transmits to the EP.
7. Not least the selection of case studies, the problems of assigning causality, the degree of receptivity of the Council and Commission to amendments on specific issues and so on.
8. By mid-1992 the European Environment Agency had still not been established. The Council, having agreed to the regulation on the creation of the Agency, has been unable to reach agreement as to where the Agency's headquarters should be located.
9. The EP passed a resolution in 1983 (OJ C 68/32, 14 March 1983) calling upon the Commission to submit an annual report on the monitoring of the implementation of EC law. In turn the Legal Affairs Committee based its monitoring of member states' legal compliance upon these annual reports.

REFERENCES

Arp, H.A. (1992), 'The European Parliament in European Community Environmental Policy', *EUI Working Papers*, No.92/13, Florence: European University Institute.

Brittan, L. (1992), 'Subsidiarity in the Constitution of the EC', Robert Schuman Lecture, 11 June, Florence: European University Institute.

Budd, S.A. and A. Jones (1990), *The European Community: A Guide to the Maze* (3rd edn.), London: Kogan Page.

Bouguignon-Wittke, R., Grabitz, E., Schmuck, O., Steppat, S. and W. Wessels (1985), 'Five Years of the Directly Elected Parliament: Performance and Prospects', *Journal of Common Market Studies*, Vol.24, Vol.1, pp.39–59.

Capotorti, F., Hilf, M., Jacobs, F.G. and J.P. Jacque (1986), *The European Union Treaty*, Oxford: Clarendon Press.

Collins, K. (1991), 'The European Environment Agency: The Opinion of the European Parliament', *Proceedings of the 32nd/IPRE Symposium*, Brussels: International Professional Association for Environmental Affairs.

Corbett, R. (1989), 'Testing the New Procedures: The European Parliament's First Experiences with its New "Single Act" Powers', *Journal of Common Market Studies*, Vol.27, No.4., pp.359–72.

de Rouffignac, P.D. (1991), *Presenting Your Case to Europe*, London: Mercury.

Earnshaw, D. and D. Judge (1993), 'The Sweeteners Directive: From Footnote to Inter-Institutional Conflict', *Journal of Common Market Studies*, Vol.31, No.2.

EC Documentation (1990), *Environmental Policy in the European Community*, Luxembourg, Office for Official Publications of the EC.

EP (1985), *A New Phase in European Union*, Luxembourg: European Parliament General Secretariat.

EP Rules of Procedure (1992), *Rules of Procedure* (7th edn.), Luxembourg: European Parliament.

EUR 12902 EN (1990), *Green Paper on the Environment*, Brussels: DG XI Commission of the European Communities.

Haigh, N. and D.Baldock (1989), *Environmental Policy and 1992*, London, Institute for European Environmental Policy.

HL 226 (1985), *European Union*, House of Lords Select Committee on the European Communities, Session 1984–5, London: HMSO.

HL 53-II (1992), *Implementation and Enforcement of Environmental Legislation*, House of Lords Select Committee on the European Communities, Session 1991–2, London: HMSO.

Jacobs, F. and R. Corbett (1990), *The European Parliament*, London: Longman.

Johnson, S.P. and G. Corcelle (1989), *The Environmental Policy of the European Communities*, London: Graham & Trotman.

Kirchner, E. and K. Williams (1983), 'The Legal, Political and Institutional Implications of the Isoglucose Judgments 1980', *Journal of Common Market Studies*, Vol.22, No.2, pp.173–90.

Lake, G. (1991), 'Biotechnology Regulations. Scientific Uncertainty and Political Regulation', *Project Appraisal*, Vol.6, No.1, pp.7–15.

Lodge, J. (1984), 'European Union and the First Elected European Parliament: The Spinelli Initiative' *Journal of Common Market Studies*, Vol.22, No.4, pp.377–402.

Lodge, J. (1986), 'The Single European Act: Towards a New Euro-Dynamism?' *Journal of Common Market Studies*, Vol.24, No.3, pp.203–23.

Lodge, J. (1989), 'The European Parliament', in J.Lodge (ed.), *The European Community and the Challenge of the Future*, London: Pinter.

Nicoll, W. and T.C. Salmon (1990), *Understanding the European Communities*, London: Philip Allan.

Nugent, N. (1991), *The Government and Politics of the European Community* (2nd ed.), London: Macmillan.

PE 116.085/fin. (1988), Report of the Committee on the Environment, Public Health and Consumer Protection on the Implementation of European Community Legislation.

PE 119.413 (1988), Report of the Committee on the Environment, Public Health and Consumer Protection on Limit Values and Quality Objectives for Discharges of Certain Dangerous Substances, Luxembourg: European Parliament Session Documents.

PE 139.166/fin. (1990), Report of the Committee on the Environment, Public Health and Consumer Protection, on Measures to Protect the Ecology of Tropical Rainforests, Luxembourg: European Parliament Session Documents.

PE 140.600 (1990), *Fact Sheets on the European Community*, Luxembourg, Office for Official Publications of the EC.

PE 143.032/final (1990), Report of the Committee on the Environment, Public Health and Consumer Protection, Commission Proposal for a Council Directive amending Directive 76/464/EEC on Pollution Caused by Certain Dangerous Substances discharged into the Aquatic Environment of the Community, Luxembourg: European Parliament Session Documents.

PE 144.135/fin. (1990), Report of the Committee on the Environment, Public Health and Consumer Protection, on a Community Strategy on Waste Management, Luxembourg: European Parliament Session Documents.

PE 145.367/fin. (1991), Report of the Committee on the Environment, Public Health and Consumer Protection, on Economic and Fiscal Instruments on Environment Policy, Luxembourg: European Parliament Session Documents.

PE 146.246/fin. (1991), Report of the Committee on the Environment, Public Health and Consumer Protection, on the Commission Proposal for a Council Regulation Establishing a Financial Instrument for the Environment, Luxembourg: European Parliament Session Documents.

PE 152.137.fin. (1991), Report of the Committee on the Environment, Public Health and Consumer Protection, on the Commission Proposal for a Council Regulation on Eco-Labelling, Luxembourg: European Parliament Session Documents.

PE 152.144 (1991), Report of the Committee on the Environment, Public Health and Consumer Protection, on the Implementation of Environmental Legislation, Luxembourg: European Parliament Session Documents.

PE 151.226/A/fin. (1991), Report of the Committee on the Environment, Public Health and Consumer Protection, on the Commission Proposal for a Council Regulation on the Supervision and Control of Shipments of Waste within, into and out of the European Community, Luxembourg: European Parliament Session Documents.

PE 200.380 (1992), Committee on the Environment, Public Health and Consumer Protection, Notice to Members, Judgement of the Court of Justice of 11 June 1991 – Titanium Dioxide, Luxembourg: European Parliament, Directorate-General for Committees and Delegations.

Peters, B.G. (1992), 'Bureaucratic Politics and The Institutions of the European Community', in A.M.Sbragia (ed.), *Euro-Politics: Institutions and Policymaking in the 'New' European Community*, Washington, DC: Brookings Institution.

Pinder, J. (1991), *European Community: The Building of a Union*, Oxford: Oxford University Press.

SEA (1986), *Single European Act*, Bulletin of the European Communities, Supplement 2/86, Luxembourg, Office for Official Publications of the EC.

Thomas, S.T. (1992), 'Assessing MEP Influence on British EC Policy', *Government and Opposition*, Vol.27, No.1, pp.3–17.

Vandermeersch, D. (1987), 'The Single European Act and the Environmental Policy of the European Economic Community', *European Law Review*, Vol.12, pp.407–429.

Wilkinson, D. (1992), *Maastricht and the Environment*, London: Institute for European Environmental Policy.

Williams, S. (1991), 'Sovereignty and Accountability in the European Community', in R.O Keohane and Hoffman S. (eds), *The New European Community*, Boulder, CO: Westview Press.

WIP 91/071/176 (1991), 'Evaluation de l'impact du Parlment sur les politiques communitaires dans les dernières années', Luxembourg: European Parliament Directorate General for Research.

WIP 92/01/142 (1992), 'L'influence du Parlement européen dans la procédure legislative à la lumière de l'adoption de quatre directives ou réglements dans les secteurs des affaires sociales et de l'environnement', Luxembourg: European Parliament Directorate General for Research.

The Implementation and Enforcement of European Community Environment Legislation

KEN COLLINS and DAVID EARNSHAW

The credibility and acceptability of European Community environment legislation depends to a large extent on its implementation 'on the ground'. This paper considers the problems facing member states when they come to implement Community environment legislation. In recent years greater attention has focused on this aspect of the EC environmental policy process.

The first and second sections of the study consider respectively the state of implementation in the member states and those characteristics of the Community legislative process which have an impact on implementation. The final two sections assess Community enforcement mechanisms and the means through which implementation may be improved. It is suggested that a centralised Community inspectorate, though probably desirable, is at present politically unrealistic if not possibly inappropriate. The development of the alternative 'inspection of inspectors' concept is outlined.

Policy implementation, like policy formulation, is a fundamentally political process on which the success or failure of individual policies depends. Nevertheless, decision-makers and public authorities in general tend to neglect policy implementation and policy delivery as they inevitably become absorbed in the legislative process itself. At European Community (EC) level this problem is particularly acute. On the one hand it is essential for the Commission to maintain the impetus of new legislation; on the other hand the relationship between the member states and the Community implies limitations on the role of Community institutions in policy implementation. Implementation is conducted at arm's length from the legislative process, with many decision points [*Pressman and Wildavsky, 1973*] existing between agreement of legislation and its implementation on the ground. EC environment policy is also relatively young and until the introduction of the Single European Act in 1987 lacked an explicit legal basis. This may have contributed to a climate in which Community policy makers concentrated on the creation of legislation at the expense of implementation [*Macrory, 1992:350*]. While the processes of initiation, scrutiny, amendment and agreement of EC environment legislation are important, Community legislation will not be worth the paper it is printed on if policies break down or obligations are not fulfilled at the implementation stage.

It is only in recent years that attention has started to focus on the implementation of EC environment legislation. In the Fourth Environmental Action Programme (1987–92) the Commission declared that henceforth it would place greater emphasis on the problem of implementation (and in its resolution on the Fourth Programme the Council of Ministers asked the Commission to send to it and Parliament regular reports on implementation); in the Fifth Environmental Action Programme a full chapter is devoted to implementation and enforcement. A number of well-publicised infringement proceedings commenced by the Commission against member states has also turned the spotlight on the implementation of environment legislation, as has the increasing number of complaints which are now made to the Commission about the poor implementation of EC environment legislation. Since 1988 the European Parliament has adopted no less than ten resolutions (seven on the basis of detailed reports) on the implementation of environment legislation. The European Summit in Dublin in June 1990 declared that 'Community environmental legislation will only be effective if it is fully implemented and enforced by member states', while in October 1991 an informal meeting of the environment Council of Ministers was devoted to implementation, at the instigation of the Dutch Presidency. The Maastricht treaty on European Union includes a declaration stating that 'each Member State should fully and accurately transpose into national law the Community directives addressed to it within the deadlines laid down therein', and in May 1992 the House of Lords Select Committee on the European Communities published a major report on the implementation and enforcement of EC environment legislation.

The implementation of EC environment legislation proved particularly controversial in the debate over the concept of subsidiarity that resulted from rejection of the Maastricht treaty in the Danish referendum in spring 1992. Given prominence in the Maastricht treaty, the principle of subsidiarity refers to the Community taking action 'only if and insofar as the objectives of the proposed action cannot be sufficiently achieved by the Member States and can therefore, by reason of the scale or effects of proposed action, be better achieved by the Community' (Treaty on European Union, article 3b). Some Community governments have been reported as interpreting subsidiarity in a way that could place relatively strict limits on the role of Community institutions, in particular the Commission, in monitoring and enforcing the implementation of Community law. As we shall see, however, the record of member states in implementing EC environment legislation might actually point to the need for rather greater Community intervention in its monitoring and enforcement.

The aims of this study are threefold: first, to examine why the implementation of EC environment legislation has taken on greater importance in recent years; second, to outline the reasons for inadequate implementation, where this occurs, of EC environment legislation by member states; and third, to assess possible mechanisms to improve the implementation of EC environment legislation. Many practitioners and commentators (see, for example, EP [*1990b*]; Clinton-Davis [*1992:201*]) have argued that improving member states' implementation of EC environment legislation is dependent on the creation of an EC environment inspectorate. However, it is suggested here that better implementation is not exclusively, as often portrayed, a matter of creating forthwith a centralised EC environment inspectorate in the strictest sense. No matter how desirable it is to monitor implementation and extend at EC level the mechanisms available for enforcement, such a proposal is probably politically unrealistic in the short to medium term.

The reasons for poor implementation of EC environment legislation are complex and diverse. Not least, the current structure of decision-making within the Community and the characteristics of public administration in the member states can have an important impact on the potential for successful implementation. The difficulties member states face in implementing environment legislation might only be partly ameliorated through increasing the Community's oversight of their activities. It will be seen, rather, that while Community involvement in implementation is necessary, an EC inspection function can be expected only to develop gradually and will need to work in cooperation with member states' own enforcement and inspection bodies.

The paper is divided into four sections. In the first section the state of implementation in the member states in set out. In the second those characteristics of the EC's legislative process that have an impact on the implementation of EC environment legislation are examined. The third section assesses Community enforcement mechanisms. Finally, this contribution examines ways in which the implementation of EC environment legislation might be improved.

The State of Implementation in the Member States

The implementation of EC environment legislation may be said to comprise three components. First, it entails the transposition into national law of Community directives by means of introducing and adapting national policies, legislation and administrative mechanisms to conform with EC law. Second, this formal legal transposition should lead to practical results and measurable impact. Hence, implementation entails more than merely the adoption of national legislation, even where it reflects perfectly the obligations contained in a directive [Haigh, 1986a: 4]. Finally, enforcement and monitoring mechanisms should exist to ensure that implementation is accurate and complete.

The 1980s have witnessed a dramatic increase in the volume of infringement proceedings brought by the Commission for member states' non-implementation of EC environment legislation. Table 1 reports infringement proceedings commenced against member states in the environment

TABLE 1
INFRINGEMENT PROCEEDINGS 1982–90

Year	Partial compliance	Non-notification	Poor Application	TOTAL
1982	1	15	–	16
1983	10	23	2	35
1984	15	48	2	65
1985	10	58	1	69
1986	32	84	9	125
1987	30	68	58	156
1988	24	36	30	90
1989	17	46	37	100
1990	24	131	62	217
TOTAL	163	509	201	873

Source: *Eighth annual report to the European Parliament on Commission monitoring of the application of Community law*, Dec. 1991.

sector. The table distinguishes between different kinds of failings in implementation: partial compliance indicates that the measures introduced at national level do not fully incorporate Community law; non-notification refers to those cases where member states have failed to notify the Commission of their national measures; while poor application refers to shortcomings in implementation in practice.

There has been a steep rise in infringement proceedings commenced due to non-notification. This reflects the increasing frequency with which member states have delayed implementing EC legislation. The directive on environmental impact assessment (85/337/EEC), for example, was required to be incorporated in national law by July 1988 but was only implemented during 1990 by Greece, Portugal and Germany and during 1991 by Luxembourg [CEC, 1991a: 206]. Of the nine environment directives which entered into force in 1990 the UK incorporated only one into national law by the appropriate date [HL 53-I, 1992: 12]. In practice few of the infringement proceedings commenced due to non-notification are pursued further as member states usually adopt national measures and forward them to the Commission.

Several factors may lead to national legislation failing to comply with EC measures. First, the range and complexity of existing national laws can lead to considerable difficulty when it is necessary for them to be adapted to the requirements of Community law. In the case of the UK over 20 items of legislation were required to implement the directive on environmental impact assessment (and in the Commission's view implementation still remained incomplete). As Macrory comments [1992: 355], some environment directives also 'cut across conventional boundaries of administrative and legal responsibility', which may lead to the need for national legislation to be adopted in different sectoral and jurisdictional areas. Second, concepts contained in many directives are 'bound to result in different definitions when given effect in each member state' [HL 53-I, 1992: 14].

Third, there is a variety of national and subnational administrative structures within the Community through which Community law must be implemented. Differences between member states are bound to result when their legislative and administrative processes are required to fulfil objectives set elsewhere. Fourth, member states' 'legislative culture' may also prevent early compliance with Community legislation. Member states may have a tradition of lengthy consultation aimed at building consensus; a concern for constitutional rectitude requiring time-consuming review of legislative proposals; or an emphasis on legal certainty encouraging highly detailed legislation [IEEP, 1992a: 168]. Finally, member states may also on occasion judge that non-compliance is politically expedient. The UK government's delay in both formally and practically implementing the drinking water directive is a prime example. In this case UK government policy was designed to create a more favourable climate for the privatisation of the water industry in England and Wales.

Federal and quasi-federal systems of government within member states can lead to particular difficulties in implementation. Two of the 12 member states (Germany and Belgium) are federations; in two others (Italy and Spain) the regions enjoy a substantial measure of autonomy.

Implementation of EC legislation may be a source of tension between central government, responsible for negotiating legislation at EC level, and regional government, which often possesses competence for its formal and practical implementation. Local and regional authorities may be suspicious that EC legislation could centralise into a government's hands some powers that had previously been devolved to them [*Haigh, 1986b*]. In Germany, for example, environment policy is a policy area where some competition has tended to exist between Bonn and the Länder. The latter are conscious that EC legislation could reinforce the power of Bonn at the expense of their own [*Boehmer-Christiansen, 1992: 194*].

The gradual devolution of power in Belgium means that it is now the three regional governments – Flanders, Wallonia and Brussels – that are primarily responsible for transposing EC environment directives into law. Central government provides only national coordination of the implementation process. In some cases it seems that Belgian central government is even unaware of implementing measures adopted by the regions. In a case brought by the Commission against it for failure to notify measures implementing directive 76/403/EEC (on polychlorinated biphenyls and polychlorinated terphenyls), for example, Belgium did not mention in its defence regional rules known by the Commission to have been adopted but not officially notified [*CEC, 1991a: 209*]. Indeed, an added complication in Belgium is that some national measures remain in force in addition to regional legislation [*CEC, 1991a: 209*]. Sometimes central government has even annulled regulations established at regional level on the grounds that they impinge on its competences but then omitted to put national legislation in its place.

Infringement proceedings brought by the Commission demonstrate the existence of major differences between member states in their compliance with EC environment legislation. Table 2 reports the degree of infringement of Community environment legislation by member state. The table shows the procedures decided upon and current at the end of 1989. From the table it is clear that Greece, for example, has one of the best records for conformity of its national legislation with the requirements of Community directives. This is due to the incorporation of the text of directives usually word for word into national law (a practice also followed by Ireland and Luxembourg). Nevertheless, Greece also records the second highest score for poor application and the highest score overall for non-notification. Measures are put in place slowly (though relatively accurately) and often fail 'on the ground', due to shortcomings in the application of legislation by regional and local administrations which lack qualified staff, equipment and other resources

[*CEC, 1991a: 211*]. Similarly, the practical application of law is particularly poor in Spain and Italy; in the case of the latter the Commission [*CEC, 1991a: 213*] has stated rather bluntly that 'regional or local authorities often find it difficult to organise or monitor the effective application of the rules'. Though Portugal faces similar problems in the organisation of administration it seems nevertheless to have been relatively successful (see Table 2) in implementing Community directives.

TABLE 2
INFRINGEMENT PROCEEDINGS DECIDED UPON UP TO 31
DECEMBER 1989, BY MEMBER STATE

Country	Partial Compliance	Non-notification	Incorrect application	TOTAL
FRG	14	4	11	29
Belgium	10	11	26	47
Denmark	–	1	4	5
Spain	15	4	38	57
France	15	1	28	41
Greece	2	12	31	45
Ireland	4	5	9	21
Italy	7	8	25	40
Luxembourg	4	3	5	12
Netherlands	14	4	6	24
Portugal	2	3	9	14
UK	6	4	21	31
TOTAL	90	60	213	362

Source: *Commission report on implementation of EC environment legislation, Commission of the European Communities*, Feb. 1990.

The best performance overall in implementation is achieved by Denmark. In all three stages of implementation referred to in Table 2 Denmark has a better record than other member states. This is a similar picture to that of Denmark's record on implementation in other areas of policy [*CEC, 1991a: 57–61*]. The reasons for Denmark's exemplary record lie in its high level of environmental awareness at both public and official levels; highly effective implementation and monitoring systems; and the close involvement of the Danish parliament, through the Danish delegation in the Council of Ministers, in the negotiation and adoption of new environment legislation. Where discrepancies do exist between Danish and Community environment law it is almost entirely as a result of a deliberate choice made by the Danish government based on a determination to protect the environment.

Germany and the Netherlands are often regarded as possessing a level of awareness about, and a national predisposition towards, environmental issues similar to that existing in Denmark. However, their record on implementation is less satisfactory. In both countries a well developed and sophisticated system of legislation and administration relating to environmental protection results in a lack of motivation to adapt existing national measures fully to new Community requirements. The Commission has suggested that the view may also often exist in the Netherlands that its own measures already conform with Community legislation even where this is not the case [CEC, 1991a: 214]. At the end of 1991 the Netherlands had still not implemented the 1980 directive on the protection of groundwater against pollution (80/68/EEC) despite a judgement of the Court of Justice against it in 1988. Similarly in Germany, the main concern could be to amend existing environment legislation as little as possible when Community directives are transposed. In areas of policy where the Länder implement EC environment legislation variations can also exist in the speed with which measures are adopted as well as in content. Some Länder, for example, lag seriously behind others in designating special protection areas for the conservation of wild birds under directive 79/409/EEC [CEC, 1991a: 211].

France, like Denmark, has a very good record on notifying the Commission of measures adopted to implement Community directives. The conformity and correct application of these measures is less satisfactory. An important issue in relation to implementation by France, which also impinges on other member states – most notably the UK, the Netherlands and Germany – is the tendency to transpose EC directives by means of administrative circulars. Such circulars tend to be subjective, grant excessive discretion in interpretation, and often lack transparency. The Commission (and the European Parliament) has long contested the use of circulars, guidance notes and similar instruments of administrative law to transpose Community legislation (see, for example, EP [1988a]; CEC [1991a]). It is argued that administrative circulars interpret legislation but do not implement it. This view has been supported by the Court of Justice. In recent years France has moved towards the Commission's position and started transposing EC legislation by statute [CEC, 1991a: 212]. Other member states have generally followed suit [HL 53–I, 1992: 13].

Table 2 demonstrates vividly that the effective practical implementation of obligations arising from Community environment directives undoubtedly gives greatest cause for concern. Nearly two-thirds of infringement proceedings relate to unsatisfactory application in practice of Community law. It is not surprising that the practical implementation of Community environment legislation should be regarded by the Commission [CEC, 1991a: 221] as the 'most pressing problem' in the process of implementation. In some cases the borderline between incomplete legal transposition and a member state's failure to implement EC legislation in practice can, however, be blurred, with failure to introduce the necessary implementing legislation resulting in specific, practical and often localised infringements of Community law. The implementation of the environmental impact assessment directive in the UK is a case in point.

In the Commission's interpretation the UK's implementing legislation contained several omissions and inaccuracies [CEC, 1991c]. The main problems concerned the application of the directive to projects for which application for development had been made but consent not granted before the entry into force of the directive; omission from the implementing legislation of the obligation to ensure that an appropriate impact assessment is conducted for several kinds of development project; and the granting of excessive discretion to UK authorities to decide projects subject to the directive.

The incorrect formal transposition of the directive gave rise to doubts about the practical application of the directive in the case of a number of specific development projects, including a salmon farm in Arran, a liquid petroleum gas installation at Grangemouth, a hospital incinerator in South Warwick, the London–Channel Tunnel rail link, the M11 link road in East London and, most notably, the proposed M3 motorway across Twyford Down. In the case of the Commission's action [CEC, 1991b] against the UK over implementation of the drinking water directive, the UK government's long-term partial legal transposition of the directive has resulted in a situation where some 4,536 individual practical infringements of the standards set out in the directive are officially acknowledged to exist in local drinking water supplies. In such cases it is the underlying failure of member states to introduce national implementing legislation which gives rise to failure to implement EC legislation in practice.

The distinction between infringement proceedings brought for poor practical application as opposed to incomplete legal transposition can be important. General proceedings taken against a member state for incomplete transposition are one thing but, as Macrory comments [1992: 356], 'action initiated in respect of a particular project may have considerable local political impact, possibly even bringing pressure to suspend or bring to the halt construction of the project in question'.

There has been a significant increase in infringement proceedings brought for incorrect practical application of Community environment legislation. Table 1 shows that up to the end of 1985 just five proceedings had been commenced for problems related to practical implementation (no such proceedings were commenced prior to 1983). In 1990 no less than 62 infringement proceedings were commenced for poor practical application of environment directives. Of those proceedings in hand at the end of 1989 213 out of 362 were in respect of failure to apply legislation effectively (Table 2). At the end of 1990 it was 218 out of 371 [*HL 53–I, 1992: 17*]. There is no doubt that the practical application of EC environment legislation, as opposed to its formal legal transposition, has taken on greater importance during the 1980s. This trend was marked in 1988 by the European Parliament producing its first reports which considered in some detail the practical implementation of EC environment legislation [*EP, 1988a; EP, 1988b*]. As stated in one of the Parliament's reports [*EP 1988a: 19*] 'there is some evidence that the Commission is itself also turning its attention to the practical implementation of environment legislation'. The record of infringement proceedings from the early 1980s to date demonstrates that although practical implementation may once have taken second place to formal, legal compliance [*EP, 1988a; Hanf, 1991*], the focus has now shifted towards the former.

The European Community's Legislative Process and Implementation

It has been argued that there ought to be a link between policy implementation, policy delivery and the formulation of policies if those policies are to be successful [*Richardson and Jordan, 1979: 153*]. In the words of Pressman and Wildavsky [*1973: 143*] implementation should not 'be conceived of as a process that takes place after and independent of, the design of policy'. Similar sentiments have also been expressed by participants in Community environmental policy-making. In a 1988 resolution on the implementation of EC legislation relating to water the European Parliament (OJ C94, 11.4.88, p.157) emphasised the need 'for implementation to be considered at a much earlier stage in legislative drafting'. The House of Lords Select Committee on the European Communities [*HL 53-I, 1992: 47*] expressed a similar view when it stated that 'Too much environmental legislation is formulated and drafted with insufficient attention to its eventual implementation'. A number of aspects of the Community's legislative process have an impact on the successful implementation of measures agreed by it.

The Preparation of Proposals

The Commission is of course the principal actor in the initiation and preparation of proposals for Community environment legislation. Within the Commission its Directorate-General for Environment, Nuclear Safety and Civil Protection, DG XI, is primarily responsible for drafting most proposals in the environment field. In some policy areas DG XI officials will work closely with other directorates general also involved: with DG III (Internal Market and Industrial Policy) for example, in the case of motor vehicle exhaust emissions. Responsibility for initial drafting of most proposals for Community environment legislation rests with some 350 (mostly temporary) DG XI officials. This is clearly a very small, albeit highly productive, bureaucratic resource, particularly if considered in relation to the size of national environment ministries, other directorates general and the corpus of EC environment legislation which has been produced since the mid-1970s. However, DG XI is considered to require additional staff; to be less influential within the Commission than other directorates general; and its priorities sometimes confused [*IEEP, 1992b: 26–30; EP, 1992a*].

The scientific and technical basis of draft legislation has often been questioned. Indeed, considerable agreement exists among environmental pressure groups, scientists and environmental agencies that the Commission needs to improve considerably its consultative procedures so as to have access to a wider and more satisfactory range of environmental data and advice on the basis of which proposals can be formulated [*EP, 1988a: 39; HL 53-I, 1992: 10*]. There is likely, after all, to be a clear relationship between the potential for policy implementation and a well drafted directive which commands the support of specialists. Nevertheless, consultative procedures employed by the Commission are at best *ad hoc* (see, for example, Mazey and Richardson in this volume). As a consequence they tend also to be opaque. Only very rarely does the Commission formally list organisations and individuals consulted during the drafting of legislative proposals or even publish scientific data and technical information on which proposals are based. The quality of legislative drafting by DG XI has also sometimes been criticised. No equivalent exists in the Commission to, say, UK parliamentary draftsmen. The House of Lords Select Committee on the European Communities [*HL 53-I, 1992: 9*] reported critically that within DG XI just ten officials provide general advice on legislative drafting as well as being responsible both for ongoing legal work in connection with the preparation of new legislation and for monitoring implementation in 12 member states, comprising 15 or 16 different legal systems, in nine languages.

Criticisms are also frequently made that the Commission's scientific advisory committees, though a relatively formal component of pre-legislative consultation, are poorly organised and allowed insufficient time to deliberate fully [*EP, 1988a: 40*]. Some members of the Commission's scientific committees have suggested that the Commission often seems incapable or unwilling to employ its advisory committees effectively [HL 227, 1985: 56–7]. Similarly, little information is available about the agendas, deliberations and conclusions of advisory committees. It is also relatively rare for authorities likely to be responsible for practical implementation to be involved in discussions with the Commission during its preparation of proposals. Nor is it probable that those organisations and individuals most likely to be affected by the implementation of EC environment legislation will be aware of the Commission's intentions during the early stages of legislative drafting. This tends to prevent the creation of a favourable climate for swift practical implementation once legislation is agreed.

The Process of Negotiation in the Council of Ministers

Decision-making within the Community brings together the member states in 'an intensity and size of organised cooperation that are unparelleled in other international organisations' [Wallace, 1982: 113]. Bargaining between member states is often remarkably complicated, the interactions between national elites complex, and agreement often difficult. Member states' policy articulation in the Council of Ministers usually has its roots in their domestic political environment. Council negotiations therefore usually aim at decisions which are acceptable to relevant groups in member states' domestic policy community and consistent with national traditions and practices [Bulmer, 1983]. For some member states this will entail influencing the policy process in such a way as to increase the stringency of proposed environment legislation. For others it could mean the opposite.

One example that shows these processes at work is the Commission's 1986 proposal for a Council directive relating to discharges of aldrin, dieldrin, endrin and isodrin ('drins') into the aquatic environment (COM (86) 534). Drins are toxic, persistent and bioaccumulative organochloride pesticides. Following a Commission-sponsored study of the environmental effects of drins, a proposal was submitted which envisaged a 5ng/l quality objective for drins and a 0.15mg/kg standard for drins in fish flesh. A report produced by the European Parliament marshalled considerable evidence to demonstrate that one member state – the UK – sought to influence Council discussion on the basis of 'levels of drins currently found', rather than on the basis of scientific or environmental criteria [EP, 1988a: 42–6]. Its objective was to avoid having to introduce in the UK a quality objective for drins which would have entailed the introduction of new measures to comply with it. The UK sought 'a standard which could be met in the majority of UK waters' [Department of the Environ-

ment, 1987]. It could of course be argued that UK officials were in fact taking likely future problems of implementation into account, a laudable objective indeed, if it were true. However, by proposing a total drins concentration of 50ng/l and deletion altogether of the fish flesh standard, the UK government differed in opinion not only from its own authoritative Water Research Centre but also from the House of Lords Select Committee on the European Communities which concluded that 'the dangers posed by drins to the United Kingdom environment lead us to consider that there is no safe limit value for the drins, and their use should, in the foreseeable future, be eliminated altogether' [*HL 6, 1987: 25*].

Despite member states' articulation in Council of often deeply entrenched preferences based on national circumstance and practice, negotiation in Council remains best characterised as a search for consensus. Even with the entry into force of the Single European Act in 1987 (which introduced qualified majority voting in Council on proposals for environment legislation related to the completion of the internal market) most environment legislation has up to now been adopted unanimously. In cases where qualified majority voting is available the tendency persists for Council to seek overall consensus. This search for unanimity among the Twelve increases the possibility that EC environment legislation will be vague, ambiguous and sometimes superficial. Scientific credibility and precision are likely to be sacrificed in order to achieve consensus. This may also on occasion result in the incorporation of irreconcilable views into Community law. Directive 76/464/EEC, on pollution caused by dangerous substances, is a case in point. The Council's agreement on this directive, rather than representing a compromise, has been viewed as 'a last ditch expedient included in the Directive to gain the unanimous agreement required for its approval' [*Taylor et al., 1986: 227*]. All member states except one preferred to set specific uniform emission standards for discharges of dangerous substances to the aquatic environment, whereas the UK preference was for environmental quality objectives permitting a range of emission standards [*Haigh, 1984: 96–104*]. Agreement between these opposing viewpoints was not possible and accordingly both approaches were included in the directive, allowing member states to disregard one approach for the other. Hence the dispute was left unresolved but settled temporarily.

Without exception negotiation within the Council of Ministers, whether in its working groups, COREPER or in formal Council meetings, takes place outside the public domain. This has a direct effect on the implementation of legislation it adopts. In the first place it encourages policy-making which emphasises intergovernmental bargaining, often

over unrelated issues. This kind of bargaining is hardly likely to contribute to the certainty or coherence of Community environment legislation (see, for example, EP [*1988a*]; EP [*1992b*]. Second, it provides the
opportunity for Council to adopt declarations and statements to its
minutes interpreting if not qualifying legislation. These usually remain
confidential between governments and the Commission. Such 'secret'
legislation can have serious implications for satisfactory implementation
(see, for example, Haigh [*1984: 53–4*]). The Commission acknowledged
the difficulty in its 1991 report to the European Parliament on the
application of Community law where it stated [*CEC, 1991a: 217*], for
example, that several member states derogate from the requirements of
the directive on the quality of surface water (75/440/EEC) on the basis of
a declaration to the minutes made when the bathing water directive
(76/160/EEC) was adopted. Hence it is possible for member states and, in
particular, their enforcement agencies, local authorities and other
bodies, to embark on the implementation of legislation which has been
agreed through considerable horsetrading and which is only clarified in
intent by reference to generally inaccessible interpretations.

The Form of Community Legislation

Over 90 per cent of Community environment legislation is in the form of
directives. Though very few regulations have been adopted in the environment field it is possible to discern in recent years a trend towards
their greater use. Community legislation on the production and importation of ozone depleting chlorofluorocarbons (1988 onwards), the export
and import of dangerous chemicals (1988), the evaluation and control of
environmental risks of existing chemicals (1992), the EC eco-labelling
scheme (1991), and the establishment of the European Environment
Agency (1990) have, among others been adopted as regulations. Although 'superficially attractive' [*HL 53-I, 1992: 16*] the greater use of
regulations as part of the solution to difficulties faced in implementing
directives is not widely supported. Member states would be reluctant to
sanction the creation of a body of law at EC level which may conflict with
extant national legislation. Similarly, the flexibility and respect for local
legal and administrative traditions and procedures implicit in the use of
directives are probably highly desirable in a political sense at present. The
use of directives can be viewed as an expression of the principle of
subsidiarity in the Community's legislative processes. The House of
Lords Select Committee on the European Communities [*HL 53-I, 1992:
47*] considered, however, that there may be 'scope for some increase in
the use of regulations'. In addition, the possibility could be raised of
greater use of regulations, albeit in a more closely delineated range of

policy areas, should Community competences be more tightly drawn in future through a more resticted application of the concept of subsidiarity.

It is a basic principle of Community law that when directives are adopted they are to be implemented uniformly by the member states (though in some directives different timescales have been specified). For the first time in the Maastricht treaty on European Union a provision is formally incorporated in Community procedure allowing for temporary derogations from environmental legislation where a member state considers the costs of particular measures to be prohibitive. The Maastricht treaty also allows for financial assistance from the new Cohesion Fund to be made available to compensate the member state(s) concerned. Under the terms of the Maastricht treaty any member state may seek such a temporary derogation so long as the legislation to which it will apply is based on Article 130s(1) of the treaty (that is, under the treaty, passed by a qualified majority in Council and adopted in cooperation with the European Parliament but excluding the large number of environmental measures based on Article 100A); and costs which are deemed disproportionate to the member states' public authorities will have to be incurred to implement the measure. Where these two criteria are met the Council may grant a derogation from the legislation. This provision is a radical departure for Community environment policy, the full impact of which it is at present impossible to assess. It may, however, open the door to Community environment legislation which explicitly accepts different national standards of environmental protection [*Wilkinson, 1992: 12*].

It might also lead to the Council negotiating not only the content of legislation but also, for some member states, its speed of implementation. If the provision is applied widely it could make for considerably greater differentiation in the application of EC environment legislation, making enforcement much more difficult. In support of the provision it can be argued that it will encourage Community institutions to take greater account of economic costs during the formulation of environmental policy. It might also expedite decision making by allowing a member state otherwise likely to oppose a particular measure instead to support it though with a derogation.

The Enforcement of EC Environment Legislation

Responsibility for the implementation of EC legislation rests primarily with member states. Nevertheless, it is clear that wide variations exist in their implementation of EC environment legislation. The Commission can have recourse to formal legal procedures under the treaties, supplemented by a complaints procedure, to ensure member states' compliance. It has also pursued the idea of 'osmosis' between it and national authorities as a way of encouraging implementation. In addition, the European Parliament has also played an important role in monitoring implementation.

Formal Procedures

Each directive agreed by the Council of Ministers specifies a time limit (occasionally several time limits) by when its provisions are required to be incorporated in national law. Member states are also required by directives to notify the Commission of the measures taken. Twice before the implementation date the Commission reminds member states of the requirement to adopt and notify national measures. Monitoring of the communication of national measures by the Commission's directorates general is reasonably routine and involves little political oversight from the college of Commissioners itself. The process can be complicated where individual directives require many separate items of national legislation to implement them. For this reason the Commission now requests member states to specify the provisions of national law in which each article and clause of a directive is implemented. The Commission has had little success in encouraging member states to produce for it synoptic tables cross-referencing national provisions with EC directives [CEC, 1991a: 221].

The Commission has recourse to Article 169 of the EEC Treaty where it considers that a member state has failed to comply fully with the provisions of Community legislation. This entails a three-stage procedure: first, the Commission informs the member state (by means of a '169-letter') that it believes an obligation under the treaties has not been fulfilled and requests its observations; second, if the Commission remains dissatisfied a reasoned opinion is forwarded to the member state; finally, proceedings may be commenced before the Court of Justice.

These formal stages set out in the treaty do not do justice to the extent and scope of correspondence and negotiation which is likely to occur prior to the Commission embarking upon each step. For its part, the Commission regards Article 169 proceedings as available only 'when all other means have failed' [CEC, 1991a: 205]. Even before starting out on the first stage of the Article 169 procedure the Commission will have extensive bilateral exchanges with national authorities. In September 1991, for example, the Commission forwarded to the UK government a 169-letter relating to the UK's failure to comply with the drinking water directive (80/778/EEC). The despatch of this 169-letter was preceded by no less than ten exchanges of correspondence between the Commission and the UK government and three meetings between Commission and

UK officials [*CEC, 1991b*]. Similarly in the case of the Commission's action against the UK government over the environmental impact asessment directive, some 12 exchanges of correspondence took place and at least one meeting of officials [*CEC, 1991c*]. The charge that is sometimes made that the Commission sails headlong into infringement proceedings would therefore appear not to be justified. On the contrary, the Commission's decision to pursue infringement proceedings is made only after considerable discussion with national authorities. Moreover, in all cases other than the non-notification of national measures each formal stage of the process requires a specific Commission decision to proceed [*CEC, 1991a: 206*].

Relatively few infringement proceedings progress further than the 169-letter stage. In many cases the receipt of a 169-letter is sufficient to encourage a member state to bring its national measures into line with Community legislation. Reasoned opinions and referrals to the Court of Justice 1982–90 in the environment sector are reported in Table 3; and in Table 4 169-letters, reasoned opinions and referrals initiated during 1990 are broken down by member states.

One issue that has been of concern, particularly to the European Parliament (see, for example, EP [*1988a*]; OJ C326, 16.12.91, p.189), is the transparency of Commission enforcement procedures. Until 1989 the Commission was reluctant to acknowledge infringement proceedings against member states prior to the reasoned opinion stage. Commission annual reports to Parliament on the application of Community law, for example, reported only those 169-letters relating to member states' failure to notify national measures, as well as reasoned opinions and referrals to the Court. Letters of formal notice to member states concerning omissions in implementation were not identified, on the grounds that the purpose of the first stage of the Article 169 procedure, rather than bringing a member state to account, is intended to afford it an opportunity to regularise its position [*EP, 1990a: 31*].

In recent years, prompted no doubt by increased emphasis on the implementation of directives required to complete the internal market, as well as by the European Parliament's criticism that many infringement proceedings are kept away from public view, the Commission has increased the information made available to the public about the opening of infringement proceedings. In a resolution adopted in November 1991, following the political furore which surrounded the Commission's 169-letter to the UK government on environmental impact assessment, the European Parliament requested that the Commission 'institute forthwith a procedure whereby Article 169 letters forwarded to Member States are henceforth sent also, for information, to Parliament' (OJ C326, 16.12.91,

TABLE 3

REASONED OPINIONS AND REFERRALS EXECUTED IN 1990, ENVIRONMENT SECTOR

Country	Reasoned Opinions	Referrals
Belgium	6	2
Germany	2	2
Denmark	--	--
Greece	4	--
Spain	7	2
France	1	4
Ireland	3	1
Italy	7	1
Netherlands	5	1
Luxembourg	1	--
Portugal	1	--
United Kingdom	2	1
TOTALS	39	14

Source: *Eighth annual report to the European Parliament on Commission monitoring of the application of Community law*, Dec. 1991.

TABLE 4

NUMBER OF PROCEEDINGS INITIED, BY STAGE OF PROCEEDINGS, ENVIRONMENT SECTOR

Year	Letters of Formal Notice	Reasoned Opinions	Referrals to Court
1982	16	7	--
1983	35	1	--
1984	65	33	2
1985	69	26	23
1986	134	11	10
1987	159	24	3
1988	93	71	11
1989	101	26	21
1990	167	39	14

Source: *Eighth annual report to the European Parliament on Commission monitoring of the application of Community law*, Dec. 1991.

p.189). By summer 1992 the Commission had not responded to this proposal. It is, nevertheless, recognised as having some force, particularly as there are unlikely to be commercial or similar interests affected by disclosure. The House of Lords Select Committee on the European Communities [*HL 53-I, 1992: 46*] agreed with the European Parliament's approach. It stated:

> The simple solution . . . is to make public all formal correspondence between the Commission and Member States concerning the investigation of complaints – that is Article 169 letters, Reasoned Opinions, and the responses to both. These documents have a formal legal charcter and like other legal documents should be publicly accessible.

The Complaints Procedure

In its investigation of the implementation of Community environment legislation the House of Lords Select Committee on the European Communities stated [*HL 53-I, 1992: 17*] that 'Without information it is impossible to assess whether compliance takes place, the effectiveness of legislation, or to gauge what further action may be called for'. Yet the Commission has no systematic means to collect information itself. This presents less difficulty in the case of formal transposition (as member states are required to communicate national implementing measures) than it does with practical implementation. Whilst many environment directives specifically require member states to forward reports on implementation to the Commission at regular intervals few do so promptly. When such reports are submitted they have tended to present only a very partial record of practical implementation [*CEC, 1991a; HL 53-I, 1992*]. As a result the Commission is almost entirely dependent on EC citizens bringing to its attention the alleged failure of member states to implement in practice Community environment legislation.

In recent years there has been a dramatic increase in the number of complaints received by the Commission. The Commission has received complaints about poor implementation of environment legislation from non-governmental organisations, local authorities, embassies and even national authorities, as well as private individuals [*CEC, 1991a*]. The Commission's intention, announced in the Fourth Environmental Action Programme (COM (86) 485, p.10), to encourage 'private persons, non-governmental organisations or local authorities to bring instances of non-compliance to the attention of the Commission' appears to have been successful.

The tendency of citizens to use the Community as an avenue of complaint has apparently kept pace with the Community's growing

TABLE 5

NUMBER OF COMPLAINTS AND CASES DETECTED BY THE COMMISSION'S
OWN INQUIRIES

Year	Environment Complaints	Environment Cases detected	Total Complaints	Total Cases Detected
1982	10	--	352	112
1983	8	--	399	192
1984	9	2	476	145
1985	37	10	585	244
1986	165	32	791	293
1987	150	38	850	260
1988	216	33	1137	307
1989	465	60	1195	352
1990	480	42	1252	283

Source: Eighth annual report to the European Parliament on Commission monitoring of the application of Community law, Dec. 1991.

TABLE 6

COMPLAINTS REGISTERED IN THE ENVIRONMENT SECTOR, 1990

Belgium	17
Denmark	3
France	47
Germany	56
Greece	40
Ireland	19
Italy	33
Luxembourg	3
Netherlands	7
Portugal	19
Spain	111
United Kingdom	125

Source: Richard Macrory, 'The Enforcement of Community Environmental Laws: Some Critical Issues', Common Market Law Review, Vol. 29 (1992), p.364.

involvement in national political life. EC environment policy, which records high levels of public support (see, for example, *Eurobarometer* [*1991: 28–31*]), has been an important part of this process. The number of complaints registered by the Commission in the environment and other sectors 1982–90 is reported in Table 5. The table also demonstrates that the Commission's own monitoring and enforcement mechanisms have not, it seems, evolved at a similar pace to public activism. When broken down by member state (Table 6) it is also clear that the number of complaints received is related to a member state's tradition of environmental activism and political protest [*Macrory, 1992: 364*] as well as a readiness to use national legal remedies [*HL 53-I, 1992: 29*].

The timescale for action to be taken by the Commission on the basis of complaints or of its own inquiries is very long. Over three years may elapse between a decision to commence proceedings pursuant to Article 169 and a judgement by the Court of Justice. Even once decisions have been taken to progress through the stages of the Article 169 procedure, many months can pass before execution of the decision. In the case of the 169-letter to the UK government on environmental impact assessment, the Commission decided in March 1991 (nearly three years after the deadline for implementation) to commence proceedings; it was not until October 1991 that the letter was despatched. Such delays can be important when infringement proceedings concern specific projects as environmental damage may occur during the course of investigations. The long timescales involved also provide an opportunity for national authorities to claim (possibly in the face of public opinion) that national rules are actually in order and that reports of Commission investigation are inaccurate.

'Osmosis' with National Authorities

In its Fourth Environmental Action Programme the Commission announced (COM (86) 485, p. 9) its intention to intensify its dialogue with national and regional administrations 'so as to promote a more fully harmonised understanding of and approach to both legal and practical questions concerning implementation'. The Commission's Director General for Environment has since spoken [*HL 135, 1987: 55*] of 'osmosis between national and Community institutions' to achieve this objective. Several meetings, both bilateral and multilateral, take place each year between the Commission's services and national authorities to discuss implementation of environment directives. Occasionally these have involved local and regional authorities as well as national authorities. There is a danger that the Commission could pursue close informal relationships with national administrations when recourse to legal procedures for ensuring compliance might be more appropriate. This concern has certainly been expressed by the European Parliament (OJ C94, 11.4.88, p.156). On the other hand it is important that the Commission should not appear to act peremptorily. Closer dialogue with national authorities and enforcement agencies is one of a number of mechanisms than can contribute to better implementation of Community environment legislation.

The European Parliament and Implementation

The European Parliament began to take an interest in implementation shortly after being first directly elected in 1979. In a resolution adopted in 1983 Parliament requested the Commission to submit annual reports on the failure of member states to fully implement Community legislation (OJ C68, 14.3.83, p.32). The Commission acceded to this request and submitted its first Annual Report on the monitoring of the application of Community law in 1984. Similar reports have been submitted annually. These are referred by the Parliament to its Committee on Legal Affairs and its specialised committees for their opinions. The Legal Affairs Committee produces an annual report on the basis of that submitted by the Commission and the opinions received from the other committees. In September 1990 this procedure was formally incorporated in the Parliament's Rules of Procedure (rule 29c) alongside provisions relating to Parliament's consideration of the Commission's Annual Legislative Programme and its Annual General Report (OJ C260, 15.10.90, p.85). The Commission's decision to prepare Annual Reports made an important contribution to improving the Community's oversight of implementation. Parliament was an important catalyst in this. However, Parliament's monitoring of implementation on the basis of the Commission's Annual Reports tends to emphasise formal legal transposition rather than practical implementation. The sheer range and often complexity of Community legislation makes it difficult for Parliament to exercise detailed or effective supervision over the implementation of Community legislation in its entirety.

The European Parliament's Committee on Environment, Public Health and Consumer Protection therefore took a further step in January 1987 when it decided to produce two major reports on the implementation of environment legislation. Submitted to plenary and adopted by Parliament in 1988, each of these reports dealt with a single environmental medium (air and water) and concentrated on practical implementation (OJ C94, 11.4.88, pp. 151–8). The major part of the report on the implementation of EC legislation relating to water comprised three case studies which considered the practical implementation of the directives on aquatic pollution caused by dangerous substances (76/464/EEC), drinking water (80/778/EEC), and bathing water (76/160/EEC). These were landmark reports which signalled a motivation on the part of the Environment Committee not only to uncover disparities and omissions in the implementation of EC environment law but also to oversee the Commission's exercise of its enforcement function in the environment field. Since 1987 seven reports on implementation have emanated from the Environment Committee. In addition to these reports three resolutions on implementation have been submitted by the Committee and adopted by Parliament's plenary (see also Judge in this volume). The Commission has co-operated closely with the Committee, for example, by responding specifically and point by point to its reports on implementation [see EP, 1990a]. On implementation as on other issues Parliament and Commission have formed a combined front when necessary against Council and member states.

On occasion it has been proposed that Parliament establish a specialised committee devoted to monitoring the implementation of EC environment legislation, either as a sub-committee of the Environment Committee [HL 53-I, 1992: 43], an entirely separate committee on implementation, including environment legislation among its competences (OJ C 94, 11.4.88, p.154), or as a temporary committee of inquiry on the implementation of environment legislation. None of these proposals has received significant support among Members of the European Parliament, within the Environment Committee, or from the major political groups in the Parliament. The Environment Committee's record on implementation suggests that a special committee is unnecessary, at least so long as the Committee continues to give priority to this aspect of its work and to produce reports on implementation at regular intervals. In addition, the Parliament is conscious of the administrative and resource implications of such a proposal [HL 53-I, 1992: 25]. Finally, the principle that implementation is related intrinsically to policy development has been a major theme of much of the Committee's monitoring of implementation (see, for example, EP [1988a]; EP [1992b]). It is recognised within the Environment Committee that the creation of a separate parliamentary body intended to monitor the implementation of environment legislation would run counter to its interest in considering implementation as part of the environmental policy-making process.

Improving Implementation and Enforcement

A number of measures can be envisaged that might improve the implementation of EC environment legislation. As noted at the outset, central to discussion of improving implementation is the idea of granting to the Commission powers of environmental inspection. The problem is that such a proposition is probably unrealistic at this stage in the development of the Community. As we shall see, a possibly more appropriate refinement of the inspection concept, involving a Community inspection audit mechanism (in other words the 'inspection of inspectors') has gained ground. Improving member states' reporting requirements, the setting up of the European Environment Agency, enhancing citizens' access to national courts, and some of the innovations introduced by the Maastricht treaty might also contribute to better implementation.

National Reporting Requirements

Information is one of the most important keys to the full and practical implementation of Community environment legislation. Monitoring the practical implementation of environment directives is particularly dependent on the systematic availability of reliable information on the environment. However, it is clear that the information available to the Commission (and often member states) is inadequate. The House of Lords Select Committee on the European Communities, in its report on implementation, noted [HL 53-I, 1992: 17] that 'The lack of information was perhaps the most pervasive theme of the evidence presented to us'. The Commission is entirely dependent for information on occasional studies on aspects of implementation contracted to consultants and environmental institutes, reports submitted by national authorities under specific directives, and complaints. Studies produced by consultants are useful but usually only provide a 'situation report on the implementation of a specific directive at a particular moment' [IEEP, 1992a: 170]. They are hardly a satisfactory substitute for long term data compiled systematically on the basis of comparable criteria in each member state. Complaints also possess limitations, in that they arrive randomly, their transmission is related to national traditions of political protest, they often focus on national environmental interests [Macrory, 1992: 365], and they are themselves dependent on the availability of information – both of environmental conditions and standards and of procedures for complaint. The receipt and processing of complaints may also detract Community officials from systematic cross-national monitoring and enforcement of implementation, particularly when resources are limited.

Neither is the requirement, incorporated in many directives, that member states submit regular reports on the measures taken to implement specific directives satisfactory. In the Commission's view [CEC, 1991a: 208], national reports have tended 'mainly (to) contain summary descriptions of the administrative and technical measures already in place or recently adopted. Consequently, they provide little useful information on the practical application of Community environment measures'. From the point of view of an environmental non-governmental organisation which assessed one member state's reports under an environment directive, national submissions 'have been late, incomplete, to a degree disingenuous and not widely canvassed in draft form with non-departmental sources of expertise' [RSPB, 1992: 145]. They are also dependent on the monitoring and reporting capabilities of national authorities. In some directives the requirement to submit reports to the Commission is completely absent (such as in the drinking water directive (80/778/EEC)); in others the requirement is formulated very loosely. In the environmental impact assessment directive, for example, it is stated simply (in article 11) that 'Member States and the Commission shall exchange information on the experience gained in applying this Directive'. Finally, some directives limit the Commission's right to publish information submitted by member states, others require publication of a Commission report.

In 1990 the Commission submitted a proposal (COM(90)287) intended to improve the consistency, content and frequency of the reports submitted to it under environment directives. Adopted in December 1991 this directive ('standardising and rationalising reports on the implementation of certain Community Directives relating to the environment' (91/692/EEC)) fixes at three years the interval between national reports under 30 directives, staggering the three year period for different environmental media. The Commission is required to publish a Community report on the implementation of each directive within nine months of receiving reports from member states. In the case of the bathing water directive (76/160/EEC) the 1991 directive provides for a consolidated Community report to be produced within four months of receipt of the member state reports. This is intended to result in the Commission's report on bathing water quality (produced annually since 1988) becoming more timely.

Probably the most significant aspect of the 1991 directive is that in future national reports submitted under the directives affected by it will be drawn up on the basis of a questionnaire produced by the Commission. Hence the Commission will be in a position to design and set out its information requirements itself. It could therefore be less dependent on information member states deign to submit. On the other hand, a 'commitology' procedure is established for member states to approve the Commission's proposed questionnaire. Commitology refers to the subordination of Commission executive decisions to committees of national civil servants (see Jacobs and Corbett [1990: 207–12]). Through this mechanism member states can be expected to keep a close eye on what information the Commission proposes to extract from them. Nevertheless, the framework for systematic reporting created by this directive is important in improving the availability at Community level of information on practical implementation during each three year reference period.

The submission of reports by the Commission, compiled on the basis of national reports, also requires improvement. Many Commission reports are produced late, if at all. In a resolution adopted in 1991, the European Parliament (OJ C326, 16.12.91, p.189) stressed the importance it attaches to the prompt presentation of such reports. A rolling calendar listing deadlines for the submission of Commission reports to Parliament in the environment (and public health and consumer protection) field is now produced for its Environment Committee, enabling it to take action when Commission reports on implementation become overdue.

The European Environment Agency: Towards Inspecting the Inspectors?

In May 1990 the Council of Ministers agreed to the creation of a European Environment Agency (EEA) and an associated European environment information and observation network (regulation 1210/90). The idea of a EEA was first raised formally by Commission President Delors in his programme statement to the European Parliament in January 1989. The role which it was intended the EEA could play in improving implementation through gathering and processing environmental information was clear. Delors stated [*CEC, 1989: 14*] that 'The object of the exercise will be ... to give us a network responsible for measurement, verification, certification, information and sounding the alert'. The Council regulation establishing the EEA sets out (in article 1(2)) its basic objectives as being 'to provide the Community and the Member States with objective, reliable and comparable information at European level enabling them to take the requisite measures to protect the environment, to assess the results of such measures and to ensure that the public is properly informed about the state of the environment'. Although the basic mission of the EEA is restricted to the collection, collation and analysis of environmental information, particular priority among its principal areas of activity is given to the collection of 'information which can be directly used in the implementation of Community environmental policy' (article 3(2)).

The EEA is not (at least yet) a nascent European environment inspectorate. The reluctance of member states' governments to support the idea of an environment inspectorate established at EC level is almost universal. It would entail investing Community institutions with a degree of involvement in national environmental monitoring and policy which at present member states would not countenance. The need to respect the principle of subsidiarity also implies that it is probably appropriate for the Community first to explore other approaches to better enforcement of EC law before embarking on the creation of a European environment inspectorate. The principle of subsidiarity has figured as a formal basis for Community environment policy (in Article 130R) since the introduction of the Single European Act; in the Maastricht Treaty its application is made explicit across the entire range of Community activity. It is also likely that in future greater attention will be paid to subsidiarity. The idea of an EC environment inspectorate is therefore probably still premature.

In its Opinion on the establishment of the EEA the European Parliament (OJ C96, 17.4.90, p. 114) demonstrated that it had considerable expectations about the role which the EEA should assume. Parliament saw the EEA taking a central place in the development of EC environment policy. For the time being these expectations are certain to be frustrated. On the other hand Parliament was successful in forcing the inclusion, among the tasks of the EEA, of the development of 'uniform assessment criteria for environmental data to be applied in all member states' (article 2(iii)). The Council's agreement was also won to a review of the EEA's tasks two years after its creation (article 20).

The development of 'uniform assesment criteria' is important as it provides a basis for the EEA to become involved gradually in the design, organisation and improvement of environmental monitoring by the member states. It suggests that the EEA could evolve from its current status as a relatively passive recipient of information towards having an increasing involvement in the coordination of environmental measurement and inspection in the member states. In essence the idea can be expressed as 'inspecting the inspectors': it does not envisage the EEA itself taking on an inspectorate role but does encompass the EEA performing an oversight or 'audit' function in relation to the methodologies employed by regulatory authorities in the member states. The review of the tasks of the EEA two years after its creation underlines the dynamic interpretation which can be made of its future role in monitoring implementation. Indeed, the EEA regulation (article 20) states that 'associating (the Agency) in the monitoring of the implementation of Community environmental legislation' will be among those areas where further tasks will in future be decided upon.

The Commission might only give qualified support to the idea of the EEA taking on an audit inspectorate function. During the negotiations over the creation of the EEA the Commission was reluctant to assign monitoring or inspection functions to the EEA. Apart from the difficulty

that it would have faced winning support in Council for such a development, the Commission also sought to defend its own role. It wanted to
ensure that functions envisaged for the EEA were clearly distinct from,
even if complementary to, its own role. The Commission emphasised that
the treaties give it specific responsibilities and prerogatives for the
implementation and enforcement of EC environment legislation. In view
of this it is also doubtful that the Commission was in a position in any case
to sanction what could amount to a transfer of power to a new body.

The Commission's view is that the role of the EEA is to generate
environmental data and to improve its quality and comparability. It
prefers to regard the question of the EEA's role in monitoring implementation postponed until the review of its operation two years after its
creation [CEC, 1992: 77]. In addition, it can also be objected that the
Commission is accountable to the European Parliament and as such
exercises its responsibilities subject to its oversight and scrutiny. Notwithstanding the European Parliament's nomination to the EEA
management board of two scientific personalities, the EEA will be much
less amenable to democratic control. Although it could be the case that
the EEA will prove to be an ally of the European Parliament and
responsive to its concerns [HL 53–I, 1992: 41], the introduction of
functional agencies such as the EEA raises important questions about
accountablity, control and oversight, particularly where agencies may
acquire powers of inspection or regulation (as in the case of the proposed
European Medicines Agency), however restricted.

The idea of developing a Community audit inspectorate is now quite
widely supported. Some member states, for example, have explicitly
taken up and promoted the concept of an inspectorate or audit agency
overseeing the work of national environment inspectors. In the view of
the UK government such an inspectorate should operate under the
responsibility of the Commission. Former UK Environment Minister
Michael Heseltine stated [HL 53–II, 1992: 183]:

> We see the inspectorate and the Agency as separate. The inspec-
> torate would report to the Commission. The powers of enforcement
> lie with the Commission ... We see it as an inspectorate inspecting
> the national inspectors that are responsible for monitoring and
> reporting on the Directives of the Community already in existence.
> The work of the Environment Agency will be ... to collect and
> compare statistics and to make reports.

In contrast the House of Lords Select Committee on the European
Communities has argued strongly [HL 53–I, 1992: 41] that the functions
and powers of a EC audit inspectorate should be clearly distinguished

from the Commission's own enforcement functions and that 'the logical home for an environmental inspectorate on the lines indicated is the European Environment Agency'. The Select Committee considered that inspectorate functions would dovetail neatly with the EEA's functions while institutional separation of an inspectorate from the Commission would enable it also to scrutinise more effectively the Commission's own role, in particular in respect of the environmental impact of other Community policies.

Rather than enter directly the discussion over the functions, role and location of an EC audit inspectorate, the Commission (in its Fifth Environmental Action Programme [*CEC, 1992: 75*]) refers instead to its intention to establish an 'implementation network' coordinated by the Commission. The creation of a network of member states' enforcement agencies is an idea which is obviously closely related to that of an audit inspectorate. The concept of an inspection network was first raised at the October 1991 informal environment Council and broadly agreed in principle. In the Commission's view (though based heavily on the conclusions of the informal Council) it would be intended primarily to exchange information and experience and aim at 'the development of common approaches at practical level under the supervision of the Commission'. Despite referring to this network rather loosely as an '*ad hoc* dialogue group' the Commission acknowledges that its central priority would be to promote consistency in the practical application of EC environment legislation.

Both the Commission's idea of an implementation network and the audit inspectorate concept aim at standardising, coordinating and improving the consistency of environmental inspection in the member states. Both would also provide at Community level information about the national inspection and monitoring regimes currently in operation. This would increase the visibility of national environmental regulatory regimes and possibly prompt the improvement of national inspection systems where there are shortcomings. The House of Lords Select Committee on the European Communities considered that an EC audit inspectorate would act as a 'watchdog' over the policies and performance of national regulatory authorities in the member states, particularly in the implementation of EC environment legislation. This goes further than the Commission's implementation network concept. Indeed, it has also been argued [*HL 53–I, 1992: 41*] that the audit inspectorate should have powers to verify the practical implementation of EC environment legislation and the data collected by national authorities.

Inspections and spot checks by Commission officials have in the past caused some controversy [*HL 135, 1987: 76–8*]. The objective of an audit inspectorate, however, particularly if located within the EEA, would be to co-operate with and assist national inspectorates. The Commission would retain its responsibility for enforcement, possibly acting on the advice of the EEA. While any attempt to improve and monitor the quality of member states' national environmental inspection regimes is likely to run up against the difficulty that member states will be jealous of their own functions, it might be possible to avoid the kind of conflicts between the Community and member states which have resulted from Commission enforcement activities in the past should the basic rationale of an audit inspectorate be to work closely with member states' own agencies and contribute positively, though pro-actively, to their inspection activities.

The Decision-Making Process

Attention was drawn earlier to the impact on implementation of the Community's legislative process. It was argued that some features of the way legislation is designed, drafted and agreed contribute to problems when it comes to be implemented. There is some evidence that the Commission has recognised that it is necessary to consider implementation as part of the process of drafting legislation. Indeed, the Commission acknowledges in its Fifth Environmental Action Programme [CEC, 1992: 75–7] that among the reasons for poor implementation are the need for unanimous agreement in the Council of Ministers; a lack of overall policy coherence due to the development of legislation in an *ad hoc* manner; and a too narow range of legislative instruments available to it. Along with the implementation network mentioned above the Commission therefore proposes the creation of two bodies which are intended to lead to improved implementation of EC environment legislation. The first is a consultative forum comprising representatives of industrial and business sectors, regional and local authorities, trade unions and environmental non-governmental organisations. Through this body the Commission intends to improve the preparation of legislation by increasing the exchange of information between these groups and the Commission. Secondly, the Commission proposes to constitute an environmental policy review group (modelled on the Committee of Directors-General of Industry) comprising representatives of the Commission and the member states at Director-General level, to examine environmental policies and measures. The Commission sees this body as filling the gap which results from exchanges between member states and the Commission usually only occurring over specific proposals and infringement proceedings. The consultative forum could lead to an increase in the visibility of Commission policy development. It might go some way to preparing the ground for the implementation of legislation which, as discussed earlier, rarely happens at present. The forum might also result in a more open and less *ad hoc* aproach to consultation. Similarly, the policy review group extends the idea of 'osmosis' with national authorities. In a similar vein the Commission also apparently intends to promote practical follow-up on all new environment legislation through training programmes, seminars and workshops involving member states' officials [*CEC, 1992: 76*].

The most serious difficulty associated with Community decision-making is the procedures used by Council to agree legislation. The need for unanimous agreement often leads to legislation based on political compromises and bargains which is difficult to put into practical operation. The Maastricht treaty extends the scope for using qualified majority voting in Council though it also complicates both the choice of legal base and the decision-making procedures which apply. There is considerable agreement that the changes introduced to the EC's legislative process by the Maastricht treaty are bound to cause confusion and delay [*EP, 1992c; Wilkinson, 1992*]. For environment legislation the co-operation procedure (see Judge in this volume) becomes the standard legislative procedure (though with some important exceptions). The new co-decision procedure will apply to environment legislation related to the internal market and environmental action programmes. Co-decision in particular is likely to result in much greater public discussion about proposed environment legislation. More information will come available about the positions adopted by individual member states and their bargaining strategies. By boosting the legislative powers of the European Parliament the Maastricht treaty also goes some way to redressing the Community's democratic deficit. Removing the ability of member states to block agreement on Commission proposals indefinitely will speed up agreement (as it has in other areas of Community policy) and prevent the gradual dilution of standards through lengthy negotiations in the Council of Ministers.

On the other hand, extension of qualified majority voting could mean that member states are more frequently obliged to adopt and implement policies to which they are opposed. As Wilkinson notes [*1992: 14*], this could lead to non-implementation becoming 'a problem even more serious than it already is'. Nevertheless, the extent of this should not be overestimated. The Single European Act has already reduced the range of legislation to which unanimous decision-making applies. Between 1989 and 1992, for example, a majority of Commission proposals in the environment sector were subject to the co-operation procedure (and therefore qualified majority voting) as they were related to the completion of the internal market and therefore based on Article 100a of the treaty. The gradual redress of the imbalance in the legislative powers of the Council and Parliament, especially through the co-decision procedure, will also root Community measures in future in a firmer democratic base.

The Council of Ministers could make a further contribution to improving implementation by itself demonstrating an interest in uniform implementation of environment legislation. The House of Lords Select Committee on the European Communities has proposed [HL 53–I, 1992: 42] that the Council regularly review compliance with environment legislation. The Select Committee suggests that consideration of implementation should routinely be placed on the Council agenda and considered on the basis of reports from the Commission and the EEA. In a sense the Council has already made progress in this direction by devoting its October 1991 informal environment Council to the question of implementation. The idea presupposes a willingness among the Twelve to discuss their own failings. It might be that the inter-governmental nature of discussions in Council would deter member states from undertaking future reviews of implementation in that forum.

Enforcement Through National Courts

In several member states access to the courts, particularly in respect of the practical implementation of environment legislation, is fraught with difficulties. Litigation can be expensive, the possibility of judicial review restricted and rules relating to locus standi a major hurdle. Some member states, such as the Netherlands, Germany and Denmark, possess well established procedures for individuals to seek remedies before administrative tribunals and courts for public bodies' non-implementation of environment legislation. In the United States virtually every statute relating to the environment enables 'citizens suits' to be brought under it. The possibility of bringing cases before national courts in environmental matters is important as it raises the possibility of enforcing Community legislation through local, regional and national processes. It would also encourage public participation in environmental protection. Furthermore, an important reason for the growth in the number of complaints to the Commission is the difficulty often of pursuing cases for infringement of EC environment legislation in national courts.

A Community measure enabling environmental non-governmental organisations and private individuals to bring cases for practical infringements of EC environment legislation in national courts would be an important measure which the Commission might usefully consider. This could be achieved through, for example, establishing a general right for Community citizens to take action in national courts over decisions of public bodies in environmental matters. In addition, decentralisation of the complaints procedure might also be envisaged, to allow individuals to lodge complaints over non-implementation with a body in the member state concerned [*CEC, 1991a: 222*]. Complaints would be referred from it to the Commission only if national authorities failed to comply with Community law. Whilst this would have the advantage of reducing the concentration of complaints at Community level it could also have the less desirable effect of erecting a barrier between the citizen and Community institutions.

As in the case of other measures which could lead to improved implementation, the possibility of improving access to national courts is highly dependent on the availability of information about the environment. The difference is that for the use of legal procedures at national level to be effective it is particularly important for private citizens and environmental organisations, as well as public authorities, to have ready access to environmental data. Better information and easier access to it will come about through implementation of the directive on freedom of access to environmental information (90/313/EEC). This directive will be particularly important in those member states which have had the least easy access to information about the environment and the pressures it faces. Lastly, it is not just information about environmental quality that is important but also the ready availability of information about standards set in EC legislation and Community and national environmental policy making processes [*EP, 1988a: 47*]. This points to the need for better diffusion of information about Community legislation and policy making.

The Treaty on European Union

It was noted above that the Maastricht treaty has introduced into Community environment policy the possibility of temporary derogations from legislation where member states are likely to incur substantial costs due to implementation. This could lead to greater variability in the environmental standards applied by member states and, put another way, sanction some member states not to implement Community legislation while others do. The treaty also established a 'cohesion fund' through which those member states with a per capita GNP of less than 90 per cent of the EC average (Greece, Ireland, Portugal and Spain) may apply for Community financial assistance for projects in the environment and transport fields. The fund could be important in helping to meet the costs of Community environment legislation in poorer member states, where implementation may be constrained by lack of resources. However, the fear has been expressed [*RSPB/WWF, 1992*] that there is an inherent tension between the financing by the fund of major infrastructure projects which might put the environment at risk and its support for projects intended to improve the environment. Certainly, environmental criteria should be built into the operation of the cohesion fund to ensure that the environmental impact of infrastructure projects is fully assessed.

The Maastricht treaty also amended Article 171 of the EEC treaty relating to judgements of the European Court of Justice. Under the Maastricht treaty the Commission may seek imposition of a fine on a member state which persists in flouting Community law after a first judgement of the Court against it. The possibility of instituting economic or financial penalties against member states for non-compliance, possibly by suspending Community subventions, has often been raised. The disadvantage of this idea is that its impact would fall unfairly on the Community's least prosperous member states and regions. While hardly likely to result in substantial financial penalties, the possibility of fining member states for failure to comply with Court judgements increases the range of action available to the Commission to bring moral pressure to bear on member states. After all, it is highly unlikely that fines imposed by the Court would have a major impact on national exchequers. Put differently, 'Fines would probably have to be set at astronomical levels in order to produce results' [HL 53–I, 1992: 46].

As well as seeking fines the Commission might also make greater use in future of Article 186 of the EEC treaty which allows the Court of Justice to order interim measures pending its final decision. As noted above, Commission investigations can take years and in the meantime environmental damage might occur. In the 'Leybrucht case' (case 57R/89) the Commission in July 1989, for the first time in a case involving the implementation of environment legislation, applied for interim measures to halt work on a development project underway in Germany which threatened environmental damage. The Commission argued that the project contravened directive 79/409 on the conservation of wild birds and should be halted forthwith pending a final judgement. On that occasion the application failed as the Court considered that the time elapsed (three years) between the Commission's receipt of a complaint about the project and its application to the Court for urgent measures suspending work pending the Court's final decision could not justify it granting interim measures. This adverse judgement could lead the Commission to be more cautious about future applications to the Court for interim measures.

Conclusion

There is no doubt that Community environment legislation raises problems for member states when they come to implement it. These problems result partly from the policy process through which Community legislation is formulated and partly from difficulties encountered within member states' own policy processes when faced with the need to implement legislation agreed at Community level. Since the mid-1980s more attention has been devoted to the implementation of EC environment legislation and to the consideration of ways through which implementation can be improved. Part of the reason for this is that the Community's role in environmental policy-making is now much more central. It is no longer possible to consider national and Community environmental policy as separate and distinct entities. Community policy now largely provides the framework and impetus for environment legislation in the member states. The problem of implementation has taken on greater importance as Community legislation has become a more vital component of member states' environmental protection policies.

In the environment field it is clear that the development of Community monitoring and enforcement mechanisms has not kept pace with the expansion of its legislative role. Such mechanisms are necessary at Community level to ensure that legislation is uniformly applied and that it achieves its objectives. As shown above, however, it may not necessarily be the case that Community enforcement mechanisms have to take the form of a centralised force of Community environment inspectors. The development of EC environment legislation is strongly supported by individuals, amenity groups, environment organisations and local and regional authorities, which look to the Community to set high standards of environmental protection. Poor implementation runs the risk of reducing the credibility and acceptability of Community environment policy. Although greater attention is now being devoted to improving implementation, the fundamental difficulty remains the reluctance of member states to acknowledge the need for the Community to possess a more significant role in monitoring and enforcing policy as well as in developing policy.

REFERENCES

Boehmer-Christiansen, Sonja (1992), Evidence submitted to House of Lords Select Committee on the European Communities, Session 1991–92, 9th Report, *Implementation and Enforcement of Environmental Legislation* (HL 53–II), pp.193–6.

Bulmer, Simon (1983), 'Domestic Politics and European Community Policy Making', *Journal of Common Market Studies*, Vol.XXI, No.4, pp.349–63.

CEC (1989), Statement on the broad lines of Commission policy, presented by the president of the Commission to the European Parliament, Strasbourg 17 Jan. 1989, *Bulletin of the European Communities*, Supplement 1/89.

CEC (1991a), 'Monitoring of the application by Member States of environment directives', Annex C to Commission of the European Communities, Eighth Annual Report to the European Parliament on the application of Community law – 1990, *Official Journal of the European Communities*, C338, 31 Dec. 1991.

CEC (1991b), Article 169 letter from the Commission of the European Communites to the Secretary of State for Foreign and Commonwealth Affairs, 26 Sept. 1991: directive 80/778/EEC.

CEC (1991c), Article 169 letter from the Commission of the European Communities to the Secretary of State for Foreign and Commonwealth Affairs, 17 Oct. 1991: directive 85/337/EEC.

CEC (1992), *Towards Sustainability: A European Community Programme of Action in Relation to the Environment and Sustainable Development (Fifth Environmental Action Programme)*, COM(92)23 final, 27 March 1992, Vol.II.

Clinton-Davis, Stanley (1992), Evidence submitted to House of Lords Select Committee on the European Communities, Session 1991–92, 9th Report, *Implementation and Enforcement of Environmental Legislation* (HL 53–II), pp.200–201.

Department of the Environment (1987), Minutes of meeting of UK Environment Consultative Group, 28 Jan. 1987.

EP (1988a), Report of the Committee on Environment, Public Health and Consumer Protection on the implementation of European Community legislation relating to water, Doc. A2–298/87, PE 116.085, 14 Feb. 1988. Rapporteur: Ken Collins

EP (1988b), report of the Committee on Environment, Public Health and Consumer Protection on the incorporation into national law of Community directives on the improvement of the quality of the air, Doc. A2–315/87, PE 119.132, 26 Feb. 1988. Rapporteur: Siegbert Alber.

EP (1990a), Notice to Members, Committee on Environment, Public Health and Consumer Protection, Implementation of Environmental Legislation, PE 137.207, 15 Jan. 1990.

EP (1990b), Report of the Committee on Environment, Public Health and Consumer Protection on the proposal from the Commission for a Council Regulation (EEC) on the establishment of the European Environment Agency and the European Environment Monitoring and Information Network, Doc. A3–27/90, PE 133.757, 5 Feb. 1990. Rapporteur: Beate Weber.

EP (1992a), Working Document of Committee on Environment, Public Health and Consumer Protection concerning the staff situation at the Commission's Directorate General for Environment, Public Health and Consumer Protection and the Commission's Consumer Policy Service in 1992 and 1993, PE 156.269, 11 March 1992. Draftsman: Hemmo Muntingh.

EP (1992b), report of the Committee on Environment, Public Health and Consumer Protection on the implementation of environmental legislation, Doc. A3–0001/92, PE 152.144, 6 Jan. 1992. Rapporteur: Jacques Vernier,

EP (1992c), Opinion of the Committee on Environment, Public Health and Consumer Protection on the results of the intergovernmental conferences, PE 155.239, March 1992. Draftsman: Ken Collins

Eurobarometer (1991), No.36, Dec. 1991; Brussels: Commission of the European Communities.

Haigh, Nigel (1984), *EEC Environmental Policy and Britain*, London: Environmental Data Services.

Haigh, Nigel (1986a), 'Keynote Speech: Overview – Problems and Perspectives', *EEB Seminar: The Implementation and Enforcement of EC Environment Legislation*, 27–28 Oct. 1986.

Haigh, Nigel (1986b), 'Devolved Responsibility and Centralization: Effects of EEC Environmental Policy', *Public Administration*, Vol.64, No.2.

Hanf, Kenneth (1991), 'The impact of European policies on domestic institutions and

politics: observations on the implementation of Community environmental directives',
paper prepared for presentation at ECPR Workshop on National Political Systems and
the European community, University of Essex, 22–27 March 1991.

House of Lords Select Committee on the European Communities, Session 1987–88, HL 6
(1987), 1st Report, *Correspondence with Ministers*.

House of Lords Select Committee on the European Communities, Session 1984–85, HL 227
(1985), 15th Report, *Dangerous Substances*.

House of Lords Select Committee on the European Communities, Session 1986–87, HL 135
(1987), 8th Report, *Fourth Environmental Action Programme*.

House of Lords Select Committee on the European Communities, Session 1991–92, HL 53
(1992), 9th Report, *Implementation and Enforcement of Environmental Legislation*,
March 1992; Volume I: Report (HL 53–I); Vol.II: Evidence (HL 53–II).

IEEP (1992a), Evidence submitted by the Institute for European Environmental Policy to
House of Lords Select Committee on the European Communites, Session 1991–92, 9th
Report, *Implementation and Enforcement of Environmental Legislation*, (HL 53–II),
pp.168–173.

IEEP (1992b), Institute for European Environmental Policy, *Assessment of the Fourth and
Fifth Environmental Action Programmes*, study produced for European Parliament
Committee on Environment, Public Health and Consumer Protection, April 1992.

Jacobs, Francis and Richard Corbett (1990), *The European Parliament*, London: Longman.

Macrory, Richard (1992), 'The Enforcement of Community Environmental Laws: Some
Critical Issues', *Common Market Law Review*, Vol.29, pp.347–69.

Pressman J.L. and A. Wildavsky (1973), *Implementation*, Berkeley CA: University of
California Press.

Richardson, Jeremy and Grant Jordan (1979), *Governing under Pressure: The Policy
Process in a Post-Parliamentary Democracy*, Oxford: Martin Robertson.

RSPB (1992), evidence submitted by the Royal Society for the Protection of Birds to House
of Lords Select Committee on the European Communities, Session 1991–92, 9th report,
Implementation and Enforcement of Environmental Legislation, (HL 53–II), pp.138–
149.

RSPB/WWF (1992), *The Cohesion Fund and the Environment*, note by the Royal Society
for the Protection of Birds and World Wide Fund for Nature International, March 1992.

Taylor, D., Diprose, G. and M. Duffy (1986), 'EC Environmental Policy and the Control of
Water Pollution: The Implementation of Directive 76/464 in Perspective', *Journal of
Common Market Studies*, Vol.XXIV, No.3, pp.225–46.

Wallace, Helen (1982) 'National Politics and Supranational Integration', D.Cameron (ed),
Regionalism and Supranationalism, London: PSI, pp.111–126.

Wilkinson, D. (1992), *Maastricht and the Environment*, London: Institute for European
Environmental Policy.

Index

Notes on the Contributors

David Judge is Reader in Government at the University of Strathclyde, Glasgow, Scotland.

Philipp M. Hildebrand is a doctoral candidate at Lincoln College, University of Oxford, and International Institutions Fellow at the Center for International Affairs at Harvard University for the spring semester of the academic year 1992–93.

Albert Weale is Professor of Government at the University of Essex.

Andrea Williams is Research Officer in the Department of Government at the University of Essex.

Jan van der Straaten is Senior Lecturer in Environmental Economics at Tilburg University, the Netherlands.

Frank Boons is Research Fellow in the Centre for Environmental Studies at Erasmus University, the Netherlands.

Sonia Mazey is Lecturer in Politics and Fellow of Churchill College, University of Cambridge.

Jeremy Richardson is Professor of European Integration and Director of the European Public Policy Institute at the University of Warwick.

Mark N. Franklin is Professor of Political Science at the University of Houston, Texas.

Wolfgang Rüdig is Senior Lecturer in Government at the University of Strathclyde, Glasgow, Scotland.

Elizabeth Bomberg is Lecturer in the Department of Political Studies at the University of Stirling, Scotland.

Ken Collins is Labour Member of the European Parliament for Strathclyde East, and Chairman of the European Parliament's Committee on the Environment, Public Health and Consumer Protection.

David Earnshaw is Researcher for the Chairman of the Committee on the Environment, Public Health and Consumer Protection, European Parliament.